D1554391

COLUMBIA NORTHWEST CLASSICS

Chris Friday, Editor

COLUMBIA NORTHWEST CLASSICS

Columbia Northwest Classics are reprints of important studies about the peoples and places that make up the Pacific Northwest. The series focuses especially on that vast area drained by the Columbia River and its tributaries. Like the plants, animals, and people that have crossed over the watersheds to the east, west, south, and north, Columbia Classics embrace a Pacific Northwest that includes not only Oregon, Washington, and Idaho but also British Columbia, the Yukon, Alaska, and portions of Montana, California, Nevada, and Utah.

Mountain Fever: Historic Conquests of Rainier
by Aubrey Haines

To Fish in Common: The Ethnohistory
of Lummi Indian Salmon Fishing
by Daniel L. Boxberger

Mexican Labor and World War II:
Braceros in the Pacific Northwest, 1942-1947
by Erasmo Gamboa

Boys of Boise: Furor, Vice,
and Folly in an American City
by John Gerassi

Gyppo Logger
by Margaret Elley Felt

GYPPO LOGGER

MARGARET ELLEY FELT

With a Foreword by Robert E. Walls

UNIVERSITY OF WASHINGTON PRESS

Seattle and London

Copyright © 1985 by Margaret Elley Felt
Originally published in 1963 by Caxton Printers
First paperback edition published in 1985 by Maverick Publications
University of Washington Press paperback edition published in 2002
Foreword by Robert E. Walls and Afterword by Chris Friday
Copyright © 2002 by the University of Washington Press
Printed in the United States of America

Library of Congress Cataloging-in-Publication Data
Felt, Margaret Elley.
Gyppo logger / Margaret Elley Felt ;
with a foreword by Robert E. Walls.
p. cm. — (Columbia Northwest classics)
Originally published: Caldwell, Idaho : Caxton Printers, 1963.
ISBN 0-295-98166-0 (alk. paper)
1. Felt, Margaret Elley.
2. Loggers' spouses—Washington (State)—Biography.
3. Loggers—Washington (State)—Anecdotes.
4. Logging—Washington (State)—Anecdotes.
I. Title. II. Series.
SD537.52.F46A3 2001 634.9'8'09797—dc21   2001035598

All rights reserved. No part of this publication may be reproduced
or transmitted in any form or by any means, electronic or mechanical,
including photocopying, recording, or any information storage or
retrieval system, without permission in writing from the publisher.

The paper used in this publication is acid-free and recycled from
10 percent post-consumer and at least 50 percent pre-consumer waste.
It meets the minimum requirements of American National Standard
for Information Sciences—Permanence of Paper for Printed Library
Materials, ANSI Z39.48-1984. ⊗ ♻

Photographs by Gus Pasquarella.

This book is respectfully dedicated
to the three men in my life, in memoriam.

WALTER ORIE ELLEY (1890–1963),
my father, who taught me to appreciate and
enjoy the great out-of-doors as he loved
the Idaho mountains during his lifetime.

HORACE WOODRUFF FELT (1913–1997),
my favorite gyppo and my husband for fifty-seven years,
who conned me into the gyppo logging game.

EDSON M. CASE,
our late attorney and good friend,
who got me out of this gyppo logging business
more or less intact—with only a few gray hairs
and a slight nervous condition to show for my
fifteen years as the working wife of a gyppo logger.

CONTENTS

FOREWORD

"THE UNIVERSE IS MADE OF STORIES, NOT ATOMS,"
the poet Muriel Rukeyser once declared. The timber industry is a splendid example of this observation: an industry of markets and machines, trees and timber towns, but ultimately an industry constituted in the public sphere as a grand, heroic narrative with tales of working-class struggles, nature's subjugation, and even corporate foresight. Margaret Elley Felt's *Gyppo Logger,* originally published in 1963, did not attempt to contradict this overly romanticized epic. It did, however, present a story almost universally overlooked in the industry's history: the emergence of family-based, independent contract loggers in the post-World War II timber economy, and the crucial role of women within that economy.[1] More specifically, *Gyppo Logger* told a story of the interrelated transformations of occupational culture and the region's physical environment. In its intimate portrait of one household's economy, the book demonstrates how gyppo wives remade the formerly masculine terrain of logging through their unpaid but vital economic activities in both private and public forums, activities that contributed to the production and reproduction of gyppo businesses and the social world of which they were a part. And it was, arguably, the success of these family businesses that facilitated the dramatic and rapid physical

redesign of Northwest forests from old-growth stands to the "tree farms" of industrial forestry.

In telling this story, Margaret Elley Felt drew upon the inherent power of autobiographical narrative, a literary form that is compelling and accessible to a broad audience, and one that is also essential to our comprehensive understanding of the past. As subjective and personal sources, autobiographies and memoirs that originate from women and the working class have tremendous historical value both in the way they reveal the dynamic relationship between private and public life, and in the way they illuminate historical changes from the perspective of people who lived through them. However, the value of *Gyppo Logger* is further enhanced by its autoethnographic qualities: a first-person narrative that places the self within a specific social context, in this case one woman's unique description of the social and economic life of a male-dominated occupational subculture with which she is intimately familiar and willing to analyze according to its gendered contours.[2] By creatively shaping this mode of self-representation, Felt introduced an authoritative woman's voice into a world of lumbering that previously had been limited to the stories of men. In so doing, she moved women from the margins of the industry's recent history to its center, and produced a story that helped to demythologize the Bunyanesque West and the prevailing ideology of gender that constructed it.

During the past few decades, logging has been an industry riddled with controversy, particularly in the Pacific Northwest. The industry has used science and managed order to improve the process of growing trees for the commodity production of timber. However, historians have documented how the U.S. Forest Service mismanaged a resource in its trust, exceeding sustainable yields in its optimistic zeal to satisfy timber interests. Environmental activists have been quick to assert that job losses in timber-dependent communities have been due to automation and the rapid liquidation of old-growth reserves, rather than to harvest restrictions imposed to protect endangered species. Scientists and the general public have increasingly objected to turning forests into monocultural tree farms on aesthetic, ecological, and economic grounds.[3] But in the rush to assign blame, antagonists have often conveniently caricatured the logging work force as either ecologically insensitive Bunyanesque brutes or victimized martyrs to the consumer demands of the American public; consequently, information crucial to our historical understanding of this political dilemma has been obscured. Western historians, in particular, have now begun to pose questions that will enhance our comprehension of the social and cultural complexity of the relations between human communities and the resources on which they have depended. Their approaches promise nuanced understandings of the subtleties of environmental transformation missing in earlier works. For example, Richard White asks how occupational communities know nature through their labor, especially through the everyday intimacies of that work/nature relationship, and Katherine Morrissey asks what a gender-conscious history of work and nature in western forests might look like.[4]

Gyppo Logger provides an excellent place to begin addressing these vital questions. Felt's discussion of the gendered relationship among work, economy, class, and occupational culture evokes striking historical parallels to women's central role in the family economies of other industrial and agrarian settings.[5] Her description clearly shows how women's productive and reproductive labor in both public and private settings were fundamental to the

success of family, community, and regional economies.
Moreover, the author's commentary on her own attitudes
toward the forest around her as a productive and regenerative landscape is highly suggestive of the breadth of
class-based meanings that nature holds for American
women, a diversity that certainly complicates many
ecofeminist arguments about women's connections to the
natural world.

The book's principal focus is on one Washington State
family's role in the emergent gyppo economy that followed the 1930s, when "logging fever" ran epidemic.
Brother joined brother and sons joined fathers to establish their own small companies of two to twenty employees who cut, logged, and hauled timber on a contract basis for larger companies, mills, and a variety of other timber owners. Such entrepreneurial aspirations to financial
independence were clearly in the interests of large timber
corporations, who saw an opportunity to mitigate the
strength of an increasingly unionized and contentious
work force that was based on traditional wage labor. Fur-
thermore, they reduced their own expenses by contract-
ing independent loggers with an interest in upward mo-
bility, who were resistant to unionization and willing to
bear the costs and risks of timber production. Changes in
logging technology were in the gyppo's favor, with the
wide availability of more mobile and affordable machinery such as trucks and tractors, and the development of a
dense network of roads which provided access to formerly
untouched stands of timber, especially on federal and
state lands. Log markets also expanded, driven by post-
war demographic shifts in the Far West and a booming
home construction industry which increased demand for
trees from thinning and salvage operations and for second-growth timber and formerly unmarketable species

such as hemlock. This combination of entrepreneurial conservatism and new technology and markets, along with a pliant and relatively powerless union, made the industry even more efficient at the capitalist transformation of the forest into an industrial tree farm.[6]

Women had long contributed to the timber industry through occasional employment in the woods and mills, especially during wartime. But after 1945, as Felt's experiences demonstrate, they became integral to the emergent division of labor in communities dominated by contract loggers, an unpaid source of labor that husbands took advantage of in a competitive climate, a practice Felt gently critiques when she remarks on her husband's "conniving to keep the gyppo's wife on his payless payroll" (p. 217). It was often a hard life, with no certainty of future rewards. There were the predictable domestic duties, which included the responsibility of raising children who frequently grew into the business as unpaid or underpaid labor for the family economy. But there were additional jobs, as when women drove to town for parts and supplies, administered first aid, maintained and operated trucks and machinery, cooked for small camps, and generally provided an "uplifting influence" (p. 166) on camp morale and behavior. Many wives also supplemented household income during winter or summer shutdowns by harvesting and bundling Christmas trees and collecting non-timber forest products such as ferns, berries, mushrooms, fir cones, and cascara bark. Such harvesting activities represented a more subtle transformation of the forest landscape and contributed to a gendered knowledge of nature through work of the kind that Morrissey and White urge us to discover, knowledge that affirms the woods as a resource with more immediate and sustainable regenerative potential.

Perhaps most important for the gyppo family economy was the fact that wives often served informally as their business's chief financial officer (sometimes as a legal partner), as they learned to maintain payrolls, collect and pay bills, meet creditors and bankers to secure loan extensions, cater to the needs of visiting company officials inspecting the results of contractual agreements, arbitrate labor disputes, become resources of financial and regulatory knowledge, and generally participate in volunteer activities (such as arranging benefits for injured loggers) that helped keep gyppo families afloat through the mercurial fluctuations of the seasons and the timber market. Of course, few women did everything, and some preferred—or were instructed—not to do anything, but most performed at least some of these important tasks. In short, the energy and skills of women like Margaret Felt made it feasible to run a business founded on marginal capital; consequently, they began to transform the occupational culture within the private and public realms of individual families and communities.[7]

Equally instructive is the progress of Margaret Elley Felt's career as a conservation advocate following the writing of her original article in the *Saturday Evening Post* and *Gyppo Logger,* the latter of which received numerous favorable reviews in regional newspapers, occupational trade journals, and even the *Journal of Forestry.*[8] Her newly gained public prominence inspired her to run, albeit unsuccessfully, three times as a Democrat for the Washington State Legislature. As a writer and publicist, however, she was far more successful. When her husband Horace retired from the woods in the early 1960s, Margaret was free to pursue new interests. Both her familiarity with logging and her early written defense of industry practices led her to the Washington State Department of

Natural Resources (DNR), where she worked as a public
relations officer with the Commissioner of Public Lands,
Bert Cole, and forester Al O'Donnell. During her seven-
year tenure in Olympia, she often served as a liaison between the state and local landowners who learned to trust
her knowledge of timber, wildfire, and ranching issues. It
was a role for which she was well-prepared, an extension
of her previous experiences as an unofficial mediator for
her family logging business.

Felt also wrote extensively for a general public audience about the necessity and promise of sustainable forestry, and eventually produced two books published by
the DNR: *Capitol Forest: The Forest That Came Back*
(1975) and *Yacolt!: The Forest That Would Not Die* (1978).
Underlying both of these books (and other popular books
she would later write profiling the lives of logging personalities) is the central theme of her natural resource
philosophy, which she describes as "conservationist": forests, and nature in general, have tremendous regenerative
powers, and with proper human intervention can provide
endlessly for the multiple needs of the general public. It
is a position borne of the mixed emotions of personal
working-class experiences and of exposure to the corporate ideals of industrial forestry. Consider, for example,
her own gendered connections to the process of forest
transformation. On a daily basis, she closely observed selective and clearcut logging practices over a long period
of time, witnessed the failures and successes of reforestation, and even participated by replanting trees herself
when necessary. Debates with her husband and male co-
workers over the fate of beautiful old-growth stands eventually convinced her to become "more sensible" and relin-
quish her preservationist "idealism" for a realization that
"timber is a crop." She loved family camping trips in

centuries-old groves, and ached with sadness when
watching the same trees felled; yet, as a wife and mother,
she felt tremendous appreciation for the paychecks that
followed soon after, supporting both her family and her
burgeoning career as a writer. Such experiences led naturally to her role as a spokesperson for the tree farm ideal.[9]

As a woman empowered socially and politically by her
experience in and out of the woods, Margaret Elley Felt
was hardly unique. The women of logging entered into
the public sphere in many capacities following the Second World War, writing letters in newspapers and trade
publications on issues that affected the industry, serving
in auxiliaries for timber-related unions and associations,
and lobbying politicians on behalf of their
communities.[10] It is not surprising, therefore, that over
the past twenty-five years women in Northwest logging
towns have drawn upon their technical knowledge of the
industry, and upon a moral authority of agrarian and entrepreneurial idealism, to organize resistance against what
they perceived as the ascendancy of urban environmental
concerns. As owners of small family businesses and tree
farms, leaders of local grassroots organizations, and even
candidates for political office, they have initiated protests
to focus attention on environmental restrictions they
deem unfair, and have become voices for their communities in media engagements, hoping to re-gender the
terms of environmental conflict (with its emphasis on
masculine representations of Bunyanesque work), and remind the general public that production and consumption issues are inseparable from those that concern family
survival. Only time will tell how successful they have
been in their efforts. But without question, their presence
serves to remind us that the making of the modern forest,
and debates over the meaning and value of nature, have

never been solely male enterprises that occurred primarily
in corporate boardrooms and university forestry classes.
On the contrary, this process has always been a joint en-
deavor, involving both men and women, that often took
place in working-class settings as well: in the woods, the
kitchens, and the cafes of timber towns throughout the
Northwest.[11]

As the only book ever written by a woman who has
nearly done it all in the world of woodsworkers, *Gyppo
Logger* makes a unique contribution to the fields of
women's, labor, and environmental history. As a historical
document, and a well-written story, it fits superbly in the
growing body of literature that portrays the historical
gendering of work and life in the West—studies that
have been slow to emerge but that greatly enrich our
wider understanding of human experience in the
region.[12] With the reprinting and reassessment of memoirs such as this one, and the development of promising
oral history projects, the prospects for achieving a better
understanding of women and the woods are bright
indeed.[13] Such work will further demonstrate that the
history of the West is hardly just the story of men, and
that a western woman's place was frequently, as Margaret
Elley Felt put it, "wherever she wants to be."

ROBERT E. WALLS
October, 2001
Lafayette College
Easton, Pennsylvania

NOTES

1. The origin of the term "gyppo" is clouded by the usual problems of folk etymology, but most explanations either assert that
small contractors "gypped" their employees with low paychecks or

assert that transient operators led a "gypsy"-like existence. See, e.g., Matthew S. Carroll, *Community and the Northwest Logger* (Boulder, CO: Westview Press, 1995), 39-40, 69-70.

2. The importance and subversive potential of such autobiographies and autoethnographies have been explored in many recent works, but see especially Deborah E. Reed-Danahay, ed., *Auto/Ethnography: Rewriting the Self and the Social* (Oxford: Berg, 1997).

3. For two recent summaries of the Northwest timber wars that give voice to the participants, see William Dietrich, *The Final Forest: The Battle for the Last Great Trees of the Pacific Northwest* (New York: Simon and Schuster, 1992); Beverly A. Brown, *In Timber Country: Working People's Stories of Environmental Conflict and Urban Flight* (Philadelphia: Temple University Press, 1995). See also, e.g., Paul W. Hirt, *A Conspiracy of Optimism: Management of the National Forests Since World War Two* (Lincoln: University of Nebraska Press, 1994); Nancy Langston, *Forest Dreams, Forest Nightmares: The Paradox of Old Growth in the Inland West* (Seattle: University of Washington Press, 1995).

4. Richard White, "'Are You An Environmentalist or Do You Work for a Living?': Work and Nature," in *Uncommon Ground: Toward Reinventing Nature,* ed. William Cronon (New York: Norton, 1995), 171-85; Katherine G. Morrissey, "Engendering the West," in *Under an Open Sky: Rethinking America's Western Past,* ed. William Cronon (New York: Norton, 1992), 138.

5. On women and the family economy see, e.g., Ava Baron, ed., *Work Engendered: Toward a New History of American Labor* (Ithaca: Cornell University Press, 1991); Carol Groneman and Mary Beth Norton, eds., *"To Toil the Livelong Day": America's Women and Work, 1780-1980* (Ithaca: Cornell University Press, 1987).

6. A history of gyppo logging remains to be written, but for several recent ethnographic and historical accounts see, e.g., Carroll, *Community and the Northwest Logger;* Charlene James-Duguid, *Work as Art: Idaho Logging as an Aesthetic Moment* (Moscow: University of Idaho Press, 1996); William G. Robbins, *Hard Times in Paradise: Coos Bay, Oregon, 1850-1986* (Seattle: University of Washington Press, 1988).

7. There are many brief articles on women in the pre-1950s timber industry to be found scattered in trade journals, but for two of the more accessible articles see Mary Hornaday, "Women in the Woods," *American Forests* 48 (November 1942): 496-98, and Anna

Lind, "Women in Early Logging Camps," *Journal of Forest History* 19 (July 1975): 128-35.

8. Gordon D. Marckworth, review of *Gyppo Logger, Journal of Forestry* 62 (April 1964): 280.

9. Margaret Elley Felt has written or edited a total of thirteen books, and has written articles for a diverse range of newspapers and popular magazines. I am grateful to members of her family, especially daughters Kimberley Moller and VickiAnne Davis, and to her friends Al O'Donnell and Pearl Severn, for providing much information on Mrs. Felt's life. Additional information comes from a personal interview conducted by the author with Mrs. Felt on November 4, 1999. Her books on logging include *Gyppo Logger* (Caldwell, ID: Caxton Printers, Ltd., 1963); *Capitol Forest: The Forest That Came Back* (Olympia: Washington State Dept. of Natural Resources, 1975); *The Enterprising Mr. Murray: Pacific Northwest Logger* (Weiser, ID: The Author, 1978); *Yacolt!: The Forest That Would Not Die* (Olympia: Washington State Dept. of Natural Resources, 1978); *The Story of a Logger, Frank D. Hobi: He Did it the Hard Way* (Bend, OR: Maverick Publications, 1984); *Maurice G. Hitchcock: The Flying Lumberjack!* (Bend, OR: Maverick Publications, 1985); *Rivers to Reckon With: Rivers on the Western Edge of the Olympic Peninsula* (Forks, WA: Cockerell and Fletcher, 1985); and with Diane Ellison, *Reach For the Sky* (Bend, OR: Maverick Publications, 1986). Her first publication, "I'm a Gyppo Logger's Wife," appeared in the *Saturday Evening Post* (August 30, 1952): 32-33, 57-59. Two of her edited works of history include *Ira E. Shea, The Grange Was My Life* (Fairfield, WA: Ye Galleon Press, 1983) and *Daughters of the Land: An Anthology* (Bend, OR: Maverick Publications, 1988), the latter a collection of histories of Native American women. Finally, she is also the author of three novels: *Come West with Me* (Bend, OR: Maverick Publications, 1990); *Not a Cloud in the Sky* (Bend, OR: Maverick Publications, 1990); *Blowdown!* (Bend, OR: Maverick Publications, 1991).

10. Documentation of women's participation in the private household economies of gyppo logging and their emergence into more public and political roles is contained in my own work-in-progress, "Women and the Woods: Engendering Work in the Western Forests."

11. On logging women in the "wise-use movement" see, e.g., Jacqueline Vaughn Switzer, *Green Backlash: The History and Politics of Environmental Opposition in the U.S.* (Boulder, CO: Lynne Rienner,

1997). On American women and nature more generally, one might refer to any number of Carolyn Merchant's books, but also see, e.g., Vera Norwood, *Made from This Earth: American Women and Nature* (Chapel Hill: University of North Carolina Press, 1993) and Glenda Riley, *Women and Nature: Saving the "Wild" West* (Lincoln: University of Nebraska Press, 1999).

12. The literature on women's history in the West is vast, but for an excellent recent collection of women's voices from the West see, *The Western Women's Reader,* ed. Lillian Schlissel and Catherine Lavender (New York: HarperCollins, 2000). On the related problem of stereotypes and Western women's history see, e.g., Beverly J. Stoeltje, "'A Helpmate For Man Indeed': The Image of the Frontier Woman," *Journal of American Folklore* 88 (Jan.-Feb. 1975): 25-41; Joan M. Jensen and Darlis A. Miller, "The Gentle Tamers Revisited: New Approaches to the History of Women in the American West," *Pacific Historical Review* 49 (May 1980): 173-213.

13. Historian Deborah Sutphen, working with the Center for Columbia River History, has already conducted oral history research for a "Women and Timber" project; a summary of that research and selected transcripts are now available on the Internet. See http://www.ccrh.org.

What Is a Gyppo?

A GYPPO ISN'T MADE; HE'S BORN. BORN A LOGGER, but with that virus of independence in his veins. My gyppo came by his love of logging honestly. He's the son of a logger, brother of a logger, and has several uncles who follow the logging game. Born in a tent in a small logging settlement on Vancouver Island, British Columbia, he knew nothing but logging almost from his first lusty breath. As boys, Horace (Sonny) and his younger brother Wayne made miniature donkey engines from spools and thread. Later, they swiped the bobbins from their mother's sewing machine for drums and blocks to enlarge the scope of their fern-patch "logging" operations. During school vacations, as they reached their teens, they began learning the logging game in earnest, breaking in on various jobs with their father's gyppo outfit. They punked whistles, fired and punched donkey, and tended hook. Finally they both learned to drive the logging tractors their father purchased for his logging operations in 1934. During that time they both became good tractor mechanics. They could scatter the parts to the four winds and put them back together again, and make them run. Horace got so he'd throw away the extra parts and his machine would still run, but Wayne was more on the careful side.

For the next ten years, Sonny drove and repaired logging cats over most of the western slopes of the Cascade Mountains. Wayne got a job with a large timber concern as cat mechanic.

I first met Sonny in the summer of 1934, but he thought sixteen a trifle young, so he waited for three years before asking me for a date. Then we went together for another three years before our marriage in 1940. It was probably the scrappiest courtship on record, for it was during that time we were going together that I discovered how far apart our viewpoints were on the subject of logging.

I was born in the sandhill country of Idaho, and the green forests of Washington fascinated me with their majestic beauty. I would look up into the tall giants where the sun came shimmering through the thick green branches, caught in the spell of their beauty, and sigh. Then I'd hear Sonny sigh, too, and I'd smile gently, thinking he was caught up in the same magic.

Then, "Geez, what a logging show!" He'd breathe, and we were at it again.

We argued loud and long about the methods of logging, wasteful and otherwise; about the reforestation, and saving certain stands of timber for posterity. Neither of us ever gave an inch, so neither of us ever won the argument. His viewpoint was strictly commercial and mine strictly aesthetic. I couldn't see a tree felled without a definite feeling of loss. The vacant space it left in the skyline haunted me for days. Consequently, I couldn't see anything in the commercial viewpoint that wasn't destructive. The only way Sonny could see a tree 150 feet tall, five feet through on the stump, was felled, bucked, and loaded on a truck to be dumped in the millpond. In spite of these differences, we were married.

Sonny was working for his father at the time, on what was to turn out to be his last gyppo logging operation. Our first home was a seventeen-foot house trailer with lovely Philippine mahogany on the inside and red leatherette on the outside. By the end of the first year of marriage, we had the heady experience of being parents of twins for almost two days, when we were pitched into sorrow by the loss of the smallest twin. Vicki Anne, weighing less than five pounds, was the survivor. Her tiny two-and-a-half-pound sister, Barbara Susan, lived only a day and a half. It was our first and greatest sorrow, but Vicki's rapid gain after her three weeks in the incubator helped a great deal. She soon became the roundest little kewpie of a baby we ever saw. Her eyes turned to a deep shining brown, with flyaway brows, a tiny mouth with upturned corners, and fat rosy cheeks. We thought her the most beautiful baby ever born.

The day we came home from the hospital, Sonny drew his last paycheck from his father's defunct logging operation and used most of it to bail us out.

For the next two years we lived in the trailer house wherever Sonny worked. I washed diapers on the banks of the Skykomish River, on the way to Stevens Pass over the Cascades, and at various other places. At Selleck we parked our shining little trailer house in the midst of a decaying ghost town which had once been a small but prosperous mill town. On the highway leading to the Paradise side of Mount Rainier, not too far from where we now live, Vicki hit me in the mouth with her bottle and broke off one of my best teeth.

It was when we lived on Snoqualmie Pass that an event occurred that Sonny hasn't lived down to this day. Sonny likes his hickory shirts stagged off at the bottom and hemmed, and that time I had nothing on hand but pink thread. Some of his logging cronies still remember and talk about him showing up with his shirttails hemmed in pink.

At the end of two years, Sonny took a job driving cat far back in the mountains, where we couldn't follow him, so we parked our trailer in a vacant lot at the little town of Algona, and Sonny traveled in and out each weekend by train.

During this time we met Mother Morris. She took care of youngsters for working mothers daytimes, and although she was a little dubious about taking on the care of a two-year-old girl, she finally agreed to try it, and I went to work in an office.

Mother Morris and I became fast friends, and soon I became almost a fifth daughter to her. And Vicki became the little granddaughter she had never had, though she had two grandsons.

Once, when Vicki was about four, Mother Morris wrenched her knee. I thought I should take my child to my own mother until she was able to get around again.

"Oh, my goodness, no!" Mother Morris protested. "I really need her now. She can carry notes to my neighbors when I need help—and did you see how she filled my coal scuttle and brought in the kindling?" Sure enough, the little rascal had filled the big coal bucket by taking trip after trip to the woodshed with her little sand bucket, and she then brought in load after load of kindling. Mother Morris' daughter Thelma came out from Seattle every evening after work, but it was Vicki who took care of her during the day, until she was up and around again.

But smoothly as things were going, it wasn't my idea of marriage. I wanted to stay home and take care of my own baby, and have a husband who came home to meals. Nothing could be simpler— but I had married the one man in the world (or so it seemed to me) with whom such an arrangement was impossible.

Once I did manage to lure him away from the woods, but not for long. Finally yielding to my constant "Why must you work at logging? Why can't you come home every night, like other husbands?" he gave in and went to work in the shipyards. It was during the war, and men far less capable than Sonny were working in these alien surroundings. He worked there for exactly three weeks —and they were the longest three weeks of my life. He was miserable.

What made it worse, he worked swing shift. Each night he would come home and keep me awake talking, talking, talking. He hated the crowded regimentation of the shipyards. The concrete sidewalks hurt his feet. (He preferred the deep mud of the woods.) The boss was always breathing down his neck, yet there wasn't enough work to keep all of those thousands of people busy on any eight-hour shift. (Sonny likes to work, and likes the satisfaction of knowing he earns his pay. Besides, being busy makes the time go faster.) Finally, even I could see that the shipyard was no place for that son of a logger.

"Okay—go back to your beloved logging woods," I said. And he did.

I was beginning to realize that a man with a family had a good many years ahead of him as breadwinner, so he should be allowed to follow the work he liked. I had seen too many women dictate the kind of work their husbands should follow, even though it might be tedious and hateful, just because the wife desired it for some reason or another. Since a man had to work and provide for his family, he should have the right to choose the job that made him the happiest. Thank goodness, I had "come to" in time to avoid the crime of depriving him of that right!

So Sonny turned in his brass and went back to the woods. We sold the trailer and bought a lovely old place called Tall Timber, directly across from Grandma Felt, on North Lake. Again, Sonny came home only on weekends, but this time it was worse than before. There was so much to be done around the place that we had little time for enjoyment of each other's company. And I was just as busy catching up on the housework for the week, washing, ironing, baking, and keeping our clothes in shape for the week to come.

The difference was that now we had our own home, in a lovely setting, and I began to feel that we were putting down roots and getting somewhere. But by the end of our first two years on the place I realized that again Sonny and I were at opposite poles, this time in our aims and purposes about our home. It didn't take long for me to realize that all he could see about the place were those lovely tall trees that gave the place its name. He had fairly drooled every time we had driven through the trees over the winding road that wound about on purpose to miss the huge virgin firs. Now I learned that all along he'd been planning how he could outconnive me and log them on his weekends at home!

"Look, Margaret, isn't that one a beaut? Four foot through if it's an inch. Betcha I could get three good number one peelers out of that one," he'd conjecture.

A peeler is a log of good-enough grade and size to be "peeled" into sheets and made into plywood. I had no intention of allowing *my* trees to become plywood panels on someone's wall. They were going to stay right where they were!

"Now what would you have when you got through?" I'd ask him in return. "Just a few bucks in your jeans and a bunch of stumps on our beautiful lots. Can't you ever look at a tree without thinking how it would look all bucked and in the millpond?"

It was the same old argument, and neither of us had yet given in. But Sonny's campaign was the creeping kind that took advantage of every single opening. First, I mentioned wanting a garden. ("Incidentally, I'd still like to have a garden.")

"Of course you shall have a garden," my gyppo

husband agreed. "You'll need more sun, of course.
Nothing could grow under the shade of those big
firs—and that maple standing on the south line
should come down." And before I could get my
breath and voice an objection, he had cut down the
first ones—right across Mr. Day's squashes, which
didn't enhance our relations with our nearest neighbor. Then he cut a smaller fir or two, and I called
a halt. I had a big enough garden patch, thank you.

Next, it was a garage we needed. Sonny decided
that he just *had* to remove at least three trees to
make it safe in case a high wind came along. I protested about the stumps, so he promised to remove
them, too.

By that time Sonny had bought his first cat. At
last he was to have the fun of logging some trees
of his own. He not only removed the stumps, as
he had promised, but in his enthusiasm for the
project he ran right through my pathetic little garden with the cat. I can still see those puny little
sticks and the string, with which my first crop of
pea vines had been held up, disintegrating beneath
those ruthless churning cat tracks. What was worse
was the look of unholy glee on my husband's face
as he happily pursued his favorite occupation.

For some time I withstood the argument he put
up about taking out a weird, fascinating clump of
cedars and hemlock near the edge of the lake. I even
accused him of sacrificing trees in order to get in
good with Mr. Day, for the squashes he had squashed.
His excuse for wanting to cut them was that since
the root system was so shallow and near the water,

that clump of trees might blow down on Mr. Day's porch.

One day in midsummer, as I was swimming away out in the middle of the lake, I happened to look toward shore and saw him cutting trees like mad. I screamed my protests, and headed for shore. By the time I could get there, the first tree had hit the water and they, Sonny and a friend, were starting on another, laughing like a pair of hyenas over how they had outsmarted me.

"Now this is enough!" I exploded. "This has got to stop! You've cut down a dozen trees for what you've called good reason, and if you keep on you're going to positively *ruin* this place!"

"Yes, dear, yes, dear," my logger agreed, and they desisted for the time being. But by that time I was beginning to learn that any time I won an argument about cutting trees, it was only because Sonny was backing up for a better start next time.

It wasn't two months later that our neighbor on the north decided to build himself a little stucco home right in the shadow of the best of the remaining timber on our acre and a half of ground. This neighbor loved trees as much as I. He had never completely cleared his lots, though he had owned them for years. He felt badly about our trees, but said if we would top them he wouldn't worry about a high wind sending them through the roof of his new house.

"Oh, no," said my gyppo, rubbing his hands together, his plans as transparent as glass. "Topping trees kills them eventually, so we'll just take them out."

Sadly, I went out to the entrance to our place and took down the lovely carved sign that said "Tall Timber." The logger had won again.

We didn't make much money on those logs, for he had no way to haul them. So we sold them to a scalper friend of ours, who made the money that might have helped a little to salve my hurt.

This is the prelude to how I came to be driving a heavy truck over a bumpy mountain road at midnight, making a seventy-mile haul from Tacoma back into the heart of the Cascades, where our camp was located. I was bone weary, and was eagerly looking forward to getting into camp and tumbling into bed. I was watching for Sonny, expecting to meet him on his favorite bulldozer, out rebuilding the road from camp after the washouts left by recent hard rains. Still, I wasn't prepared for the strange sight that greeted me as my truck breasted the next hill and drifted down onto the flat where stood the remains of our first logging camp, now abandoned. There was Sonny (judging by the glowing tip of his cigar) behind the controls of his tractor. Just in front of the dozer, with their backs to the wall of a deserted building, cowered a group of men. Evidently they were hunters who had bedded down there for the night, and I guessed that they had been rudely awakened by what they must have taken for a fire-eating monster. I jumped from the truck just in time to hear one of them yell at my husband, "What the hell are you doing, building road at midnight?"

It was a good question, and I couldn't blame him

for wondering. But having been married to a logger for fifteen years, half of them in business for ourselves, I knew the answer. I could simply have said, "He's a gyppo logger," but that wouldn't have told the bewildered hunter much, unless he already knew what it takes to make a gyppo.

You start off with an impulsive, stubborn, hardworking guy who's got the logging virus in his veins; add a couple of pieces of haywire equipment purchased on extended credit; introduce him to a "loggin' show"—a stand of timber—and you've got your gyppo. He's the small businessman of the logging game, the salvage man behind the big logging operations, the go-getter of small operations; and he may have begged, borrowed, or stolen to get his start. In the past there have been plenty of dishonest ones, and there may still be some who'd cheat you out of your last power saw, which accounts for the tainted name of "gyppo." It has even been said that the honest ones go broke faster, which makes all survivors suspect.

At best, the gyppo is underfinanced most of the time. He's continually plagued by forest fires and the hot, dry weather that forces him to suspend operations because of fire hazard; by deep snow and machinery breakdowns; sometimes by a lack of good loggers, or a shortage of flatcars to carry his logs to the mill; and always by a surplus of creditors. To keep his head above water at all, he runs his logging outfit all day, welds his machinery back together between supper and darkness, then, when the moon is up, builds road for the supply truck. But in spite of all his troubles, he can usually grin when someone refers to him as "that damned gyppo."

If he weren't that kind of a guy, he wouldn't be in business at all.

As for his wife ——— Well, it's no life for a softie, but you can bet your bottom dollar that there's never a dull moment!

"Strictly Gyppo"

IT WAS SEPTEMBER, 1945, WHEN SONNY LAUNCHED into business for himself, and I quit my office job to become his handyman. It was inevitable, in view of his background and his years of working for his father's gyppo outfit, that Sonny would become a gyppo too. He disliked working for anyone else. He grew more and more restless as the years of skinning and repairing of cats for other people over the western slopes of the Cascades galled upon him.

"If I could just get some financial backing, I'd buy me a cat and go road building, or get some timber to log," was his frequent plaint.

Helmer Gustafson, one of his best friends, for whom he drove dozer several times, was a logging-road contractor, and Sonny longed to follow in his footsteps. But we didn't have much to offer any bank for security for a loan, and we knew no one with enough private capital who could back us, so we just continued to talk about it without actually making any moves toward doing it.

Finally, in the summer of 1945, I got tired of this same old lament, and suddenly heard myself saying, "Look, my love, what have we got to lose by looking into the possibilities of going into business for ourselves? We've got the equity in our house and lots, and a 1941 automobile. I'm willing to take a chance, if you are. Surely it won't hurt to try."

The words were still echoing in the room when we were on our way. The first banker we talked to informed us that if we would consider buying war surplus equipment he could consider backing us. Sonny shook his head.

"That's nothing but junk," he said tersely. The banker merely shrugged his shoulders and dismissed us.

We went to a second bank, and spoke at length with another banker. He seemed a bit more favorable toward backing us for a start in the land-clearing business. We even made an appointment to have our property appraised. It wasn't much, but it was a toe inside the door, anyway.

On the way home, Sonny suddenly remembered that an old friend of ours, A. B. Joslyn, was going to be a stockholder in a new bank soon to be organized.

"Let's go see him," he suggested. There was no need for me to answer. With my gyppo, to think is to act. I went along for the ride.

A. B. was busily repapering the dining room of his home, and when we came in, he laid aside his paste brush to greet us cordially.

"Glad to see you, Horace, Margaret," he said. "Been cleaning up the house for Mrs. J. Sit down. Sit down." We sat down.

At that time our friendship with A. B. dated back almost ten years. Perhaps it was Sonny's thoughtfulness in making a trip to Cle Elum in 1936 to see A. B. and his wife when they were hospitalized fol-

lowing an auto accident that made him receptive
to our problem that day. He listened kindly to our
ideas and made notes occasionally as we talked to
him. Then he abruptly said, "I think perhaps I could
provide the necessary capital for such a venture."

We were very much surprised, for it was his connection with the new bank we had in mind; not
a personal loan from him. But as it happened, it
was the luckiest break we could possibly have had.
No bank could have extended the lenient credit that
A. B. Joslyn offered us, and has continued to offer
down through the years. He has come to our rescue
time after time when the going got rough. It took
not only a mutual trust, but a good deal of blind
faith for A. B. to invest his money with a couple
of crazy kids who had logging on the brain and a
rugged determination that wouldn't be beaten, even
in the face of almost certain disaster; but without
A. B. we couldn't have gone into business at all,
much less survived the lean years that were to follow.

From September, 1945, to April, 1947, we contracted to clear land, build private roads, and do
preliminary landscape work for literally hundreds
of people. During this period I got a real indoctri-
nation into being a gyppo logger's wife. I took the
place of a truck driver, driving the "whoopee" or
service truck, taking the oil, grease, and fuel oil
from job to job; I even manned the grease pump
from time to time, and greased the rollers on the
cat at night. There were twenty grease fittings on
the track rollers, and other miscellaneous ones Sonny
was very particular about not missing. There was
nothing I disliked more than trying to pump the

lever up and down on a grease gun filled with cold grease, while standing on the foot pedal to keep the gun from flopping over on its side. Good for the waistline, but devilish hard on the disposition. I'd rather have been home washing dishes and ironing clothes any day.

I was also general errand boy, bill collector, and bookkeeper, as well as wife and mother. Vicki Anne went with me almost everywhere, even occasionally when I hauled dynamite. This I usually picked up in my car because—of all reasons—it had better springs! "The better for hauling dynamite," my gyppo said. We would order it by telephone, and then I would drive to Tacoma, take an isolated, twisting road up some gulch far from any habitation, and pick up box after box of 30 per cent stumping powder, big rolls of black fuse, and a tin box or two of percussion caps. I never did find out for certain why this particular powder should be known as "30 per cent."

"Thirty per cent of what?" I asked. But the only answer I ever got was that it represented the strength of the stuff. Sixty per cent is the type they use for blasting rock, so 30 per cent was the type needed for blasting stumps out of the ground. This explanation was given with the patient expression of a good father trying to explain something incredibly simple to a moronic child, so I dropped it.

Whatever its strength, my imagination worked overtime on these little dynamite-gathering expeditions. Every bus, every car, every vehicle on the road seemed headed directly at me and my precious load of dynamite. I always pictured myself being blown sky high without enough left of me to pick up in a basket for decent burial. I once told Sonny that in case such a thing happened, I wanted my old friend Sherm Blackwell, from whom I'd once taken a few flying lessons, to fly over Highway 99 and drop a few rose petals in my memory.

Sonny scoffed at my fears. He handled the powdered death as casually as most people handle powdered milk. In fact, he was an overconfident powder monkey at times. He didn't believe in using a knife or pincers to crimp his fuse into the dynamite caps. He used his teeth. That way, he claimed, you knew just how much pressure you used.

Being present at the setting off of the blasts on a land-clearing job was one thing I always tried to avoid, but I didn't always succeed. Sonny was a firm believer in using lots of dynamite for blowing stumps. He claimed that digging out stumps wrecked a tractor quicker than anything he knew of. Many of the stumps we were called on to remove were from two to four feet across, and had root systems that must have reached to Indo-China, at least.

After he had spent a day or so digging holes under some hoary old stumps and filling said holes generously with dynamite, and attaching caps and fuse, he would take me out with him to act as flagman. (If telephone or electric lines were in the near vicinity, we would first call their servicemen to stand by for possible damage.) I'd hold back the traffic (not always easy to do, as some people were hard to convince of the danger), watching fearfully while my husband and his helper ran from one stump to the other, lighting the long black fuses. The fuses would sputter, and the minutes were short by the time the men had reached the shelter of the tractor or were a safe distance from the area. Before that first stump blew, the seconds seemed endless. Then we would all count the shots as the dirt and debris flew high into the air. Then we'd compare counts. Maybe one wouldn't go off. How long should we wait before investigating? A dormant blast can do considerable damage to an overconfident powder monkey, and after all, I reminded my gyppo, I had but one husband to give to the land-clearing business.

One time Sonny was using an antique knife (a bone-handled pocketknife with a curious little feathered arrow on the metal part) that had been handed down from his great-grandfather, the one who fought on the Confederate side in the Civil War. (It was thought in the family that this knife had been used in disposing of a Yankee or two.) After using it to cut fuse that day, Sonny laid it carelessly on top of the stump he was blasting, and lit the fuse. After he had gained protection under the winch of his cat several yards away, he remembered the knife, and the Hail Columbia I would give him if anything happened to it. He dashed back to the stump, retrieved the knife, and made it safely again to his cat by the time the stump went shooting into the air.

He had many such narrow escapes, not all of which occurred in the course of his work. One of our projects was digging a well on our home place. (When we first moved there, we pumped water for washing and bathroom use from the lake, and carried water for dishes and drinking from our neighbor's well next door.) The deeper we went in digging our well, the more hardpan we hit, and the less sign of water. We had to loosen this rocklike soil by using occasional sticks of dynamite. First, Sonny would drive, by brute strength, an iron bar into the ground; then he placed a stick of dynamite in the hole, attached fuse and cap, and departed for the upper regions via the old ladder and waited for the blast to go off. Then, giving the fumes time to disperse (they give one lovely headaches!) he would again descend to dig out the loosened soil, which he loaded into a bucket for me to pull up with a windlass. (He still claims I dropped it on him once, on purpose, but I can't seem to remember that.) This process was repeated for several monotonous feet, and Sonny got braver and braver with the sticks of dynamite, and took greater chances as the well (or hole, rather) got deeper.

One day he placed four sticks of dynamite in a big hole and lit the fuse. The fuse was short, but it would do, he decided. He made a leap for the ladder. The first rung gave way. His feet dangled right above the sputtering fuse. He lunged again. The second rung broke. Then he began to get a bit worried. He considered smothering the sputtering fuse, but the instinct to get away from the danger was stronger. The ladder was old and shaky —and Sonny was getting that way fast! Later, he said he wouldn't have given a plugged nickel for his chances when that second rung broke.

His third try for footing on the ladder was successful, and he made it to the top of the twenty-five-foot well just as the blast went off. Whoosh!

The ladder came out of the well almost the second he stepped off onto solid ground. He certainly had his guardian angel working overtime that day. It was Sunday, too!

I didn't blame him a bit when he walked over to his dozer, started the motor, and began scooping up dirt to fill in the dry well. We continued carrying our water from the next-door neighbor, and I shifted my activities to secretaryship of the association for getting our own cooperative water system. Two years later, we succeeded.

Sonny knew his dynamite much too well for the comfort of his more scary friends. One time a group of friends came up to camp to spend the weekend. It proved to be one they'd never forget. They ate vast quantities of steak and sweet corn on the cob, drank copiously of the cold beer, fed the corncobs to the big black bear that was hanging around camp at that time, and just had a good time generally. When the fun waned a bit, Sonny brought out his favorite "firecrackers," attached fuse and cap, laid them out in the open on stumps, and lit the fuse. The noise was greater than the danger, and Sonny laughed like a fiend at our weekend guests huddling in the dining room, waiting for his return to normal, afraid to go to bed or step outside.

It was even more fun to wait until Cookie or someone was in the john, and then set off a stick right behind it, and see the occupant come bursting out, wild-eyed with terror. Another time, it took just one unlighted stick of dynamite tossed in the middle of the table to clear the dining room double-quick, so the cook could get the dishes washed.

Weekends were no occasion for rest. It merely became the time when we could catch up things on the homeplace. What time wasn't required for repairing equipment was spent in digging out stumps and leveling and improving our lots. When Sonny's chokerman wasn't around, I was called in to pinch-hit. Sometimes I was the lowly chokerman and he was the important cat skinner. Other times I was the lowly cat skinner while he bossed things from the ground where he choked the logs. Had I been aware of the insidious campaign underlying these requests for "a hand," I would never have climbed on the seat of a cat or set a choker.

As it was, such terms as "choking a log," "going ahead on the main line," "yarding in a turn," became familiar to my ears. But that terrible profanity that loggers excel in using!—I would look skyward at such outbursts and wonder if there would be a side door to heaven for loggers to slip into, where the use of the Lord's name in vain wouldn't be judged by normal standards.

In addition to my daytime duties in the land-clearing business and being pressed into the mechanical department after hours, or on Saturday when I was trying to pay a bit of attention to my house and child (but with poor results), things like this were always happening. I'd just get a batch of cookies in the oven when I'd hear a call from the yard. "Hey, Ma, come help me."

The first few times, I dropped everything and ran, thinking he was caught under something and needed help; but I soon wised up. Thereafter, I'd merely wipe the flour off my hands and walk out warily to where a pair of calked boots were sticking out from beneath the small dozer. Then something like this would happen:

"Yes, dear, what do you want?" (Knowing very well I wasn't going to like it.)

"I wantcha to drive the cat back and forth so I can see how the dofunny goes around the dingle-fuss." His voice was muffled from his position far underneath the cat, but I got the idea.

"With you under there? Oh, no!"

This brought my well-greased, be-dieseled husband from under his ailing tractor. I noted with no pleasure that he had some new holes in his good stagged-off hickory shirt, eaten, no doubt, by battery acid. That morning, he had been almost presentable-looking in clean shirt and jeans. (It always irked him to have me "wash the life out" of his stagged-off jeans, as he expressed it, but I still did it often enough to provide him with clean clothes.) Now, he ran greasy hands through his standing-up hair and glared at me, his brown eyes almost black in his sudden temper.

"I don't wantcha to run over me. I just want you to drive the cat back and forth in the same place. Can'tcha do that for me?" He was the patient papa again, and I the not-too-bright child. So I held onto my dress skirt with one hand, trying to keep as clean as possible (a physical impossibility around a cat, and I knew it), climbed upon the tracks and around the steering levers, and sat down heavily in the cat seat. I was hoping this wouldn't be as disastrous as the time two weeks before, when I stopped the cat by slipping the clutch, and burned all the facing off. I'd had no choice when the gully behind me had yawned as deep as Grand Canyon and I didn't know for sure how to stop the thing. That fiasco had lowered my husband's regard for my intelligence, however, and earned me the dubious title of "grease monkey" as we stood on our heads for nearly fourteen hours, taking out the burned clutch and replacing it.

Now, Sonny pushed the starter for me, after making sure it was out of gear, and refreshed my memory on where first gear forward and low reverse could be found. So I ran it forward and backward, with my husband lying supinely beneath the belly of the thing, nervously watching his feet appear as I went forward and disappear as I went backward. By the time he yelled at me to stop, I was a nervous wreck. After he pushed himself out from under the cat, and was safely standing beside me, I began to climb off.

"Just another minute — I want to tighten this sprocket nut. Drive it ahead a few feet," he ordered.

Oh, no! That was the little deal that had brought about my trouble before, with the clutch.

"But I've got cookies in the oven," I protested.

"It won't take but two jerks of a dead lamb's tail," he assured me. So I sighed and put the cat in low gear, watching his hands for signals. He was using the flat iron wrench he had designed for tightening sprocket nuts which utilized for turning power the forward movement of the tractor, while all he had to do was hold them with the wrench.

My cookies were burning. I could smell them.

"I want to put the blade on now, so just guide

the cat between the dozer arms. Won't take a minute," he said. This time, I yelled at him.

"Are you kiddin'? I couldn't guide this thing between the house and the garage, and they're thirty
feet apart! Besides my cookies are burning! Can't
you smell them?"

Sonny sniffed the air in the direction of the house,
and shook his head. So I set my mouth in that grim
line my temper bring on, and jammed the cat into
first gear again. But one look at the tiny space between the waiting dozer blade arms, and a second
one at my husband's face, told me I'd better take
it easy or I'd never get back to my cookies.

Gently—so very gently—I eased the cat forward,
calling upon all my half-knowledge of operating
automobiles, trucks and tractors, and inched between
those two dozer arms, surprising even myself. I
jiggled the connecting arms on the cat up and down
until Sonny could slip the pins into place; then I
jerked the gearshift into neutral and bailed down
off that cat. I'd had it!

From my kitchen black smoke was rolling in a
heavy cloud, which was soon joined by blue smoke
from me as I deposited the charred cookies in the
sink. My husband came in just in time to hear what
I thought of cats *and* loggers *and* one woman's logger in particular. He chuckled.

"Now just what good would a skinny little cookie-
bakin' woman do me in my business? Couldn't drive
a cat, or help me lift a gas barrel or a cat battery.
Bet it isn't every woman who can drive a cat and
put it between the dozer arms on the first try. Most
cat skinners can't do that well." So he went on

sweet-talking until first thing I knew I was over my "mad" and was laughing over the charred cookies. To be certain the next batch would be good, I'd make him sit still a few minutes while they baked the proper length of time. Then he ate most of them, and I wasn't any farther ahead.

At the time we went into business, World War II was just over, and the discharged veterans were beginning to come home. We learned to know a good many of those men during the next few years as they worked for us. We also learned a lesson in buying equipment, that fall of 1945.

Our first bulldozer, a tractor with dirt-moving blade, we purchased second hand from a private party, and it was a good deal which we never had reason to regret. It was the purchase of a ton-and-a-half truck that taught us never to pay the full amount in cash for a second-hand piece of equipment from a dealer of doubtful reputation.

In the first place, the truck was not supposed to have been war surplus equipment. I don't remember whether the title showed this fact, or whether we overlooked it, or just what happened; anyway, the red paint began to peel off about the same time Sonny discovered the motor wasn't powerful enough to haul the little cat up a hill on a trailer.

Our fruitless visits to the dealer brought me my first real rebuff from a businessman. He told me he preferred to do business with my husband, and asked me to wait out in the car. I finally retired, sulking, to the car, but not before I had finished what I had to say about his kind and his ancestors. I think it must have been at about this point in

my career that I began to develop that thick hide
and long memory that served me so well throughout
the years. The next step was stuffing my pride in
my pocket—but that came later.

The equipment dealer refused to do anything about
that truck, and thereby gained the dubious distinction
of becoming the first on our Abominable list. He
wasn't the last, either, for we ran across a few others
of the same caliber in the same business. They pulled
a variety of tricks in their professional leeching off
the small, underfinanced businessman, the farmer,
the logger, and the road contractor. In one case,
a friend of ours had this same dealer sell a cat for
him. He sold it on a commission, for far more than
he reported to the contractor, keeping not only the
commission on the amount he reported but the whole
of the difference. Our only defense against such
characters was to remember such acts and pass the
word to others in our kind of business.

We eventually traded off our lame duck to a
mechanic friend of ours for a truck of much older
vintage with dump body and hoist. We lost about
six hundred dollars on this deal, but the new truck,
though much slower of motor, was more reliable.

We often remarked that we went into business
too late to make any of the big money in either
land clearing or logging. Such services had been at
a premium during the war because both men and
machines were hard to get. The best money Sonny
ever made while working for wages was during the
war, driving bulldozer on a government land-clearing
project. It lasted only three months, but we made

marvelous progress in paying off our debts and re-modeling our house.

After we went into business for ourselves, Sonny drove his own bulldozer for some time before the union caught up with him and demanded that he hire a driver. We preferred to break in our own driver rather than take one the union hall sent out, and it cost us nothing but money. There were broken springs, tracks, winch lines, clutches, brakes, and dozer arms. Finally our man emerged a good cat skinner. Then we got a second cat, which Sonny drove himself until the union came around again.

I think I can safely say that our first trouble in meeting our payments began when we had to hire men, under orders from the union. If Sonny and I could have run the little outfit we had at first, we would have avoided so much more indebtedness so many headaches, so many heartaches.

I have always thought it a violation of a man's rights when the union says he cannot operate his own equipment. The union doesn't help to pay for that equipment, or keep it in running order. It may provide more employment, but in our case, with one tractor, we were able to make the payments and make a living when Sonny did his own driving. With a driver, we had to pay his wages, make payments, and our own living expenses. It was impossible to do. So one tractor led to another, and another, and more liability, and more and bigger jobs, until we were forced to decide that land clearing wasn't the business for us.

"A-Logging We Will Go"

OUR NEXT MOVE WAS, OF COURSE, TO GO LOGGING. Common sense told me that. But I still hadn't changed my viewpoint about logging in the least.

The first boy I ever went steady with was a big-shouldered young logger who felled timber for a living. Then, when my folks moved from the Olympic Peninsula to southern King County, about thirty miles south of Seattle, I again found myself surrounded by loggers and sons of loggers—and in logging country. My friendship with Sonny began with an argument on the relative merits of logging and conservation, lasted through a stormy courtship which resulted in marriage, and it has been going on ever since.

Great slashed scars in the evergreen cover of the foothills of the Olympic and Cascade mountain ranges had warped and twisted my viewpoint almost beyond reason—from the logger's point of view, of course. The ruthless slashing manner in which they seemed to go into a majestic stand of timber, leaving only ugliness behind, convinced me that they were despoilers of nature, robbers of our natural resources, and completely lacking in appreciation for beauty. Barren hills, covered with the vast devastation of blackened stumps, and gaunt, unfelled snags, were tragic to me. I couldn't listen to the arguments from the logger's point of view. I often refused even to talk about it, for fear my extreme prejudice would be ridiculed.

It was with full awareness of these facts that Sonny came home one day in April, 1947, with news of a salvage logging job. At one of the big mills in Tacoma he had run across an old friend of his father. Said friend held a very good position with the company which was destined to become the Big Company in our lives for the next seven years, and he had an experiment in salvage logging in mind, for which he needed a guinea pig. Sonny had walked right into his arms.

Sonny was enthusiastic about any kind of a logging job, even if they did call it "salvage" logging. Both he and A. B. Joslyn looked it over. It was at the three-thousand-foot elevation, but during the previous winter they had lost only three weeks' work because of snow. (To my knowledge, that was the last winter on record, until we left there, that there was a more or less "open" winter.) To Sonny and A. B., it looked like a good deal. We were to get paid by the cord for logging all the hemlock and white fir marked for us by the forester who worked for Mr. Cutting Rights, as well as the down stuff, windfalls, and chunks.

Land clearing I could see some merit in, and even building roads for a logging company, perhaps; but when Sonny saw that anti-logging glint in my eye, he brought forth all the old diplomacy. He explained very carefully that the proposed job would be a method of conserving, *not* depleting, the timber supply. In that light, I could readily agree to have a try at it. I think the hope was still there, in the back of my mind, that perhaps Sonny would learn to be a little less commercial about logging, and would veer slightly more to my idealistic view. And he was likely thinking that this might be an entering wedge to convincing me that logging could be an honorable occupation.

So it was for entirely different reasons that we put our shoulders to the wheel again and went into the gyppo logging phase of our business.

A. B. backed us in the purchase of a third cat, a donkey, and a shovel loader. After this equipment was purchased, put in shape, and shipped, we plunged into the "sticker" of the deal; that of putting in and maintaining a boarding camp for our crew. This was to be just a temporary arrangement, the Big Company representative told us; just a year or so, until we moved in closer to their operation; then we could send our men to their camp to board and room. In the meantime they would send us out three old railroad cars that we could utilize for a camp of sorts, and put in a spur for them to stand on.

Judging from the looks of them, those three old railroad cars had seen service on the first railroad into the Pacific Northwest. There was a boxcar, variously used as a dynamite car and "crummy" to haul the men to work in earlier days; a baggage car, which must have been a resplendent thing in its day, with high domed ceiling (the devil's own, when it came to kalsomining it), and dozens of coats of dark red paint on the outside. The third car, a vile green by contrast to the diner, was a caboose, complete with cupola and rear platform with iron railing. After looking them over thoroughly, A. B. said he could make them do. He divided the caboose into two small compartments, one for the Felt family and one for the cook. In the dining car, he built false platforms to make the entrance smoother, and above the porch, to give pressure, he hoisted a three-hundred-gallon steel tank to be used in the gravity water system. Then he divided the car into a kitchen, in which he built cupboards and installed plumbing and a sink; a long dining room with a twenty-foot table and benches and, on the end nearest the kitchen, more cupboards and counter space. The small room at the opposite end from the kitchen was used at one time by the bull cook and another time for a head loader and his wife who cooked for us. On one side, with a door leading out from the dining room, he built a storeroom.

The crummy became a bunkhouse for eight men. The overflow was housed in tents.

It was no small chore to build such a setup into a logging camp for the convenience and semi-comfort of some sixteen or eighteen people, counting visitors, cook, bull cook, and the Felt family. Then, we had to equip it. This job fell largely to me. A. B. and I went shopping for—and found—a surplus light generating plant, which was a real stroke of luck. We also bought a big range, which we equipped with an oil-burning pot and electric fan, and a refrigerator which one of our friends had built for sale. It was a duo-temperature box, with a thirty-five-degree compartment and a freezing compartment. Besides these large items, we had to buy such things as bedding, dishes, utensils, electrical wiring, beds, groceries, stoves for heating, and all that miscellany of stuff that came to be known on the books as "camp supplies and equipment."

If you had followed us on our many treks to and from the mountain camp that first year, you would have sworn we were moving an entire village. Picture a heavily laden truck rattling its way along the twisting logging road leading to our camp, followed by a red pickup (well named). A bump, a chuckhole, and a piece of lumber falls by the wayside. The red pickup stops; the driver (me) gets out and picks up the lumber and places it carefully with a number of other items in the pickup bed, then gets back in and proceeds, watching carefully the truck driver's load ahead. By the time we reach camp I have more stuff on my truck than Sonny has on his. He was always in a hurry, and could never take the time to tie his load down securely. We hauled in tar paper, nails, glass windows, old doors, a toilet seat, a sink, tents, rope, cable, axes, saws, stovepipe, aluminum roofing for the donkey engine and drums, meat, vegetables, nuts, bolts, light bulbs, and fuel oil. Sonny named it, I bought it, and A. B. paid for it. My gyppo made many trips over those rough roads with me, and I think he enjoyed every minute of the excitement.

At last, on July 11, our camp was ready for occupancy. The sink drain worked beautifully; so well, in fact, that Sonny warned everybody to be careful lest he or she be drawn right down the pipe. The big eighty-gallon hot-water tank supplied hot

water to a fare you well; the beds were all made
up, and we were ready for the crew to arrive. I
can still hear Sonny, as he bustled about our small
new domain, humming in his tuneless little way:
"A-loggin' we will go, a-loggin' we will go, Hi-O
the Derrio, a-loggin' we will go."
I had never seen him so happy and content. Maybe, I thought, it was worth the sacrifice of a few
principles—especially such unpopular ones as mine
—to see him like this.

That first year I couldn't tell a good logger by
the cut of his clothes the way my husband declared
he could. I'd call Archie MacDougall in Seattle and
tell him to send out a set of fallers, and he'd send
out the nearest man at hand, good, bad, or indif-
ferent. He didn't have much choice. Men were
scarce and on the move. They had found a new
independence during the war years, and were hard
to interest in any job for any length of time. This
was rough on the gyppo. Although he was willing
to pay more for good men if they would stay and
produce, the loggers merely shrugged their shoulders
and said, "Sure, sure, he pays more—but dammitall,
he expects you to work harder than the bigger
outfits."
That was true, and a hardworking man was hard
to find. But the day finally came when the man
who, in that first season, threw down his gloves in
the middle of the day and walked off the job came
back begging for that same job back. By that time
we had, through trial and error, established the
nucleus of a permanent crew.

Before that was accomplished, however, we hired and rehired, fired and refired, loggers. We were always willing to give them a chance, and occasionally even a second chance. My call to Archie for a pair of fallers once brought us a pair of cowboys, complete with boots and ten-gallon hats. The heels of their cowboy boots clicked on the rails as they got out of the speeder, and someone stuck his head out and called, "Where's the corral?" We gave them a fair chance, but when it turned out that they didn't know one end of a power saw from the other, and had felled only one tree by noon, Sonny let them go.

Another time, Archie sent up a sailor. He brought an early end to his employment by almost getting himself killed. Sonny was having no blood on his hands with inexperienced help, so he "made 'er out."

More than once I picked up a couple of men Archie had sent at the local bus depot, only to find them only half sobered up. If they had a few shekels left in their pockets, I would have to round them up out of a tavern every time I made a stop. Between the fumes of snoose and stale beer, and a pair of "corks" (calked boots) falling down off the seat behind to hit me on the head, I would be about ready to hand in my own resignation by the time we got to camp.

In spite of Archie and me, however, Sonny did finally get enough of a crew to operate full-handed most of the time.

My first job, however, even before the men were

started on their logging operations, was that of camp cook.

Undoubtedly the most important person in an isolated logging camp such as ours is the cook. Lots of good, plain food, served on time, was all they desired. It made all the difference between a happy crew and a grumbling one and, in turn, the disposition of the logging crew affected the log production. The ideal situation, however, was not always easily achieved.

Since it was the middle of the season, and the labor market was as tight in the camp cook department as it was in the loggers', it was a week before the cook we had hired could come to camp.

I can truthfully say that that week I pinch-hit for the cook was one of the most miserable of my life. Any other time I might have taken it in my stride, but at that time I was slightly (four months) pregnant, and everything I attempted seemed to assume exaggerated proportions.

My talents had never run to cooking, for my mother had always said of my clumsy attempts, "I'd rather do it myself than watch you struggle with it." Of course, since my marriage I had practiced up some on Sonny. Now, confronted with having to keep an entire logging crew well fed and contented, Sonny's years of experience in logging camps came in mighty handy. He knew such things as how to set the table with setups (sugar, salt, pepper, butter, bread, for every four men), and why the cups must be turned upside down on each plate. He knew how much pancake dough to mix up, and how many cakes to have baked ahead before ringing the breakfast bell; and he knew what food to serve, and how.

One of the first things he did was grab the plates out of the warming oven, where I had put them, with a brusque, "Godelmighty, don't warm their plates! You'll spoil them, and loggers are hard enough to please as it is!"

When he ordered a dozen pies at a time, I was almost frozen in my tracks. I could turn out one or two—but twelve! But I did it.

When I insisted upon salads, Sonny declared them unnecessary. But the loggers seemed to like salads of almost every kind and description, so I won that round.

In my awkward way I got things done. The food was cooked and put on the table, and there were no complaints—but then came the aftermath. My back ached, my ankles swelled, and the sink overflowed with dishes. Even so, it might have been bearable if it hadn't been gnat season, and those blamed no-see-ums attacked me in full force, often rendering me almost helpless with their burning, relentless stinging. One night Sonny found me almost in tears. He took pity on me and dried the dishes and put them away. Then he tenderly led me off to my bed.

"That cook had better show up tomorrow," he said grimly. "You can't do this work much longer."

"Oh, I can do it," I told him wearily. "If only those blessed gnats would leave me alone!" Then I cried myself to sleep, scratching my bites and wishing I were anywhere but in Felt's logging camp.

The days when I had dreamed of being a writer seemed far, far away, in another world.

It was with real joy that I saw the cook arrive the following morning on the speeder. He was an odd-looking man, with a long scar torturing one side of his face, running from his eye to his chin. In one hand he carried a black satchel, and in the other a black steel tool case. He took over the duties of the cook easily, and with evidence of long practice began putting a roast together, rolling out pie dough, and fixing his vegetables. It was obvious that he was well in control of the situation, and I could have flung my arms around him in sheer gratitude for my liberation. Now I could go home, rest up from the past weeks of planning, building, and equipping this gyppo camp and getting it started, and just be a housewife and mother while waiting for my baby. What fun Vicki and I would have, getting ready for the little newcomer!

I did leave shortly—with a fistful of instructions for supplies, parts, fallers, gas, diesel, and tar paper. The coming of the cook had released me for my old job of driving truck and being supply sergeant again.

Hospitality at a logging camp is the accepted thing, and our camp was no exception. We always had a pot of coffee on the stove, fresh pie or cake, large bowls of fruit; and if the passerby made it at mealtime, he was welcome to stay and join us. But there was one time when we failed to be hospitable to some unexpected "guests."

I was away at the time, so didn't actually see it, but this is how it was told to me: Someone, either a recently fired logger or a mischievous rumormonger, reported to the game wardens that we served nothing but venison at our logging camp. Since it was during the summer, and definitely out of season, the game wardens had to investigate. But they must have needed a feather in their caps or something, because they made a big production out of raiding our little backwoods logging camp. A couple of them came from as far as fifty miles away to get in on the "big raid."

Four wardens drove up by auto, then stole quietly through the woods and brush to "surround" the camp; then they converged from all four directions upon our unsuspecting little cookshack.

Sonny was sitting in the dining room, drinking coffee and eating fresh doughnuts the cook had just sugared and laid out in fragrant rows. One warden came through the side door of the dining room, two from the kitchen door, and another from the opposite end of the dining room. Nobody said "We've got you covered!" but that was the impression they gave.

Sonny took his elbows off the table, looked them over calmly, and asked them what they wanted. They told him, and added, "We'll have to search this place."

"Got a search warrant?" Sonny asked. He knew a couple of the men. No, they had no search warrant, but since we ran a public eating place, they didn't need one.

"I don't run a public eating place, and I do think you need a search warrant, but go ahead anyway," Sonny said. And they did so, quite thoroughly, even looking behind the outhouses and beneath the bunk-houses. Then they came back, opened the refrigerator, and began slamming the beef and veal out onto the meat block.

"We try to keep our food fit for human consumption here," Sonny reminded them. The warden just kept mumbling to himself that this *looked* like venison, and by gosh, he knew we *served* venison. The purple stamp of government-inspected meat was in plain sight on the loin of baby beef the man was handling, so Sonny just grinned, shrugged his shoulders, and went back to drinking his coffee and eating his doughnuts.

Finally the wardens gave up, but they were quite unhappy about it. They hadn't found a trace of venison on the place.

"All I can say for you guys is you're darn lucky my wife isn't here," Sonny informed them. "She'd not only show you the receipts from the packing house in Tacoma where she bought all that meat, but she'd likely take a cleaver to you for handling it the way you did. We have to eat it, you know." He smacked his lips over another fresh doughnut.

The wardens looked unhappy, and eyed those delicious doughnuts hungrily.

"How about a cup of coffee, Felt?" one of them asked.

Sonny looked him over coolly. "I told you I'm not running a public eating house," he pointed out. "I hear there are a couple down on the highway, though, about twenty miles or so from here."

The wardens left empty-handed and still hungry. We were never bothered again, nor did we ever turn anyone else away hungry.

Salvage or Scavenge Logging

WE SOON FOUND OUT WHY THE BIG COMPANY WAS so anxious to get us into their timber. It was rough terrain, at the end of twenty-five miles of railroad. They wanted to experiment with salvage logging, but they didn't want to lose money on the deal. The solution: a contract logger to take the risk. If *he* went broke, so what?

That little "so what" was of great concern to us.

The two parties involved in this timber-cutting deal were Mr. Cutting Rights and the Big Company. Mr. Cutting Rights was the man who gave us to understand that he still retained control over the cutting rights of this timber, although he had sold the holdings—the railroad, hotel, camp, and all equipment—to the Big Company. The Big Company owned the mill in Tacoma which would utilize the available and merchantable timber on this land, and pay the man who still (according to him) owned the cutting rights. We were the little Operation Experiment in the deal between these two powerful forces, and we soon came to know just how little and insignificant we really were.

Our salvage operation covered an area that had been logged several times previously. First they had taken out the best grade old-growth peeler logs; then, down through the years, the lesser grades, until only the salvage and seed trees were left. "Salvage" was supposed to be the taking out of the usable snags, some mature white fir, considerable hemlock, and all of the down stuff that could be utilized.

This sounded fine, until we found that the forester representing Mr. Cutting Rights, and the superintendent representing the Big Company, were not always in agreement. When we had been sold on this salvage logging deal, it was the Big Company's representative who had led us to believe that much more of this type of timber could be used than they would later accept and pay for.

My first rude awakening came at the end of the first month of logging, when I went in to collect a check I had figured should be close to $3,200. Although I had drawn a couple of times, we had shipped a good many carloads of logs, and we should have had more than enough left to meet our first big payroll. By the time the scaler with the long thumb got through with our loads, however, the check was a mere $267!

The shock was almost more than I could take. All I could see was a three-thousand-dollar payroll due the next day, and only five hundred dollars with which to meet it. Whether it was the tears I barely managed to control with frequent trips to the washroom, or the sheer enormity of our situation, I finally arranged for an advance payment on next week's logs. This relieved our immediate dilemma, but it also was the road to bankruptcy. Being in debt to

the Big Company—*any* Big Company—has broken
more loggers than can be told.

It was the first step on the downward road into
debt to the Big Company. It was a number of
years before we actually paid off our obligation in
full. We were one of the few gyppo outfits who
did pay off, and one of the very few who kept our
equipment out from under mortgage to them. Several times during the next few years, the subject
of "security" was broached, but we never would
give in, and they didn't insist to the point of breaking our contract. It was a tenuous agreement for
both of us. They gave us work year after year so
we could get out of debt to them, and we stayed
with them so we could accomplish that same purpose.

But that first day I went back to camp and made
out the paychecks from Sonny's time book, and paid
the men for the month of July. We looked at each
other gravely across the green field desk he had
bought from a surplus store, and I think it struck
both of us at the same time that our position was
really rough. Looking back, I think it was the first
time that both of us were "down" at the same time.
We took turns. When Sonny was low, I was pur-
posely gay, and when I was down, he would slap
my dejected shoulders and cry, "Cheer up, Mama,
we'll make out all right!"

But that day, neither of us said anything.

About the middle of August my doctor asked me
if I was still driving a car. I told him I ran the de-
livery service to camp, seventy miles from home,
plus side trips to Tacoma, Seattle, and way points.

When he learned that the last twenty miles was over rough mountain road, he threw up his hands in alarm. Then, pulling his glasses down on his aquiline nose, his dark eyes snapping at me over the top of them, he forbade me to make like a truck driver beyond the end of the pavement.

"And in another month you'd better stop that business altogether," he said. "The idea—rough mountain roads—logging——" He went off mumbling to himself.

Secretly, his ruling made me happy. My own bed at home was much more comfortable than the one at camp, in the end of the caboose, and the roads had been getting me down. The turns and twists in that last twenty miles of logging road had multiplied beyond all reason, and the height from the road to the bottom of the canyon had trebled, at least. For some reason my heart had taken up permanent abode at the place where my tonsils should have been.

Sonny showed some disappointment in me. He seemed to think I could carry on up to the very last minute. (That's the trouble with being as big as a cow; no one believes you should take care of yourself.) I hastily assured him that I could still do a good deal of the business by telephone, when I could no longer get beneath the wheel of the car.

But there were strings on it. I agreed to keep on with my old job of running errands and running the business for the company if he would agree to my taking three days a week of writing classes at the university in Seattle. I'm sure he had fondly believed I had forgotten all about my idea of being a writer, and was surprised to find that it was still lurking in the back of my mind, only waiting for an occasion like this to spring forth again.

Early in the spring I had read in a Seattle newspaper that the University of Washington had established a reading bureau where, for a fee, they would read and criticize manuscripts. I sent in fifteen thousand words, and how Dr. George Savage ever found the least germ of writing ability in that mess I'll never know. He called me in for an interview, and talked to me about coming that summer for classes in novel writing. Before I could definitely act upon it, however, we went into the logging business, I became pregnant, and between the two events my time was thoroughly occupied. Now, with the doctor's admonition to "take it easy," the writing bug came to the front again.

Our "little stranger" was a good sport about the whole thing. "It" became used to driving over rough roads, and sleeping on poor beds; to listening to dry lectures at college, and to the tall tales of loggers at camp. We went fishing in the big swamp, and walking on the campus. (In fact, said expected was a much better sport about the whole thing than I, but we managed.) I often think that if children can be marked before birth, our youngest had an excellent opportunity. It is no wonder she can pick herself up from a hard fall and grin at her bruises. She has always been able to take things in her small fat stride.

So my baby and I stuck it out that first summer.

Before his first month was up, signs of dissatisfaction with the new cook began to sift through. The crew began muttering such epithets as "greaseball" in the direction of Scarface. The New York cuts of steak off the hind quarters of beef were disappearing, as well as entire barrels of gasoline. Somehow he was managing to load a fifty-gallon barrel of gasoline into the back end of his old coupé by himself. Someone told me later that his method of scrubbing the kitchen consisted of sluicing the floor with a bucket of water whenever A. B. or my husband was about to arrive. Perhaps it was the supply of sharp knives he kept in that black tool case, or the manner in which he wielded that wicked-looking cleaver—or just because cooks were scarce that Sonny kept him on longer than he wanted to. Then we had a bit of fortune. The head loader's wife was a good cook and looking for a job. We took a quick trip to see her, hired her, and telephoned Scarface not to return to camp that Sunday night.

Myrtle was a good cook but could only work as long as her husband felt like staying with us. When he quit we were without a cook again. Things were looking desperate with me so pregnant. Then we had an inspiration. My sister hadn't had any experience cooking in a camp but she was available so she took on the job for the rest of the season.

She soon gained great popularity with the loggers. She had been christened Mildred, nicknamed Midge by our father, but to the loggers she became Cookie. They not only began bringing her tokens of their regard like a bouquet of wild tiger lilies from the woods or a string of fish, or perhaps a lunch bucket filled with wild huckleberries, but they began to tell her tall tales of the woods.

In her naïveté she actually believed some of the fantastic stories that Morgan told her. "How'd those big dead trees get so twisted? Well, Honechile, I'll tell you. They were twisted that way by the rachetowl. What's a rachetowl? Why a rachetowl is a very special kind of owl equipped with a rachet set just above his ankles. You know what a rachet wrench is—like what the boss uses to get hard-to-reach nuts of his bulldozer—well, this owl has got the same sort of attachment. He just flies over the forest until he finds a young delicate tree and then he flies down, lights on it, and sets his rachet on it and gives it a quick twist, and there you got it; a twisted tree. Unfortunately, the tree grows up only to die earlier than any of the others in the woods, with its circulation cut off that way," he ended sadly.

When Cookie looked a bit dubious, he asked, "Haven't you ever seen a barn owl twist its head around until you thought he'd twist it right off?" Of course she had, so Morgan declared that proved his point. He looked so truthful, and had such an air of injured innocence at her disbelief, that Cookie never knew whether to believe him or not. It was some time before she found out that lightning had killed those trees after twisting them so brutally.

On one occasion even I had to give credence to one of Morgan's stories. I had driven up one night with a new sheet-iron stove, which I hadn't been able to unload. When I went out in the morning, I found the stove all dented and scarred by the claws of a bear. Some of the bread and butter, and a half of a slab of bacon were also missing.

"Saw a big black bear running off across the flat with a loaf of bread under one arm and a slab of bacon under the other," Morgan told me, dead pan as usual.

It was about this time that I started spending some time and thought upon my views on "equal rights," so-called, and if I was really being wise in demanding mine. I began to lay all the chips right out on the table and look them over. So you wanted to be treated as an equal in the business world, Mrs. Felt? Okay, so you've achieved it—along with an occasional rebuff from some businessman who refused to do business with a woman. So you wanted an equal say in your husband's business, Mrs. Felt? Okay, you've got it. The trouble is, you got a lot more than you bargained for, didn't you? Who stretches the money, who pays the bills, the wages, and taxes? Who meets the creditors, and talks for extensions on loans and notes? Yeah, and who does without, so the truck can have a new tire and the tractors new tracks? You do, Mrs. Felt. And who feels guilty because she doesn't feel well enough (because she's pregnant) to drive that load of lumber to the logging camp? How much better off this "feminist" would have been to have sat on a cushion and sewed a fine seam, and there was no time like the present to start!

By the end of each week I would just about have myself talked into taking the female road from here on, then Sonny would come home for the weekend.

He soon learned to know when one of my "difficult" turns of mind was about to make itself felt, and with that little sideways glance of his, he would begin his campaign.

"Guess there aren't many guys got a wife who can drive truck and load gas barrels and cat batteries, and yet be smart enough to run the business," he'd say. "And Lord, the way you carry a baby, no one would even suspect you're 'that way.' " Then, after getting me all softened up, he'd say, "Hon, I wish you'd go see the banker tomorrow about another loan." (And if there's anything I loathe, it's seeing bankers about loans!) But what could I say? He knew from the beginning that I'd do what he asked. He accepted me as a full partner; I could do no less. Besides, Washington is a community-property state, with a law that says a wife shall have 50 per cent of her husband's property. It also says she shall share his debts. So it was a case of sink or swim together.

Another strike against me is that I am not exactly the petite feminine type. I am tall, for a woman, and on the big-boned, husky side, with broad shoulders and deep bosom that make it difficult for me to even buy clothes that fit well. My complexion, hair, and eyes are all about the same shade of light brown (my skin a trifle lighter), and I have a wide mouth, turned-up nose, broad forehead, high cheekbones, and a determined chin. (The chin is that with which I am usually leading.) Horace is about the same height as I, but we are built so differently that he seems shorter than I. He is long of torso, somewhat heavyset, and short of arm and leg. I'm just the opposite. His complexion is several shades lighter than mine, although his hair and eyes are almost black, and he has a steady way of looking at you from those merry dark eyes, set wide apart beneath arched black brows, that he inherited directly from his grandfather Horace Felt, along with his name. His nose is somewhat stubby, his mouth generous, and when he grins that quick grin of his, and gives you a sideways glance, you know there's some devilment afoot.

My classes in Creative Writing at the university during that period were a source of great happiness to me, and made the time whiz by much faster. Sonny still kept in touch with me when I was in Seattle on class days, for there were errands I could take care of while there, so I never actually shook responsibility for our business. I had to make at least one call every week for loggers, to Archie MacDougalls, since we were having a big turnover of men that first season. Archie took special interest in our little outfit, as Sonny had hired out of his agency for several years. Archie was pulling for him in his own logging venture; also he was vastly amused by Sonny's prospects of a son to carry on his business. (Even after our second daughter was born, Archie addressed all mail to us "H. Felt & Sons." I don't believe my gyppo ever fully appreciated Archie's sense of humor.)

The autumn season took its time about arriving that year. I was beginning to get restless and impatient. I eased my aches and pains with frequent hot showers, wallowing in self-pity throughout the week and putting up a good front over the weekend when Sonny was home. By the end of the first week in November, we began "expecting" any day. My girl friend sent me a message of encouragement: "Don't worry about your baby being late. I read somewhere that it takes an elephant years and years to have a baby." I was hardly in the mood to be encouraged by such information.

Then, on the twenty-sixth of November, when our oldest was seven years of age, my blood pressure began acting up and that old ghost, toxemia, which had probably had something to do with the death of Vicki Anne's twin, was again threatening, so I was ordered to the hospital pronto. I drove down to the hospital, turned the car keys over to my sister-in-law, and somehow talked my way into the crowded hospital. Since I was in no pain or immediate danger of having a baby, they saw no reason why I should insist upon cramming myself in where there was no extra room. But they kept me.

Then, for two of the dullest days of my life, I sat around and—of all the things I most dislike to do—embroidered tea towels, putting on string beans, apples, and oranges in agonizingly small cross-stitch.

Somebody must have given me the blamed things for just such a time as this, because I couldn't imagine myself buying them. And I've never liked the things, even after all that work I put on them.

On Friday the doctor wanted to send me home, but I begged off. Any "false alarm" business was going to get me in Dutch at headquarters. My bookkeeping services were going to have to be available by the end of the month, as the first was payday.

So he let me stay, and about the middle of the afternoon Kimberly Jane was born.

That was on Friday, November 28. On Monday night, December 1, Sonny brought me the time books and I made out the payroll. My vacation was over.

There were two sides to this business of having a daughter. Two sides to Felt's way of thinking, at least, although I didn't find out about it for some time. I'd had a hint of it the day Kim was born, for when they wheeled me past the chart desk after her birth, I heard the nurse saying into the telephone, "Why, yes, Mr. Felt, your wife has just presented you with a baby girl. . . . Yes, I said *girl*." I could hear a buzzing and crackling at the other end of the line. The nurse smiled at me sympathetically, and I knew my husband must be taking it hard. Later, he came in to see me. (He has never had to walk the floor of the waiting room, like other husbands, for some reason or other. I've sometimes pointed out to him how little trouble I've been at such times.) He brought my mother, who declared she had more gray hairs because her son-in-law had given her such a wild ride. He was grinning delightedly, but I knew how disappointed he was, and hastened to assure him that the law of averages would surely make the next one a boy.

Mother threw up her hands in horror, saying, "You have enough family." (She always says that, with every grandchild.)

A few days later, Vicki told me how her father had received the news of the baby girl.

"Mama, you should have seen the way he acted,"

she said. "He threw much worse tantrums than I ever did. He stamped his feet on the floor of the pickup, and beat the steering wheel with his fists. Oh, he was awful mad!"

I laughed with tears in my eyes at her description of her father's antics—and at the birthday outfit her father had taken her out to buy the day after Kim was born. He bought her a complete logger's outfit; plaid shirt, woolen trousers (she can't stand wool), high-top shoes (without caulks, thank goodness!) and a black and red woolen blazer. The poor child could hardly carry the clothes about!

Sonny soon grew to love the baby, however, and wouldn't trade his girls for all the boys in the world. (There's no doubt in my mind, however, that he would still like to add a son to the family.) Both little girls are dark-eyed with light brown hair, but Vicki Anne is a little pixie and Kim is the squarely built, chunky replica of her father. From almost any angle, she looks and acts just like him. She can even mock his slight limp when she's in one of her comic moods.

There was a record on all the juke boxes about that time, and all the loggers played it to razz "the boss." It was "Take Her Back and Trade Her for a Boy."

Great Expectations

WE LOGGED UNTIL A WEEK BEFORE CHRISTMAS THAT first year, and we had every reason to believe we could return after the first of the year. After all, hadn't the Big Company logged all but three weeks of the preceding winter?

A day or two after New Year's, Swede and Sonny went into camp, started the shovel loader, repaired the water system, and generally put the camp in running order for resumption of work the following Monday morning. There was no snow, and Swede had even been able to drive his little red coupé into camp over the miles of usually bad road.

On Sunday night, Cookie and I went with Sonny and two or three of the men to camp. I still had our car, and I was planning to help Cookie get the new supplies of groceries put away, lunches made, beds changed—all the things that have to be done to get ready for the return of the logging crew.

About halfway in from the highway, on the main logging road, we ran into snow too deep for the car to negotiate. While Cookie and I stayed in the car, the men went ahead in the four-wheel-drive rig to see how deep the snow really was. A snow

belt through this area was deceiving at times, and
a mile or so up the road there might be no snow at all.

When the men returned an hour later, they found
Cookie and me asleep in the warm car, with the
motor running. Sonny opened the door and shook
us furiously until we awoke.

"Don'tcha know you could have gassed yourselves
in deep snow like this?" he yelled at us. "The ex-
haust pipe could have gotten plugged up."

We assured him that we came of a family you
couldn't kill with a broadax, and asked him about
the snow conditions.

"Not so good," he told us. "Three feet deep in
most places, and getting deeper. I don't know how
in the hell so much snow could come down in such
a short time."

So we started home. Five or six miles back, below
the switchback, we had another decision to make;
whether or not to leave the tractor on the truck
and trailer we had been returning to the woods.
(We had taken the tractor home with us to do some
land clearing over the holidays.) Sonny hated to
give up, but finally decided he would leave it and
come back later in the week to try to clear the road
to camp.

We were definitely in a mess. All of our supply
of perishable groceries, our fifty blankets and other
bedding subject to mildew, our supply of gasoline
and oil, and most of our equipment that might be
used elsewhere, at lower altitude (in case we could
get a job elsewhere in the event that we were snowed
out), all the things we would need were snowed in!

The next morning our crew began calling. Some

had tried to take the speeder, and found the Big Company was shut down; some had tried the same route we had, and met with the same lack of success. We had no choice but to call it all off for the winter. Taking one man with him, Sonny tried to recover most of the camp supplies and a cat or two. They were gone for five days, and I had only my imagination to tell me what had happened—was happening—to them. Anything *could* happen—and most of it did!

The night they returned they had difficulty in keeping their eyes open long enough to eat, much less tell me the tale of their adventures twenty miles from civilization, in five feet of snow, and in freezing temperatures. They were half starved, hollow-eyed, bearded, and almost exhausted. After a little hot food they took hot showers and tumbled into bed, and slept twelve hours. When they again got their eyes open, they told me what had happened.

One of them had driven the small tractor from the foot of the switchback, while the other drove the four-wheel-drive rig. Three or four miles per hour was the best progress they could make. About eight miles from camp, the balled-up snow in the sprockets of the cat broke the final drive. Then they proceeded in the four-wheel rig to where the snow became too deep for it, about two miles from camp. By this time it was dark, and they decided to stay in the rig rather than risk freezing, floundering about in five feet of snow. For a time they kept the motor running for warmth from the heater, but the gas fumes almost asphyxiated them. They even built a small fire with newspapers on the steel floor of the pickup in an effort to keep warm, but that wasn't too successful either.

At daybreak, the two of them set out for camp, dragging a couple of cat batteries to use in the small cat parked halfway to camp. They found the little cat buried deep, but managed to start the motor and took off for camp again, battling the snow in order to find the road. Just as they got in, they noticed oil running out of the sprocket and spreading itself all over the snow. The final drive was broken on this cat, too.

By this time the sun was going down, and they'd had nothing to eat since the day before, when they consumed the lunch I had sent along with them. They lit a fire in the bunkhouse heater and tried to get some decent supper.

Snowfall in the deep woods is an awesome, frightening thing. There is something ominous in the inexorable way the big, soft petals of white stuff come drifting down, to pile up in the roads, making them impassable and most of the equipment so useless. The water freezes, the fire doesn't want to burn. Cold water won't wash away the dirt and grease and soot that soon collects on your hands, face, and the kitchen utensils. It's pure misery to try to live, to cook, and keep warm, at one and the same time. The little sheet-metal stoves keep one side warm while the other side of you freezes. You pile all the heavy woolen blankets on your bed until you can hardly roll over under their weight, and you keep the heater full of wood, and that way you can keep halfway comfortable. But it is hard to go to sleep, thinking of all that great white expanse of snow between yourself and civilization. If one planned to be snowed in all winter it wouldn't be so bad, but to be caught more or less unprepared is a rough deal.

If they had known that a great padding mountain cat was slumbering peacefully beneath the bunkhouse, gleaning what heat filtered down through the floor, his big yellow eyes drowsily closing in the warmth and unexpected comfort, they might not have slept even as well as they did. They found his tracks the next day, under and around the bunkhouse. And cougars don't have much to eat in the dead of winter!

The morning after their arrival, Sonny and his pal stayed in bed until noon, when hunger forced them to brave the frigid cold to make a bit of breakfast. Then they dragged up a barrel of oil to keep the heater going, drained the water pipes, and returned to bed.

On the fourth day since leaving home, they looked out to see that the snow of the day before had begun to crust deeply enough so that their weight and that of their sled could be borne for the trips they must make to the pickup. The sled was a toboggan-like affair which they pulled by hand on the two-mile grind between the camp and the pickup with loads of groceries and cat batteries. (They had one more cat in camp, but the batteries ran down before they could get it started.) The sun came out briefly, to spread a feeble warmth and to also threaten them with snow blindness from the glitter off the snow. To alleviate this danger, they smeared soot from inside the oil stove under their eyes, which contributed greatly to their cadaverous appearance when they arrived home the next day.

With a thousand pounds of stuff to be moved two miles, it also became imperative that they get out of there as fast as possible, for more snow suddenly threatened. They finally made it, without disaster, but it was the end of our logging activities until spring.

We didn't return to camp until the first of May that year. There was still three feet of snow, and evidence to show that eight or nine feet had fallen during the winter months.

An abandoned logging camp, or any building left unoccupied in the woods, is a dreary place, with all the accumulated dampness of winter in its walls and floors. Sonny plowed the remains of the winter's snows off the roof and built and carefully tended fires in each of the buildings to dry them out. The stoves were rusty, a roof torn loose here and there, a few shakes missing. Steps had to be repaired, bedding aired, counters and cupboards scoured after the chipmunks and squirrels' messy winter jubilee (the little rascals had even rolled glasses off counters and pushed dishes off the shelves), and the waterstained walls and ceilings had to be freshly kalsomined.

On the latter job, the high-domed ceiling of the baggage car (converted to our dining car) hadn't changed a bit. Again, I ate more kalsomine than on any other painting job before or since. Cookie did most of it, however. The paint ran down our arms and formed pools at the base of our throats, but when we were finished, we had to admit that the final results were worth it.

It was very hard to keep rough floors, untiled drainboards, and the primitive furnishings of a logging camp like ours clean. It took constant scrubbing, window washing, oilcloth surfacing (wherever it could be used), and much soap and hot water. We derusted the stove and coaxed it to draw again, flushed out the hot water tank and pipes and refilled the tank with clean water, worked the balky refrigerator over, and wheedled the light plant to provide us with a little electricity. By the end of the second day, the new camp began to be about halfway livable once more.

That light plant was a real cross for poor Cookie to bear. It had a four-cylinder motor and generator, which ran the refrigerator to conserve the food, operated the fan on the kitchen range, and provided electric lights for the camp. After about eight months of sixteen-hour-a-day duty, it began to act up. Scotty was supposed to look after it, but it was a bit too modern for his experience; his knowledge of such "mo-chines" was limited to what Sonny and Swede had told him. He knew that if the brushes were in contact with the generator, it would put forth light; so he shoved so many cedar sticks against the brushes you could barely see the plant.

One day during the second season, it refused to give forth light, so I was dispatched to civilization for the necessary parts with which to repair it. It was four thirty in the afternoon when I got back, to find Cookie cooking supper for the crew on the top of the slippery barrel heater in the washhouse. How she managed to fry potatoes and hamburger steaks in that manner I'll never know. Her face was besmudged, her hair mussed, and her eyes red from the smoke. I felt like a heel for having taken all day to find the parts and get back, but she didn't complain, and the crew got fed in good order.

There were two other problems that cropped up from time to time: water and refrigeration.

Our water supply came from a small spring a thousand feet up the track from camp, which was sufficient fall to provide a gravity-type water system. The spring was dug out, and the pipe laid, and it worked quite well, providing the pipe didn't get crushed by some heavy vehicle, or filled with some obstruction, such as dead robins or water dogs. (When we moved to New Camp, there was a fast-running creek east of camp that served as an ideal source of water. Through inch-and-a-quarter pipe, it came by gravity a thousand feet down, across the camp yard, and up into the old three-hundred gallon pressure and storage tank. Any time the overflow from this tank stopped, we immediately investigated the cause. In the midst of the dry season, it was often necessary to dig a larger intake pool in the creek, so the water supply could be kept at normal level.)

The opening up of the water system was first on the agenda when starting up the camp in the spring. (It was also the last thing attended to when closing camp in the fall.) Until the pipes were dug out (and repaired, if any had burst or suffered other damage), we used snow from a nearby bank, melted on the stove, for dishwater and cleaning purposes. One May, following a winter of heavy snow, Sonny pushed four or five feet away from the camp shacks, and as late as July I found enough ice beneath pumice-stone banks to make ice cream for the crew.

Our refrigerator was an overgrown box having a thirty-five-degree temperature in the top compartment and a ten-degree compartment in the bottom. It ran by electric motor for several years, then, when it started giving trouble, Sonny substituted a gasoline motor. Fortunately, with all the meat and perishable food we had to keep on hand, we had very little trouble with it.

That first spring, as soon as Sonny could get the the big cat started, he dozed off the road so we could get the groceries and supplies in as quickly as possible. The slushy snow was still three feet deep in places, and more than once I fell through and had to yell for help. It got so that Sonny grabbed a shovel every time he heard me yell. He knew I had fallen through somewhere.

Finally, the loggers came. Some drove in as far as they could and walked the rest of the way, boots slung over one shoulder, war bag over the other. They eyed the soft, leftover snow with some disfavor, but made little comment, for they were all happy to be going back to work. Soon they were choosing their bunks and pounding nails in the walls for their clothes and mirrors. Empty apple boxes and orange crates served as cupboards, and the long shelf above the beds held the contents of their war bags or "turkeys." The union forbade the doubling up of bunks one above the other, so after eight men were made at home in the bunkhouse, the overflow was housed in tents, and in the spare room in the shop. Swede always had either a tent or trailer, which he shared with a cat driver or bull cook if the need arose.

Somehow, everyone had a place to sleep and hang his hat. Primitive, but quite adequate.

That first year of actual logging was rugged, to say the least. The one thing that likely saved us was the fact that our cats were still in good enough shape to take such abuse in logging the rough terrain.

"Jesus Peak" was one of those rugged places that logging crews like to talk about. The cat skinners named it, saying it was so high (about 4,500 feet elevation) it might be the back door to heaven. They even declared they had had words with St. Peter's assistant, who, according to them, was sergeant-at-arms at this back door. Up to that time I'd had to take their word for these things, as my pregnancy forbade my taking a cat ride up such a mountain; so all I know is they dragged many a log off that peak.

Right here I'd like to say a little about labor in the logging woods. From the days when that extra carload of logs was worth more than a man's life, to this day when the unions dictate every last word in employer-employee relations, the logging industry has come a long way. We don't want to see the old days return, when the little dictators who represented the big companies could fire seventy-five men on a Monday morning without good reason (except that perhaps they had full bellies and weren't quite as good workers as when they were lean and hungry) knowing full well there would be 150 on hand to choose from in a few hours. Neither do we like to see a few men in a well-placed union be able to throw tens of thousands of men out of work by calling a strike for some reason which makes sense to only a very few. There must be a middle road somewhere, so that the employers who are trying to do right are not penalized and victimized along with the guilty—if such there be. There must be someone with the intelligence to find that middle road. As it now stands, each side wants the upper hand, and when one or the other gets it, they wield a wicked sword.

We have been told by many (who no doubt know what they're talking about) that we treat our men too well; that we pay too high wages, feed them too good food, and treat them too well in our working relations with them. We agree only at those few times when someone takes advantage of our good nature. It has not been very long since we were wage earners ourselves, working under someone else's direction, and we remember the things that irked us most. We treat the people who work *with* us as we would want to be treated ourselves, and perhaps we'll never become millionaires but we sleep well at night, with a clear conscience on the matter of treating our employees fairly.

Every log, every board foot, is bought dearly by the blood, sweat, and tears of the man in the logging woods, whether he is the faller, the bucker, the chokerman, the cat skinner, or the loader. He is the man who goes to work in every kind of weather, when the mud is hip-deep to a tall Indian, or the hot dryness of the close, still forest makes the warmth of summer hardly bearable. He faces the sudden dangers of the logging woods that may bring death and disaster to himself and/or a fellow worker. Add to this the fact that, even today, a logger often has to live apart from his family for a week or two, getting home only for occasional weekends, while working in some remote logging camp. It totals up to a rugged life, unusual in its demands upon the men who follow logging for a living. There must be some fascination that attracts so many men who could earn an easier living, and make more money, at a steady job down in civilization.

With the gyppo, there is usually a quota to be met. Sonny knew just how much his crew could produce in a day, and he would order his flatcars accordingly. If things went well (which wasn't always the case) he loaded out four to seven cars per day, the number depending upon the setting, the length of haul, and the condition of the roads. It was his job to keep his operation running smoothly, and it took his constant attention. A broken-down cat, the loss of chokers (of which there always seems to be a lack), the shortage of a man on Monday morning, a wreck on the railroad (over which he has no control, but which can be costly to us), breakage of a tong line on the shovel, a labor slow-down—anything could, and did, happen to cut down the average output. And whatever it is, the gyppo is on hand personally to get his outfit back under control.

We were off to a typical start that season. On the twentieth of May, just a couple of weeks after we began operations, we were logging at a merry rate when the loading shovel broke down. It was a ten-day, five-hundred-dollar welding job to repair it, not counting the time lost from loading logs. This promptly got us into hot water with the Big Company's superintendent.

The house of the shovel was jacked up off the undercarriage, to facilitate the welding job, and was resting against one of the logging flats. The Supe sent for the four empty flats after a day or so, because the railroad company would charge demurrage after the third day. We let them take three cars, but not the one on which the shovel was propped. An argument ensued. The Supe raised Cain about our keeping one railroad flat tied up for the ten days we were broke down. Mr. Midway took a hand in things, and told us that a little matter of twenty-five or thirty dollars demurrage wasn't too important to the Big Company. We offered to pay the demurrage, but the Supe turned us down. However, he never let us forget his generosity on this point. It was his stepping-stone to showing us what a big man *he* was.

Even as the argument waged, the work of repairing the shovel loader was going on. The welder, a cousin of Sonny's, let me watch through an extra helmet, which protected my eyes from the blinding blue flashes of light whenever an arc was struck. If it hadn't been for worrying about the lost time, I could have enjoyed watching the flying orange sparks and the flashing blue lights through my dark

helmet. Even at night, high upon the trees about
the camp the ghostly blue light flashed spasmodically,
making a brilliant fireworks display. Sonny's shadow,
as he came across the yard, cast itself higher than
the tallest trees.

When the job was finished, they were not sure
that welding the broken undercarriage had been the
right thing to do. Maybe we should have sent for
new parts. But when it was put together, everything worked perfectly. They never had trouble
with it.

Sonny and Swede were both irked with themselves when they later realized they could have turned
the shovel completely around, and used the other
side of the undercarriage until a more convenient
time to tie it up for repairs, say during the Fourth-
of-July layoff.

Later we purchased our own welding equipment
to keep our haywire machinery in better shape. It
was too expensive to lose time in sending for a welder
with equipment, or tearing off the broken part,
laying off the piece of equipment, and sending it
to town for repair. With our own welding equipment right on the job, we lost little time in getting
the repairing done. It was still far from cheap,
however, for it was usually overtime work.

I was still errand boy for the outfit. With Auntie
Jewel, as we called her, taking care of the children,
I was able to give practically full-time attention to
keeping Felt & Co. in supplies, loggers, and whatever was needed to have the business going. My
poor old automobile squeaked protest from every

joint as I carried load after load into camp over the rough road.

We were having loading landing trouble about that time, with both loaders and shovel operators hard to find. I brought up head loader after head loader, but none pleased Sonny. By the time I brought up one that pleased him, he had lost his shovel-loader operator and had to operate the shovel loader himself. On one occasion, when one loader tried unsuccessfully to fit in a log several times, changed his mind a time or two, and had riled up Sonny's Irish disposition to the boiling point, he suddenly began hurling logs out into the brush much in the manner of an indignant elephant throwing straws to the wind. Fortunately, nobody was hurt and no permanent damage was done, but that loader was canned pronto, and Sonny started looking for head loaders and shovel operators all over again.

It was during this period that I brought up the aforementioned Scotty to build a sled for the donkey, file the saws, and do general handiwork around the camp. Scotty was a delightful character; he was a "donkey doctor" and boom builder of long experience. According to him, he was "the best durned boom and sled builder this side of logger's heaven." There was a lot of practical knowledge packed inside the old white-haired head of his, and he did us a lot of good.

Scotty was built on the stocky side, and for his age he was a very husky man. He had a perpetual quid of "W.B. Cut" in one cheek, and his smooth, ruddy face was weathered by a lifetime of outdoor work. Often his blue eyes snapped with mischief as he thought up ways to give people a bad time. He always wore a belt around his middle, even with bib overalls.

He was rather quiet the day I brought him to camp. Afterward, I figured it must have been because he was planning how to build the new donkey sled to his own specifications instead of Sonny's. (He got it done, too, as it turned out.)

Sonny had dragged in two forty-foot yellow fir logs (of which Scotty didn't approve—"Yellow fir won't last," he said) and put them in position six feet apart. From that point, Scotty hitched up his leather belt, shifted his quid, and took over. The ends had to be sniped (cut diagonally from underneath to give them a sled-runner edge) so they could more easily go through the brush and over the rough ground. This part of the operation was done one evening when the crew was sitting out behind the caboose on a stack of car stakes, relaxing and offering a lot of free advice. To the accompaniment of rapid-fire comment (Sonny is no slouch at holding his own in that), three different sets of sawyers took turns. Then Sonny and Scotty took over again.

"Quit draggin' your feet, Scotty," Sonny said.

Scotty merely spat a stream of brown juice into the pumice dust and didn't answer. Then, when they had raised a sweat, Scotty suggested that they "make way for a forty horsepower, heavy-duty Swede." Swede and Chet took over, and Scotty noted with approval the way the yellow sawdust flew.

"See what *men* can do," he said to Sonny, as he flicked a few drops of saw oil into the diagonal cut.

Then he added, "Saw won't be worth a damn when *they* get through with it."

With much waving of arms, and between streams of tobacco juice, they measured and argued about the bolts to be ordered for putting the sled together. As a result of these measurements, Sonny had a number of inch-and-three-quarter by six-foot bolts made special for the job, and brought them to camp only to find they were a foot too short. Scotty neatly sidestepped the blame.

"I just don't make mistakes like that," he told my gyppo. "You must have wrote down the wrong figgers." So they hacked out enough wood on the logs to mortise in the bolts (much to Sonny's disgust) and then went ahead with the building of the platform.

It wasn't until the entire project was complete that Scotty discovered a foot's length had been broken off his wooden folding rule, with which he had done the measuring for the bolts.

Scotty seemed to think his own work was above reproach or criticism, but he was acidulous enough about everyone else's work. About the donkey sled, he said "Well, it was as good as I could do, considering the help I had." On the manner in which one of the loggers hooked a log, he said, "What'd he do, sleep with some hook tender's daughter and think he was a hook tender?"

When all was said and done, it did seem that the donkey sled was more Scotty's handiwork than Felt's. And despite the mistakes and complications which entered into its construction, that sled outlasted old

Scotty. We used it for six seasons without it falling apart.

Scotty's favorite stories, about logging in the "good old days" when they really employed *men* in the woods, were usually of the hair-raising variety. The stock of stories he had retained down through the years was exceeded only by his supply of chewing tobacco. Back when highball logging was the method, it was considered too much of a nuisance to shut down just because some logger got himself bumped off, said Scotty, so they waited until the end of the day to bring in the dead and injured. That way, he said, no time was lost in getting out important things like logs. (Though he never actually said it, I also gathered that neither was it any trouble this way, since they had to come in for supper anyway.)

"One time," Scotty related, "I was running a yarding donkey, and they signaled to go ahead on the main line. I did, and then when the whistle punk signaled again to highball, I just poured on the steam. The turn came in fast, and I figgered it was pretty light, and when the butt riggin' and chokers came in sight I could see why. The hook tender had wrapped the line a couple of times around three dead loggers." At that point Scotty would pause and glance around at his audience to see if he was getting the proper reaction. And no matter how many times we had heard the story, someone was bound to ask, "And what did you do, Scotty?"

"Me?" Scotty's blue eyes got that devilish twinkle. "Why, I took one look, turned off the steam, grabbed my toolbox, and went off down the track to get my time," he said.

But Scotty had his crosses to bear, too, along with the rest of us. One of these was "Teeney." (We all called him "Tiny" because of his size, but to Scotty he was "Teeney.")

Teeney weighed about two hundred and thirty, and was at least six foot two in height. He was a big roughneck of a man with powerful arms and shoulders that could hold the brake on the donkey drums as it should be held. Needless to say, this amount of bulk, handled in Teeney's reckless fashion, was a little hard on the small army-type camp beds we had at camp. One by one, he caved them in, and would then move on to the next one as soon as there was a vacancy.

One morning Scotty came into the kitchen, where Sonny was sitting on a thirty-pound lard tin (which had also been squashed by Teeney, on a previous trip to the kitchen) on one side of the door, and Teeney was standing on the other side, near the hot-water tank. Scotty was red in the face and fairly frothing at the mouth as he reported "that durned Teeney's" latest broken bed.

"You'd better do something about him, Felt," Scotty said. "He's got blame near every bed in camp broke down, just pushes out the ends with his big feet and breaks down the springs. Ya won't have a decent bunk left in camp. Ya'd better tell 'im!"

Sonny was convulsed with laughter, and Teeney, unnoticed by Scotty, was trying to muffle his own laughter.

"Tell him yourself, Scotty," Sonny finally said. "He's right behind you."

Scotty took a quick look over his shoulder, turned

a brighter shade of red, sputtered like a wet fuse, and went out just as fast. But after that Teeney had to shake down his bed every night for an empty bottle, or a tin of milk or a cedar shake, before he could retire in comfort.

Scotty didn't think much of women drivers, but he got used to riding with me, and after a couple of years he even went so far as to compliment me on how I drove the ton-and-a-half supply truck over the rough mountain road, around the stumps and mudholes on the last few miles into camp. But it happened only once. He had no more than gotten the words out of his mouth than I misjudged slightly, ran up over the edge of a spreading root of a stump, and the cab of the truck bounced back and forth, hitting poor Scotty on his white head. Back on a more or less even keel again, I looked at him as he rubbed his bump. He looked back at me.

"Take it back," he muttered.

When Scotty found out how tenderhearted Cookie was, he would throw heart attacks at will to give her a bad time. He took great pains to show her how to fix his ammonia drops in case he should have an attack. (Actually, Scotty did have a heart condition which could give him plenty of trouble if he overworked, but he was always of the perverse nature which loved to plague someone.)

One day, when Cookie was looking out of the kitchen window, watching Scotty, he began slowly to wilt and tip forward on the chopping block, which he was using for a seat while filing an axe. Cookie sprang into action; then as she rushed down the steps to administer the ammonia drops, he abruptly recovered and began filing busily again. Coasting silently down the hill and around the corner came Sonny, in the four-wheel-drive rig. It was the shortest heart attack of Scotty's colorful career, and Cookie began to suspect that she was being taken for a ride.

Scotty always called himself "Jack of all trades and master of none," but that wasn't true. He had a world of practical information in that old white head of his. He rigged himself a contraption to paint the uppermost gable of our house that wouldn't have held anyone with lesser balance, and he walked about the top of that high house with the surefootedness of a cat. He helped us finish the shaking and painting of the house, and the laying of sidewalks. I'm sure we could never have gotten the house finished in such record time, during that particular dry-weather layoff, if Scotty hadn't helped us.

As usual, our "free" time at home was being utilized in making improvements around the place. Scotty worked for us for a whole week, then went home to get some weeds scythed and wood carried in for his wife. He was in an "all-fired rush," as he called it, to get everything done in time so he could return to the woods with us the following Monday.

But he didn't make it. Scotty had a sunstroke the day he scythed the weeds and hauled the wood in a wheelbarrow, and died that Friday night.

For weeks afterward I could see his vigorous old figure coming across the yard at camp, and remember so many things; the sly little stir of the hot-cake batter in the mornings; his ready supply of wit and stovewood for the kitchen range. Somehow none of us will ever forget Scotty, the donkey doctor, he of the big heart, the ready stories, and the willing and capable hand. When we discarded the old donkey sled a few years later, it was like discarding something that had belonged to Scotty, for he had made it. His personality was in that old sled, and it was the first job he had done for us. He was a grand old man.

Of Home and Family

THE IRISH HUMOR, THE TRACE OF SCOTTISH CAN-
niness, the German ability to take the rough life,
the dark eyes of the English, the olive skin from
the French—all these things show up in our two
daughters. As I watch them growing up and chang-
ing from day to day, I cannot help but recall the
words of a contemporary painter who said our
American children are the most beautiful children
in the world. No wonder, when you consider they
are such a mixture of races and nationalities.

While Vicki Anne was our only child, we lived
variously in our seventeen-foot trailer, two or three
temporarily rented cabins, and finally settled in the
house on North Lake. I always liked that house.
I knew quite intimately every square inch of it,
having painted, papered, scrubbed and varnished it
all several times over, as well as laid asphalt tile in
the living and dining rooms to smooth the caulk-
splintered floors. While Kim was being born, huge
front windows were installed, so we could look
directly out upon the lake only thirty feet or so
from our door. Upstairs, Vicki's little room had
lovely big windows that looked into the tops of
the cedar trees and over the lake.

It was while we lived at North Lake that we found our Auntie Jewel. She was from Montana, visiting friends, when I heard of her through a baby-sitting agency. The children quickly grew to love her, and when on weekends I couldn't get down from camp in time, she would bundle them up and take them with her to her friends in Auburn, where she spent her weekends.

Kim was only nine months old that first fall, and quickly caught on to how to raise her fat little arms to "Praise the Lord" when Auntie Jewel took her to her own church on Sundays. Later, we learned, to our embarrassment, that she was the spoiled little wanderer about the church while the services were going on. Everyone thought Kim was entitled to do just as she pleased. We learned this for ourselves at a Christmas gathering when our offspring went clomping about the church when everyone was supposed to be quiet, and climbed over the little railing to stand beside the minister, and dug into the great boxes of sacked candy until she found just the piece she wanted. No one paid the slightest attention. After all, she was Kim, Auntie Jewel's little pet!

Auntie Jewel didn't spoil the girls, actually, but she did seem to think they were just about perfect. I was happy to have someone who loved them so to look after them and keep them well fed and clean and well loved. It made me feel much better about having to leave them so much.

Also, I know that usually the children are safer with her than they are with us. Once, when Kim was a year old, I returned to the truck where I had left her for a few minutes, and found a full box of copper detonating caps strewn about the floor and seat of the truck. As I hastily replaced them in their tin box, I noticed tiny teeth marks on some of the caps. Like father, like daughter! Sonny had told me there was six hundred pounds of pressure behind each cap. Never again did I leave her in any car or truck we owned without first investigating the glove compartment or looking under the seat for a box of dynamite caps.

We often take three or four youngsters up to camp with us, especially during holiday seasons or when there is no school. Vicki, Roge (my small brother) and Midgie Lloy, a grand-niece of my parents who is being brought up by them, love to come to camp.

One night the two girls went fishing with one of the loggers and came home at dusk with lovely strings of fish, tired, happy, proud, and wet. I frowned as I counted noses and found my small brother missing, only to learn that he hadn't been with them. That started a search, for I had visions of him being lost in the woods or drowned in the swamp.

Half a frantic hour later we found him sound asleep in one of the bunks in the bunkhouse. He was only about eight at the time, but was snoring as loudly as any of the loggers who had stayed in camp over the weekend. Big Hank, one of the loggers, had told him that it would do him good to get his back end wet once in a while, so he had gotten himself good and wet fishing in the swamp near camp, then had come back and crawled into bed. He had remembered to take off his wet clothes, thank goodness.

Life at home wasn't exactly uneventful, either, especially for Auntie Jewel. Though the North Lake community isn't "country" in the true sense of the word, people do have chickens, ducks, cows, a horse or two, and even goats.

One afternoon, when Auntie Jewel was hanging out clothes, she looked around to see a big billygoat ready to charge her. She ran to the house, with the huge, smelly animal at her heels. She slammed the door in his face and screamed for the children. The old goat's yellow eyes glared fiercely at them through the glass of the back door as he stood on his hind legs and tried to decide whether or not to butt the door down. While they were piling chairs and furniture against the door, Sonny's sister Madge and her husband drove in and came to the rescue. After great difficulty, Chuck forced the goat's head between the bars of an iron hitch off one of our cats that was lying near the garage. The old duffer was still there when I got home late that night, perfuming the atmosphere with his extremely potent goaty smell. I called the owner of the goat, and got her posthaste after her goat the next morning. I doubt if Auntie Jewel will ever forget that experience.

Nor did she forget the time we nearly frightened her to death through mistaken kindness. Sonny and I arrived home late at night, without a key, and rather than awaken her to let us in, we decided to put the ladder up to the window of our bedroom and get in that way. She heard us, and lay paralyzed with fear in her bedroom below while we softly padded around upstairs, trying not to waken her. Finally she called out, and I answered, reassuring her. The next morning we apologized for our thoughtlessness.

I think she finally got used to the uninhibited family she lived with, and regarded us with the same tolerant affection she would feel for her own children. She still lives in Auburn, and is married to one of our old friends.

No chronicle of our life at that time would be complete without including Paddy. Those first two seasons we were at camp, Paddy was the gyppo's inseparable companion. He was a little rusty brown cocker spaniel which Vicki and her daddy had brought home two years before, when I was ill, saying he was the only one left out of a batch of puppies from which we were to have our pick. Our friends hadn't been home, but they took the puppy anyway. As it turned out, this one had been sick and was in isolation when Vicki and Sonny found him so all alone. We put him in a doll cradle with an alarm clock for company and a hot pad for warmth, and he finally grew up to his big feet, for which we had named him Paddy.

Paddy wasn't a house dog. He loved to ride in trucks and on cats, and he adored Sonny. When we went logging, Paddy went along, and he had more fun chasing little bear cubs and fawns and birds than any other little lawbreaking dog in the country. He never caught up with either the fawn or the bear cubs. The fawn could outrun him, and the bear cubs could climb trees.

It was a sight to see him run and run until he

was exhausted. When he would sit down to rest, the bears would look back over their shoulders at him and they, too, would stop to rest. When Paddy was ready to resume the chase, the cubs would take off too. A good time was had by all. It was a good thing he never ran across the old mother bear in his rambles. Morgan was always telling about one big bear whose *tracks* weighed seventy-five pounds apiece!

But Paddy had duties to attend to, for he was a gyppo's dog, and life wasn't all play. Every day he went on a tour of inspection. He'd hitch a ride to the scene of logging operations and stop off to watch this faller or that bucker at work. If a cat came in while he was there, he would climb aboard (at the driver's invitation) and take off through the woods, watching the chokermen set chokers on logs, other buckers and other fallers attending to their tasks. When they reached the landing, where he liked to be about noon, he would sit at a safe distance watching the logs being loaded on the flat-cars. When the last one was loaded, he would go and sit near the crew while they ate lunch, and he was always rewarded with the scraps.

About this time the logging train would come in, and he would climb up the steel steps into the cab of the engine, where he was always greeted kindly by the train crew. They, too, were usually eating lunch about that time, and here again he got in on the food. When the loads were switched out, the train crew would back their little engine carefully down the steep track and stop at camp to let their favorite passenger off at the cookshack. Paddy would often get to the camp by this method before Sonny got in on the truck for lunch. There must have been something about logging that made a little rusty-colored dog awfully hungry, for he usually snagged another meal here, too.

Both dog and master were so devoted to their jobs that they hated to come home weekends. Sonny stayed in camp for five weeks in a row once, and his hair needed cutting so badly that the train crew took pity on him and took up a collection.

"Here," the engineer told him as he handed him a dollar and a half in small change, "you been tellin' us for so long that you weren't makin' enough money to get a haircut, so we took up a collection for you to get one."

Sonny grinned widely, took their money, and spent it on beer that Friday night. However, he did get a haircut over the weekend, much to the crew's delight.

Another resemblance between dog and master was in their attitudes when they did come home for a weekend. They could hardly wait to leave again, and apparently they found being at home most boring. If Paddy had to stay home for longer than a weekend (which he did a time or two during hunting season) he just lay around, his nose on his forepaws, with a disgusted look on his sad face. He'd much rather have been helping Sonny run his logging outfit, and chasing the bear cubs or the fawns.

About this time, too, we decided we had ahold of a big black bear and didn't dare let go. In spite of all we could do, we couldn't seem to log enough good timber to keep the quality as high as the Big

Company wanted. On the other side, we were constantly being urged to ship *all* the logs, good or bad, we found fallen or standing. So far, we hadn't even begun to make any kind of repayment to Mr. Joslyn. He wasn't alarmed, but we knew he had expected us to do better.

It was the first year of many such years; there were compromises, more extensions of credit, and the expectations of better things to come—next season.

Hardest of all to take, I think, was the patronizing tone of the "big shots" who literally patted Sonny on the shoulder as they said, "Well, you know it takes quite a while to learn to log salvage; how to ship the right kind of stuff, you know."

We could have told them that a little more honesty on the scale would have helped. Instead, we dug our heels in harder, gritted our teeth, and just kept on going.

New Camp or No New Camp?

I SPENT CONSIDERABLE TIME AT THE LOGGING CAMP that second season. Kim was only six months old that June, and a bit small to drag up to the woods as yet, although Vicki often went with me during the summer.

We were making a collection of snapshots for Sonny's logging album, and usually kept the camera within reach. They logged in and around camp for a couple of months, making it very convenient for me to get occasional pictures of big turns of logs, of the equipment in action, and various other subjects I knew Sonny wanted.

It was this picture-taking business that almost cost the gyppo logger his wife.

When I wasn't fishing or riding around the woods with the boss, I usually lounged on the bunk in the caboose, reading, with one eye open for a big turn of logs to be brought in by the larger cat. One day I heard the clatter that denoted a turn of logs was coming. One look assured me it was of the desired size, so I grabbed my camera and dashed down the steps of the caboose. The light plant was running with its usual sputtery noises, and across the tracks, at the landing some two hundred feet

away, the loading shovel and the approaching cat
added to the general noise. There was nothing on
my mind except to beat that cat to the landing
and get my picture. I was headed for a big stump
behind the shovel that would give me a perfect shot.

I was swinging along the main track, about to
cross, when I saw my husband running toward me,
waving his arms wildly. I could see his mouth making
words, but couldn't hear what he was saying. I
waved back in friendly fashion, and instead of step-
ping across the rail, as I had intended, I continued
on my way alongside it. Sonny was still a dozen
steps from me when a big yellow speeder slid noiselessly up alongside of me—on that rail I had intended to cross! The operator was bug-eyed with
fright. He had come around the curve into camp
pretty fast, and in trying to put on his air brakes
and stop in a hurry, had forgotten to blow the
whistle.

Sonny was near collapse. The landing crew across
the track were helplessly watching what they were
certain was going to be my untimely end, but I
hadn't been in the least aware of how close I came
to getting myself "runned under," as Scotty put it.

Lee, the speeder operator, and I had great respect for each other after that. I watched my step,
and he blew his whistle when he came around the
bend—at much slower speed. My husband had saved
my life, for if he had not attracted my attention
and come to meet me as he did, I certainly would
have stepped into the path of that speeder and been
only pieces to pick up in a basket.

"And then who'd make out your paychecks?" I

kidded the fellows later, to cover their embarrassment at being so scared. "You were just worried about your meal ticket, that's all."

The speeder was a big, long, buslike conveyance on railroad wheels. It likely weighed fifty tons, and could carry fifty men. The outside was painted yellow, with the Big Company's name in big black letters. On the inside it was anything but fancy, for logger's caulks had long ago marred beyond recognition any paint that might once have been on the seats or floor. Worn steel reinforcement bands held the speeder together, and a powerful motor provided the go-ahead.

The ride to company headquarters via this speeder was an experience not to be missed. After each spine-jarring turn and bump had been absorbed by these old bones, I would vow never to cuss the cat or truck ride over the logging road again. The rails on that railroad were worn thin on the sharp turns by countless loads of logs from woods to civilization, and that didn't add to the comfort or smoothness of the ride. The fact that at each telephone, on some days, the operator would have to stop and phone ahead for clearance because somewhere along that twenty-mile stretch of road a big log train was lurking, didn't add anything to my peace of mind. Around a sharp turn we might meet a section crew, or a locie, or the rear end of a logging train. Where another reload was set up on the side track, we literally ducked beneath the heel boom of the loading rig. Rocks rolled freely down onto the track, bridges two hundred feet high over tumbling wild creeks were crossed, or a wildly racing buck deer gave us a brief thrill by staying just in front of the hurtling speeder.

But there were compensations, too. In the narrow gorges, where the stony walls were always damp, grew the loveliest of all our mountain ferns, the maidenhair, with lacy fronds. In green secret places, the thick moss and the wild trillium gave rare forest beauty. As the broader reaches of the lowlands came in view, there were abandoned log cabins among the gigantic stumps and scarlet vine maples; mute testimony to nature's healing after the ravages of man.

Then, civilization, and all the terror of the ride was behind us. The gate over the main-line railroad was reached, and we remembered only the good things about the speeder trip from camp.

Whenever I got the chance I went fishing. I fished along the clear mountain streams that entered into the swamp, in the large one that drained the swamp, and in all the big, deep holes in the swamp itself. The beavers had built several dams across the two-mile length of the Big Swamp, which accounted for its being such a fascinating place. Willows grew along the edges of the dams, and yellow grass made thick turf on the muskeg-like ground that had been used to fill some of the deeper holes that might have been deathtraps for lone fishermen like myself.

Most everyone caught fish but me. I tried it for three different seasons. The most I ever caught was four or five, and they were on the puny side. To add insult to injury, I was always falling down, scratching myself on the brush, digging holes in my shins by banging into things, and getting water in my boots. Sonny asked me once if I just lay down with my head upstream and let the water run into my boots. They were usually wetter on the inside than on the outside. My knees were rough and red from the icy water, and every exposed part of me was mottled from the dive-bombing attacks of the gnats. Somehow I never could be as nonchalant about those no-see-ums as Morgan was. He always said he didn't mind them biting him, but he was darned if he wanted them to drink his coffee!

Morgan could catch fish where nobody else could, but he would never go fishing with me and let me learn his secret. I finally decided that he must have the knack for catching fish just like other people can paint, or cook, or adz a board straight. Finally, after beating myself to death fishing in vain where everybody else caught fish, I gave up.

When hunting season started, I tried a casual hand with a gun. Fred, the Arkansaser who always "bought his teeth in bottles" to replace the false plates he had lost in some tavern, brought a .22 rifle back to camp one Monday morning, along with his usual hangover. We had great sport shooting at tin cans and beer bottles, and he was generous enough to lend me the gun to go hunting with Sonny's grandfather, Gramp Woodruff, when he came up for a bit of hunting or fishing.

Gramp, at eighty-three, was the youngest grandfather anyone ever had. He was a great fisherman and hunter, and we had many happy times together. One sunny October morning we took off up the tracks for a stroll, bringing Freddy's gun with us.

We jumped four deer, and they scampered off into the woods.

Right ahead of us was a blowdown, with its root system sticking high into the air. Gramp told me to jump up there and see if I could see the animals. Excitedly I scrambled to the top—and, sure enough, there they stood, not more than forty feet away!

"Take a shot at them, Margaret. See if you can hit one," Gramp said.

So, in typical novice fashion, I shot—several times. I never so much as ruffled their fur, or any of the brush near them. Then, suddenly realizing what I was doing, and aghast at my temerity, I scrambled down from the tree roots and went back to where Gramp was standing, fairly splitting his sides with laughter.

"What if I had hit one of them?" I sputtered. "This is an illegal gun, all four of those deer were does, and I haven't got a license!"

Gramp wiped the tears of laughter from his eyes.

"They were safe at all times, Daughter," he told me. "They were perfectly safe at all times."

I haven't been hunting or fishing since, unless you want to count a private pond with several thousand tame fish to pick from. Some of them were bound to be sucker (I mean "poor fish") enough to bite at my line. Well anyway, *one* did.

Actually, there was very little time for playing around that second season. The mire of debt was creeping up about our ears, and we often had occasion to ask ourselves if this big black bear we had by the tail was going to pull us under. Our first

season had been much shorter than we had hoped
it would be, and the second had been late in starting, so it, too, would be short. Our equipment was
being worn out on the rough terrain, and the Big
Company and Mr. Cutting Rights were still bouncing us back and forth between them in this experi-
mental game of salvage logging. When we logged
to suit the Company, the other party wouldn't let
us move to a new setting until the old one had been
cleaned up to suit *them*. Since our contract was
for logging, not land clearing, and since we were
being paid according to what we logged, or what
was actually scaled at the landing, Felt & Co. were
doing lots of no-profit business.

We ran into more trouble when we decided to
move our camp to a new location three miles farther into the woods. We consulted Mr. Midway,
our old friend who had first introduced us to the
Big Company for this salvage logging operation (and
who, poor man, was often midway in the arguments
of all concerned) and he agreed that it was the best
thing to do. He could see that we would be closer
to our logging operations and to the main stem of
the Big Company's railroad. He also knew that our
old camp had been almost ruined by the deep snow
of the previous winter, making it necessary for us
to either spend a lot of money repairing it, or building a new camp, He also agreed there would be less
fire hazard at the new location, with better chances
to get a good water supply.

As soon as he agreed, we went ahead on the assumption that no further permission was necessary. We
couldn't have been more wrong. (In those days, we

paid little attention to such things as protocol and the Supe's ego.)

It took a while for the explosion to build up. We had time to move the forty-foot shop over to the new location, and get the camp half built before the Supe made his appearance. The day he first came, Scotty was putting siding on the cookshack. What happened was relayed to me in detail later.

"What the hell's going on here?" he asked Scotty. Scotty looked around at his black-browed questioner in surprise.

"Why, Felt's buildin' a new camp here," he said.

"He's not building no goddam camp here! Where is he?"

"Over at the old camp, salvagin' some lumber."

"You can quit working right now, and go tell Felt to come and see me at headquarters," the Supe ordered. "He's not building a camp here!"

The Supe went off muttering about so-and-so gyppos who thought they could go over *his* head. Poor Scotty was frightened by this great display of angry authority, and hurriedly did as he had been told.

Sonny, Swede, and Chet were working at Old Camp, loading lumber on a truck, when Scotty arrived all out of breath. According to them, Scotty still had his hammer in one hand and a mouthful of nails, and his face was as red as a tomato from his three-mile dash.

"By golly, Felt, a feller was just over at the new camp and he said you couldn't build yer camp there," he said, all in one breath.

"Who was he?" Sonny asked.

"Didn't say—some big black-browed bas——"

"Oh," said Sonny. "Must have been the Supe."

"Well, I know he was mad, all right," Scotty told him. "Said you weren't building no goddam camp there."

Sonny went back to loading lumber.

"Ain't you going' to see him?" Scotty asked.

"No. If he wants to see me he knows where to find me," Sonny replied.

Scotty shook his head at Sonny's failure to be alarmed. Later he rode back to New Camp on the load of lumber, muttering all the way about Felt's "goddam independence." The last thing that night, he told Sonny he'd better go down and see the "black feller."

"He sure was mad," he said, shaking his white head at Sonny's stubbornness.

Bright and early the next morning, the Supe arrived. He was really roaring.

"I thought I told those carpenters to stop work," he yelled at Sonny.

"Are you paying their wages so you can order my men around?" Sonny countered. "Besides, I've got permission to build my camp here."

"Not my permission—and I don't want it here!" the Supe informed him. "Midway hasn't got the say-so about this."

"That ain't the way I understood it," Sonny said calmly. "I've got my camp damn near built, and here it's going to stay. You get ahold of Midway, and we'll settle it once and for all."

The Supe stomped off furiously. He'd see who was running this outfit, all right!

Another week went by, then one morning I was in the cookshack after the loggers, who were cold decking logs until we could start shipping, had gone to work. There was a knock on the door. I opened it to find the Supe, his heavy brows pulled down in that black expression he had when he was angry. Without so much as a "good morning," he started in on me.

"How long have you been here?"

"Why, we've been building for three weeks or more," I said in surprise. "You know that."

"Who gave you permission?" he demanded. Beyond him, I could see Mr. Midway standing nervously in the yard between the cookshack and the big bunkhouse. I felt sorry for Mr. Midway. He so obviously was feeling the pinch of being caught in the middle like this, but he just as obviously had been guilty of some buck-passing.

"Why, *he* did," I replied, then went on to tell him how we had talked the matter over with Mr. Midway, and had proceeded to build on the assumption that it was agreeable to everyone concerned.

Suddenly, I decided this matter had gone far enough. It was time to settle it, once and for all.

"Come with me," I ordered. "We'll find my husband."

The Supe followed me, stomping along in that way he had when he was hot under the collar. I had to grin a bit to myself. This was one Dutchwoman who was going to put a fellow countryman of the same descent in his place! He hadn't even tasted my temper yet.

Sonny was trying to start the pickup so he could

tow the welder down to the shovel to do some work, and his disposition was not the best. The Supe started in on him about our going over his head in a matter which he should have had full authority to act upon. In the second place, he didn't want our camp here because (of all things) we would be too close to the reload, and we, or our loggers, might steal tools and supplies off his logging operations!

He may have had other reasons, but he didn't get to state them. At the mention of stealing, I jumped in between them, boiling mad. I shook my finger in his face as I went into the matter quite logically and quite thoroughly. The truths I spoke reddened their faces and kept them that way until I was through. I told Mr. Midway that he remembered very well when and where he had given us permission to build our camp, and that he had promised to make it all right with the Supe. To the Supe I pointed out that he had deliberately let us get our camp practically built before he raised any objection, in order to give us as much trouble as he could. As for stealing from his reload, I pointed out that he hired many more loggers than we, who had just as much opportunity to pick up tools and supplies as ours had, and that his insulting remarks were going to be remembered by us for a long time to come.

When I was through, they didn't have much more to say. They agreed to the campsite, and walked off. Perhaps they were too gentlemanly to abuse me as I had abused them, but anyway, they left us alone on the camp subject from there on.

A month later, when logging season was in full swing, I had visitors. There was Mr. Cutting Rights and son, and several other big shots, at midday for coffee and pie. Mr. Cutting Rights exclaimed many times over the nice new camp we had built; so near our logging operations, near to the creek for good water supply, and other advantages over those ancient railroad cars of Old Camp. He was most generous with his praise. Then, to my astonishment, the Supe spoke up.

"I had them build their camp here," he said boldly. "Not so much fire hazard as at the old camp." He saw my mouth open, and his face reddened, but he brazened it through. I closed my mouth and contented myself with giving him a dirty look. But during the following years, as long as we logged for the Big Company, I never passed up an opportunity to say "I told you so" in every way I could, whenever I could give the Supe a bad time.

When we had decided to leave the old ruined camp to the chipmunks, we knew the labor of building the new camp was going to be a big item. For that reason we decided to build out of the materials at hand as far as possible. Our forty-foot shop, built the year before, had been of such good materials, and was so well built, that it easily withstood the three-mile drag from Old Camp to New Camp, over a crooked, rough logging road. It arrived with but a few cedar shakes missing from its sides, and a skinned place here and there. But everything else would have to be built on the spot.

Sonny set each of his crew to a separate task. Several of them went down the creek to the old railroad bridges and wrenched off great planks—

sixteen feet by four inches thick and twelve inches wide—for flooring. There would be no signs telling the loggers to remove their "corks" in any of our camp buildings. (During the years we used New Camp, there must have been an inch and a half worn off the doorways and busy aisles. We swept out great piles of wood splinters every morning after the previous day's action of those sharp "corks.") During that time, Scotty was looking for suitable cedar logs from which to make shakes and cedar roof joists. For uprights we used the regular four-by-five-inch sawed car stakes we used for high-staking our log cars.

Amy, Swede's wife, and I helped to split the shakes from the thirty-inch cedar bolts Swede and Chet cut from the big cedar logs with a power saw. The power saw ran somewhat "anti-gogglin'," as Scotty expressed it, and our shakes weren't the most beautiful in the Pacific Northwest, but the effect after they were nailed to the sides of the log buildings was that of accordion pleats. Before they became weathered by the wind and rain, they had a fresh bright color that couldn't be duplicated by any paint on the market.

To split a perfect shake from straight-grained cedar takes considerable practice, although almost anyone can split out a useable one. We split them by setting the frow (a thing that looks like Paul Bunyan's butcher knife, with the handle put on straight up and down instead of parallel to the knife) on the soft edge of the cedar bolt and striking the upper side of the frow with a hardwood mallet. It takes many shakes (you might call them oversize shingles, though shingles are sawed by machine) to cover a forty-foot bunkhouse and cookshack, sides and roof; but when the six of us concentrated on the building, we got it done in a hurry. We also built a washhouse, a shed to shelter the light plant, and a couple of necessary small outhouses. Later in the year we had a smaller four-man bunkhouse built, and in the shop we had two rooms remodeled for us and the bull cook.

By the time the camp was completed, we had quite a village. I told Sonny we should post speed-limit signs at each entrance to "Feltsville." The logging road from Old Camp went right through New Camp, across the creek, up a steep pitch, around a curve or two, and onto the main logging road of the Big Company. A number of others used the three-mile stretch of road, and everyone complained because it was so rough, but no one offered to spend any time improving it, either with cats or a few loads of gravel.

That rough road was responsible for a small personal tragedy I shall long remember. I had a pair of red shoes, of which I was very proud. They made my feet look almost dainty, and were very comfortable to wear; consequently I wore them sometimes when I shouldn't.

One day, when I drove back to camp with a heavy load of groceries, wire, and other things, I didn't bother to change them on the way in. Sonny and Earl met me at Old Camp, where they transferred my truckload to a box they had built on the gooseneck of the logging arch, to spare the truck that three-mile stretch of hard going. We started off to

New Camp, towing the arch with the cat, with Earl and the groceries sharing the arch and Sonny and me sharing the cat seat. The seat wouldn't quite accommodate both of us, so I sat very daringly upon the arm of the seat, with one arm flung around the roof support post, feeling somewhat like a princess in a daffodil parade on my precarious perch. (Only the daffodil queen sits firmly on her throne. The princesses seem to just hang on.)

It was dark, and we had no lights to show us the road through the woods. Suddenly Sonny ran up on the side of a stump. The cat lurched alarmingly to one side, throwing me, feet first, into a big mudhole. I hung on desperately with one hand. Sonny backed up, and I back-pedaled fast to keep out of the way of those heavy cat tracks. By the time Sonny got everything under control and had rescued me, my red shoes were thoroughly soaked with mud.

"Now, you sit right up there on the fuel tank where I can watch you," he said sternly as I climbed back aboard. "The idea of you falling off and darn near gettin' runned under when I haven't got you insured!"

It was the nearest thing to sympathy he was willing to offer. And my red shoes were never the same again—nor was my dignity.

In one respect, New Camp was like Old Camp. There were no windows in our sleeping quarters. (At home, we sleep with our windows wide open even in the dead of winter.) One night the wind blew the door off, so we had no door, either, after that. On top of that, Sonny gave our stove to Amy, so we had no heat to dress by in the mornings.

Sonny loved it, but not me. He loved to tell about how he would get up in the morning in the late fall, when it had snowed during the night, to find snow drifted far into the doorway and across his bed. That was a little too much for me. It was bad enough to have to stub my toes on cat rollers and batteries, finding my way in the dark to my wilderness bed, without waking up to find snow all over my bed in the morning. So after the door blew away, I found plenty of excuses to sleep at home, in more civilized circumstances.

Curiously enough, we seldom have colds, except when we do close the bedroom windows at night. Even the girls like the cold, fresh night air.

"Good training for gyppo loggers' wives," some-one once said. Well, maybe so—but even their father hopes they'll marry boys in some other occupation.

Sonny had various ways of getting the loggers out of bed in the morning. They ranged from pound-ing on a gong to blowing a siren, to building such a hot fire in the bunkhouse heaters that they couldn't stay in bed.

The gong was a three-foot length of railroad iron, and when he beat on it with a piece of water pipe, he could fairly play a tune. The loggers had to get up in self-defense.

But his dream of the ideal morning camp alarm was a siren. It must be something between a police siren and a fire-boat whistle, and it must be strong enough to fairly blast the men out of bed in the morning, in order to please him.

At last, in a surplus store, he thought he had found it. It was a small gray-painted siren that stood about eight inches high, and was operated by electricity. It took some work to get the wires strung and a crude switch of sorts hooked up, but at last it was ready. They cranked up the light plant, and Sonny touched the ends of the switch wire together. The resulting noise was something that sounded like a cross between a banty rooster and an alley cat on the back fence at midnight. Sonny was slightly disappointed, but decided to keep it anyway. It must have had a far-reaching wail, though, because the early-morning crew at the reload, half a mile away, sent over a messenger to ask what on earth was going on.

It wasn't long before Sonny began having trouble with his beloved siren. He touched the ends of the switch wires together one morning, and only a muffled sound came out. When he investigated, he found the siren wrapped in a gunnysack and stuffed with newspaper. It looked as if the morning alarm had become a bit unpopular with the crew. Eventually, he went back to the gong and the beater, and the hot fires in the barrel heating stove in the bunkhouse.

Scotty had his own method of awakening early in the morning, without an alarm clock to do the job. Just as he was ready to climb into bed at night, he would go to the door of his bunkhouse and shout into the stillness of the night, "Four o'clock in the morning." Then, according to him, the echo would travel around the swamp and return at exactly four in the morning to arouse him. Never failed, he declared.

Some Characters

DURING THE SEVEN YEARS WE LOGGED, WE HAD THE opportunity to know many loggers as they lived in our primitive boarding camp. It took a certain type of person to enjoy living so far back in the mountains for a week at a time, especially in these days of modern conveniences and fast automobiles. Many could not be content so far from taverns, so they didn't stay with us long. Others, although they were victims of what we called "Fridayitis"—that weekly urge to return to civilization on Fridays—enjoyed living in our little logging camp. They liked the people they worked with; they liked the fishing, the deep woods, the friendly atmosphere of the place, and they came back year after year to log with us.

Most of the loggers were on the younger side, and had seen service during World War II. Ralph, whom everybody called "Swede," had spent forty-four months in the South Pacific theater, going from island to island with the Army. He was on a ship that was wrecked off the northern shores of Australia, and had traveled across the desert to civilization with what equipment his company had saved from the ship. Behind the faint smile on his cherubic face, that almost shy manner, was a toughness that seldom showed. He fast became one of our most loyal and trusted loggers, as well as a good friend. Eventually Sonny came to depend upon him to run his outfit as foreman during Sonny's absence, although we couldn't afford to hire anyone as such full time.

Swede learned to drive cat and loading shovel, power saw and welder, and when something went "gunnysack" (his expression for "haywire"), he could take any machine apart and put it back together again and it would run. He had had considerable mechanical background and training, so it came natural to him to know what bolt belonged where on any machine within a short time.

Swede's six feet four was further heightened by his "corks" for even though he was officially a shovel operator, he often climbed down to help wire car stakes and otherwise get a carload of logs completed in time for shipment. He liked to "see things go," as Sonny expressed it.

More than one logger was deceived by Swede's angelic looks. There was only one way we could tell when he lost his temper. He would get slightly pink around the eyes, and remove his rimless glasses. Once, a head loader thought Swede couldn't hear the epithets he was hurling at him over the roar of the shovel motor. When Swede took off his glasses and climbed down from the shovel, the loader took off for the tall timber, until he was certain things had calmed down a bit.

Swede had a little red coupé which he could put over any kind of road, no matter the depth of the mud or the roughness of the ruts. I had a strong suspicion that he simply took out the floorboards, shoved his feet and long legs through to the ground, and operated it kiddy-car fashion. That was the only way that some of the things he did made sense. One hunting season he brought Amy, his wife, up, and over the weekend it rained torrents. So, rather than take a chance on the washed-out road, he decided to go out the three miles via the railroad. It took a little maneuvering to get the wheels up on the rails, but when it was done, he revved up the motor and they went buzzing off down the railroad track just as if they had iron wheels on that little old coupé.

He would use his own equipment recklessly, but he was always careful with ours. Swede worked with us for seven logging seasons and became a real member of our logging family.

I sometimes wondered if the men on the landing really took for granted Swede's sense of responsibility when he handled the loading rig so capably right over their heads. If he had ever killed a man, he would have left the woods. One time, during our third year, he dreamed for several nights in a row that he killed the young second loader, a boy named Ernie. Shortly after that, he was one day swinging one log against another to bump it into place, and narrowly missed crushing Ernie between the two logs. After the sweat of his shock had passed, he called Ernie over and told him about the dream. Ernie quit that night. His mother had been having the same dream.

Chet was always one of my favorite loggers. He

was our hook tender and chokerman, and finally
our head loader. He was about five foot ten, lean
of body and unhurried of movement. He consumed
a box of snuff every two days. One day, when he
ran out during the day, he asked me if I'd bring
him back a fresh box from camp, two miles away.
When I got back to camp I became involved in my
cooking duties and forgot all about the request.

When I apologized to him that night, he just
looked at me and said, "It's a good thing I wasn't
bleedin' to death and had to send you for a tourni-
quet."

The way he told of his first impression of our
logging outfit, in that dry drawl of his, would con-
vulse his listeners. I had left a note at his farm
(which was about ten miles from civilization, too)
asking him to come up to log with us; even drew
him a map with instructions for getting there. He
appeared a day or two later, his "corks" slung over
one shoulder, his suitcase in the other hand. Because of the big mudholes, he left his car out a mile
from camp and began walking, not even certain
he was near the place. By and by he met a small
tractor waddling along with a turn of logs, pads
missing off the tracks on either side, almost disappearing at times in the wide, deep mudholes. He hailed
the cat skinner, but the skinner didn't even see him.
Chet had to jump into the brush to keep from being
"runned under." He wondered if they were hiring
deaf and blind cat skinners in this outfit.

He continued up the twisting logging road another thousand feet and met another cat. This was
Swede, who stopped and directed him to the rail-

road track ahead, from where he could see the camp. Just as he was within hailing distance, a big yellow speeder came around the bend of the track and squealed to a stop. A man jumped out and ran over to a hollow log, and began yelling into it. Chet stopped, put his suitcase down, and scratched his head thoughtfully. Just what kind of a place *was* this—a cat skinner who couldn't see or hear, and had almost run him down, and now this jerk shouting into a hollow log. While he watched, the man returned to the speeder and drove off rapidly; then Chet went and peeked into the end of the log. There was a telephone, which he figured the man had used to get clearance for the speeder. Now he felt better, so picking up his stuff, he sauntered on to the cookhouse and made himself acquainted with the cook; the one with the scarred face. He found his bunk, got himself settled, and in a day or two found the informal air of the camp enjoyable; but he never did forget that first impression.

Chet worked with us on and off for several years. He put up with my vagaries, although I think he placed all women in the same category, which wasn't complimentary even to those who warranted it, much less to those who didn't. We carried on a good-natured running feud for years. When he once gave me a compliment on my cooking, it was an accolade. The particular subject was a flaky apple pie, which I didn't always manage to produce, and I heard him say to Chub, "Try that apple pie. It's the best pie I ever lapped a lip over."

One time, when I had to leave the cooking to

someone else while I was gone for a few days, I in-
quired about his health when I returned.

"I was worried, Chet," I told him. "I forgot to
leave instructions for the care and feeding of head
loaders."

"Wa-a-al," he drawled, "to tell the truth, I was
gettin' pretty worked up over it myself."

One day, while working under his "klunk," as he
called his car, he got so much grease in his salt-and-
pepper hair that he shaved his head. I was quite
put out about it, and called him "my bald-headed
friend"—which made *him* put out with *me*. Until
his hair grew out, he wore his white cap with the
"bill"—even to the table. He hated "hard hats," and
refused to wear them, despite industrial insurance
regulations, and despite the fact that loading on the
landing is considered one of the most dangerous
places in the woods to work. He stuck to red felt
hunting hats in winter and white duck caps during
the summer.

Chub and Chet were good friends. They looked
out for each other's interests at the table. They
divided the last piece of meat or pie, and it was
amazing how much coffee they could squeeze out
of a pot which they had, by eloquent shrugs and
gestures, indicated to other loggers was empty. If
they each ate more than two quarters of pie, Chet
would say that perhaps they had better quit; that
folks might talk. They could both drink plenty
and hold their liquor, although Chet never went in
for drinking to the extent that Chub did. When
Chub arrived at a tavern on Friday night, he would

immediately order a half dozen bottles of beer and empty them as fast as he could tip them up. He loved the "cafe society" of his favorite tavern—"Strongarms," he called it—and spent most of his free time there.

Chub was a big, rangy fellow with tremendous energy. He never walked when he could run (unless he had a bad hangover) and his hands and feet were large even for his frame. One time, when I ordered some number eleven caulked boots for him, he had considerable to say about the two weeks it took to get them. He had split the toe of his old pair with an ax, and he claimed the water ran in even though he greased carefully around the hole. When the new boots finally came, as big a pair of boots as I had ever had the opportunity to heft, I told him the factory had had to shut down and retool in order to make them. He just laughed that gay, infectious chortle of his, and didn't answer.

Chub showed the influence of a Russian ancestor in his deep-set gray-green eyes, the extremely high cheekbones, the high-bridged nose that had been broken a time or two, and the wide mouth and square jawline. I don't believe I ever saw him lose temper, although he took quite seriously any slight offered our little cockers. After Paddy left us, we got two; Corky (whose real name, on his papers, was Trooper), a large parti-color male, liver and white, and his dainty little mate, Black Beauty, whose little baseball-size head didn't exactly conform to everyone's notions of beauty. We took them often to camp because there was lots to eat, and they didn't get in the way, and Chub loved them. He let them sleep under his bed, and even on top of it if they wanted to. He merely grinned when Corky pulled the blankets down underneath the bunk and made himself a nest, but when some of the loggers kicked the dogs out of the bunkhouse because Corky snored, Chub immediately whistled them back in.

"You can sleep under *my* bed, Corky, and we don't care if you do snore. There's lots of snorin' goin' on around here at night." He was dead serious about taking on anyone who disagreed with him, where those dogs were concerned. We finally took them home and left them there to avoid trouble.

Chub would coax the dogs along with him when he went down to the swamp fishing, even though he would likely have to haul fifty pounds of fat cocker dog home, along with his fishing gear and hip boots.

"You know," he'd laugh as he told us, "I beat myself to death getting out on the beaver dam, occasionally going back to untangle Corky from a black-berry vine, or to help Beauty over a log; and just as I get back out on the dam and ready to cast in a big, deep, still pool, Corky gets thirsty and goes 'Slurp, slurp, slurp,' with that noisy way he has, then all the fish scurry away and I never get a bite."

After we took the dogs home, Chub's fishing ex-peditions were more productive, but I always sus-pected they were a lot less fun.

Chub always got even with me for picking on him. He dearly delighted in separating me from my weekly gambling allowance. I have very little gam-bling spirit, and always limited my losses to two dollars a week. When that was gone, I would re-

The Felt family. *Left to right:* Vicki (age eleven),
Margaret, Kimberley (age four), and Horace.

The gyppo logger at the controls building a road
with the little cat. Mount Rainier is in the background.

A pair of fallers preparing to put in an undercut so
that the tree will fall in the direction planned for it.
The fallers, Lennart Elfven and Chub Romanoff.

(Facing page, top) Coming in out of the woods
with a big turn of logs.

(Facing page, bottom) This is a Cletrac tractor
with a Carco arch bringing in a turn of logs.

(Above) The second loader unhooks the turn of logs
when it arrives at the landing.

The shovel loading rig operated by Swede Nelson
loads logs off the landing onto the railroad cars.

The next step is wiring each layer of logs as the load is
built up between the car stakes to insure safe arrival
at the paper plant in Tacoma. The gyppo and his wife
often performed this necessary task.

When the little Felt girls came to camp
they often watched loading operations with their parents.

The Felt logging operations didn't always go smoothly.
This day several machines broke down at once.
The loggers became mechanics. Swede Nelson was doing
the welding so the equipment could be patched up
and the logging operations would be going again.

. . . and (according to the gyppo) "Nothing was running
but the creek, and it was damned near dry!"

Lunch on the landing.
Left to right: Gene Waller, cat driver; Elmer Otremba, loader;
Harold Gibson, hook tender; Chub Romanoff, faller;
Margaret, the gyppo's wife; Les Van Hoof, cat driver;
Swede Nelson, shovel operator and foreman;
and Sonny Felt, the gyppo himself.

Margaret, Vicki, and Kimberley.
The girls entertained themselves in a logging camp
built out of the materials at hand.

Gambling was a favorite pastime in most logging camps. At the Felts' camp the loggers humored Margaret with a few games of blackjack until her weekly $2.00 gambling allowance was gone. Then they hardheartedly returned to poker.

Supper was the best time of day. Kimberley sits
next to her father and Vickianne is between
"Handlebars" and Chub Romanoff.

Kimberley does a little baton twirling to entertain
the loggers in the bunkhouse. This was the lead photograph
published in the article "A Gyppo Logger's Wife,"
written by Margaret Elley Felt and published in the
August 30, 1952, issue of the *Saturday Evening Post*.

The Felt family. *Left to right:* Vicki (age eleven),
Margaret, Kimberley (age four), and Horace.

fuse to risk any further. Since the loggers understood my feeling about this, they would always pretend to be highly enthused about blackjack (which was the only game my poor lame brain ever really mastered) until my money was in their pockets; then they would wholeheartedly revert to poker— a game I had tried a couple of times but found the lessons too expensive. I did get down on my knees to the dice game once in a while, though. How that Chub could breathe luck into those cubes of ivory! "Come on, dice!" he'd say passionately. "Four, five, six!" By the end of the year, his gambling money would amount to forty or fifty dollars, which he kept in a little square cardboard box with tinned corners. We called it his "ironbound box."

The last week of the season, they would always have one big, long gambling session, until one person had all the money; and it wasn't always Chub who had it, either. One year Earl, our fair-haired boy truck driver, won it. By the time he got home, he had very little to show for his gambling luck. The whole crew stopped at the tavern-restaurant and insisted he treat them. They had beer and more beer, the best steaks in the house, razor blades, aspirin, chances on the punchboard, tips to the waitress, long-distance telephone calls—everything they could think of, to spend his winnings. To add insult to injury, they "squealed on him" by telling the bartender not to sell him any beer because he wasn't twenty-one. He had to sit helplessly by, watching everyone else guzzle themselves silly at his expense.

It was a good thing Earl had such a wonderful sense of humor. He even grinned good-naturedly when he saw Chub sack up his opened but still full bottles of beer, stick extra ones in his pockets, and order a case of beer—all out of Earl's winnings.

If I had a son, I would want him to be exactly like Earl. He was a big-shouldered, fair-haired youngster of nineteen, with green eyes that crinkled to mere slits when he grinned, a golden complexion, and a marvelous disposition. He drove truck for us, and I could trust him with a blank signed check any time. He was very conscientious about his work, and if he did something dumb (which we all did at times) he just never got over calling himself a fool. Sonny grew very fond of the boy, and practically adopted him. But he was eligible for military service, so we lost him to the Air Force. (Later we heard he was in Newfoundland, was married, and had a little fair-haired son.)

In direct contrast to Earl's Scandinavian ancestry, we had a number of Indians who were good loggers. There was Herman, of an east of the Cascades tribe; talkative, friendly, and as opposite from the usual taciturn Indian as any I ever met. He loved coffee, although he claimed it shortened your life quicker, and called himself a "smoked Swede." He was well educated, well read, and conscientious about getting back to work on Monday mornings. He brought up a fellow Indian from time to time, and sometimes they were dependable and sometimes not, just like any other race or nationality.

Howard was Herman's good friend, and a fellow member of their little Shaker church on the Muckleshoot Reservation. Herman brought him up to work for us one season. He was a kind, quiet man—and dependable. Shortly after we closed camp that year, he passed away of a heart attack, and we were invited to the funeral. We sent up quantities of tinned vegetables, fruit, and staple groceries, for the big crowd of Indian folk who came from all over the state to attend the funeral.

Sonny couldn't get away, so I went alone. When I came into the small unpainted church, they gave me a seat of honor where I could look directly into Howard's peaceful face. He was dressed in a dark suit, and was wearing the leather dress gloves and white silk scarf he would evidently have received for Christmas had he lived two days longer.

All through that long ceremony, I sat there with the oddest feeling that I was far removed from civilization as I knew it. Candles were lighted on the tiny pedestals beneath small crosses that arched themselves over the end wall of the primitive little church. The ceremony itself was a touching service, combining the solemn beauty of the Catholic with the Shaker and the weird solemnity of the Indian burial ritual. The flickering candles cast a peculiar light over the shining dark faces of the hundred people who managed to get inside. For days afterward, I was haunted by the unending two-note chant, which I couldn't reproduce myself to save my life.

Herman told me that his church was criticized by other churches for not having the Bible open upon their altar during services. His reason was as logical as any I could think of.

"We worshipped the Great Spirit—God—long before we knew the Bible existed, so why should our church be condemned because we do not use the Bible in the manner prescribed by other churches?" It made perfect sense to Herman—and to me.

Herman and I had many warm discussions about the white man's influence upon the early Indians in the West. He was also well enough informed to see both sides of that age-old problem of the government's treatment of the Indians. We both agreed that our government would have fewer black marks upon its escutcheon if they had kept their promises to the Indians in all the treaties they made. Herman, however, had no bitterness on that subject.

It was Herman who remarked drily one evening how like a church the bunkhouse became when I stopped in for a chat or a short try at gambling. The language immediately improved. I didn't mind the profanity very much, for no one can beat Sonny at it when he gets started, and the profanity of a logger is usually colorful and unique.

(The worst oath I ever heard uttered came not from a logger but from a construction superintendent who used the road past our camp. He seemed to have the idea that he had first rights to the road, since he had been there first. After we blocked the road a few times, and made him come and ask us for help to get his pickup through, and plied him with pie and coffee while he was asking, we succeeded in making a friend of him.)

Chuck was a canny one with his tongue. He tended hook and broke in all the new chokermen. He knew how to get those logs out of the brush. His family and ours were good friends, dating back to the early friendship between his wife and my husband, when they were four and five years of age. Selma, Chuck's wife, and Sonny went to school together in the little town of Mineral, and later, after each had married someone else, they again met and all of us, including our little daughters, became friends.

Chuck worked with us several times, once briefly as a partner in the business. He was on the small, lithe side, with a quick step and a keen sense of humor. There was one thing I can't stand about a man, though—and Chuck did it. Whether he was at home, dictating to Selma, or at camp, telling me how to cook his eggs, he *had* to be one of those men who cook from the dining-room table.

We had one bad scene about those eggs one morning. It was a Monday morning. The night before, the road had been so bad that we couldn't come in with the truck, and I had sacked up enough groceries for breakfast and carried them in on my back for three miles—including several dozen eggs. At breakfast, I took one look at what he was doing to his eggs, and lit into him.

"For heaven's sake, Chuck, do you know that I carried those eggs in three miles on my back last night?" I exploded. He was dipping his toast daintily into the yolks a time or two, and then pushing the rest aside.

Chuck looked up. "I always eat my eggs this way, whether the hen-house is just outside the kitchen or seventy miles away," he informed me. "What difference does it make to you how I eat my eggs?"

I shut up—but I was still mad when he finally finished eating and went out to work.

I got the blame for bringing up a logger who turned out badly—like the cat driver who ran bull hook, chokers and all, around the drum of the cat, and broke the drum to bits. Felt wanted to shoot him; thought he was going to have to in order to get him off the cat before he did more damage. He lasted just an hour.

But when it came to giving me credit for finding a good logger occasionally, he never would. For instance, I sent Handlebars up to load logs, and he turned out very well.

Handlebars turned up at my front door one day, and I found myself paying more attention to the adorable black handlebar mustaches he sported than to his recitation of his experience in loading. He had them waxed to points, the most fascinating mustaches I ever saw, and he seemed quite unaware of my admiration. We finally got used to them, but he was seldom called by his right name, Elmer. He had a winning personality, a grand sense of humor, and he filled the bill completely as a head loader.

Lennart came to work for us through a brother-in-law of a brother-in-law of Sonny's. He was Swedish, well educated, and a good logger. He worked as head loader a season or two, but preferred falling with the power saw. Lennart's wife, Kay, and their baby, Katrina, came over from Sweden the first fall he worked for us, and we became very well acquainted. Both parents and baby talked Swedish, and Lennart, I discovered, even read Agatha Christie in the Swedish translation. He loved the woods, had been a forestry student in the old country, and no matter what he did during the winter months, he always wanted to come back to the woods during logging season. Lennart's careful English, his hobby of color photography, his surveying and forestry background, made him a very good witness for us once in a trial. Several times, when we would have a birthday or a New Year's party, Kay and Lennart would come, and nobody could dance the polkas, schottishes, or the good old Swedish waltzes as well as they could.

The feuds that Scotty carried on from time to time gave the camp a lot of laughs. He began the first one with Hank, the big broken-nosed Norski, partner to little Fred, the Arkansaser, who were the "best tam fallers in the state," according to Hank. Hank had his own ideas about how a falling saw should be filed, and had no reluctance about imparting those ideas even to an old saw filer like Scotty. Of course that didn't set well with Scotty, but he got even. He filed Hank's saw just right, doing a very good job on every saw, until he had lulled Hank into thinking and bragging that "now he had Scotty trained." Then one day, when there were some especially large trees to fall, Scotty handed Hank a poorly filed saw, and Hank took off with it, not thinking to examine it. About noon he came stomping down out of the woods to find Scotty, who looked as innocent as a lamb and disclaimed any knowledge of such a dull saw being turned out of *his* filing shack. Hank must have dulled it himself, he said. Hank, frustrated, grabbed up another saw (a sharp one this time) and returned to his job, muttering to himself. I doubt if anyone ever got the best of Scotty, at least for very long.

Hank's broken English was in direct contrast to Freddy's Southern accent. They loved each other like brothers, until Hank got drunk; then all bets were off until he sobered up. When Hank was drunk, Freddy said "You couldn't chisel a dime out of that big shot with ball peen hammer and a two-pound chisel."

Freddy was a little fellow, with a merry, toothless grin and twinkling blue eyes. His particular ambition, which he spoke of between paydays, was to replace his false teeth, which he had lost in some tavern down Hoquiam way some years back. Only thing, he told us, he always kept buyin' 'em in bottles.

He did accomplish his ambition that summer he was with us. Our loader and his wife took an interest in Freddy, and kept after him until he actually did have a set of dentures made. They improved his appearance wonderfully, but they weren't too successful, for he had gone without teeth for so many years that he couldn't seem to get used to them. I often wonder if that set met with the same fate as the first, if they were left in a tavern somewhere.

Freddy and Hank had been partners for several years, oddly matched though they seemed to be. Hank, for all his bulk, was the agile one, and de-

lighted in turning handsprings down the length of
a newly fallen tree. Freddy's sense of humor made
him many friends. He prefaced almost every remark
with "Wal, dip me in cider." When someone wasn't
acting normally, Freddy claimed he had "slipped his
lead."

Both Freddy and Hank liked to drink, and this
finally brought about the breakup of their partnership. Hank didn't want to return to camp drunk,
after a payday, and Freddy did. It always makes
me a little unhappy to think of that partnership
being broken up—"the best tam fallers in the state."

The last time I saw Hank was on Skid Road
in Seattle. I was walking down the middle of the
sidewalk, toward Archie MacDougall's employment
agency, when a man jumped out from the doorway
of a flophouse and grabbed me by both elbows. I
had my mouth open to scream when I recognized
Hank. He threw back his leonine head and fairly
roared at giving me such a fright. He had an Indian
partner and was looking for work, but we weren't
looking for fallers then, so I couldn't hire him.

Little Freddy, the Arkansaser, we see occasionally,
tamping a tie or lifting a rail with the section crew
on the Milwaukee Railroad.

It was a second loader we had that almost convinced me that the younger generation of American
loggers was going to be of a different breed. Bob
attended a couple of quarters of college during winter and spring, and worked in the logging woods
during the summer and fall. He was big, husky,
and very nimble on his "corked" feet. I've seen

him jump clear from the top of a loaded car to the
ground, fourteen feet below, without ill effect. He
had a Polish name and features, quite handsome, with
deep-set blue eyes and wavy black hair. I drove him
up to camp that first day, and he fell in love with
the country, the fishing, the hunting to come, the
camp, and our dog Corky.

"You can go down to the swamp fishing with
me, Corky," he crooned, stroking Corky's white and
tan coat with large, capable hands. "And come hunting season, we'll get us some grouse. Bet you can
really flush out the birds." I don't remember that
we told him that Corky was a better "eatin'" dog
than he was a "huntin'" dog, but we figured that
anyone who liked dogs was a good joe.

About a week later, Bob made a startling dis-
covery, and blurted it out right in Corky's hearing;
a most unkind thing to do.

"That dog is the *dumbest* dog I ever saw!" he
exclaimed.

I don't remember what occasioned the remark, but
I remember how Corky looked up at Bob and stalked
haughtily out of the dining car. That night, he and
Butch, our bob-tailed cat, moved out from under
Bob's bed, where they had been sleeping. I guess
Corky wasn't so dumb that he couldn't figure out
he wasn't liked for himself alone. Evidently Bob
had expected too much of our little pet.

It was a day or two later when Bob appeared in
his hot-weather stagged-off pants. They were stagged
off a bit high for Sonny's taste, resembling shorts
far more than they did a logger's stagged-off pants,

barely covering his knees. Sonny took one look, and
pointed back toward the bunkhouse.

"We aren't running foot-races today, my boy,"
he said. "You can go thataway."

"Okay," said Bob, and promptly went to the bunkhouse to get his clothes. Sonny went off muttering
to himself about "the characters you meet in the
brush when you haven't got a gun."

No roster of our logging family would be complete without A. B. Joslyn, though he wasn't a logger. A. B. was an able and shrewd building contractor and a businessman of the old school. He
knew how to make money, and he made it.

He also thought very little of women in business,
and it took several years for him to actually accept
me as Sonny's full partner in our logging setup.
When Sonny would say that he had to talk something over with me, A. B. would shake his head and
say, "For heaven's sake, why? Women don't know
anything about business."

But he finally changed his mind about that, at
least as far as I was concerned. Perhaps it was because Sonny was so persistent about including me in
on everything from the rough work to the financial
responsibility that he finally accepted me. We became fast friends, and I now feel certain that he
likes me fully as much as I like him. We make
mincemeat together, and we talk over business in
man-to-man fashion. I drive him to Seattle or
Tacoma on business trips, and worry about his health
as if he were my own family. There is a great deal
of satisfaction in making friends with a man like

A. B. Joslyn, and to overcome his prejudice against women—"the modern-day women who stick their noses into their husbands' business"—and to have earned his respect.

A. B. was an unusual person in that he was eighty-five years old at the time he first backed us in business, and he planned ahead as if he were going to live to be at least one hundred and ten. (At the time, it wouldn't have surprised me too much if he made it!) He hasn't aged much during the past ten years, except for a little loss of hearing and an occasional bout with arthritis. We've always marveled at his alert mind and his still-keen business sense. He stands straight and tall, proud of bearing, his clear eyes kind but discerning, his mustaches lending dignity. For more than fifty years he has been a building contractor, and each year he still plans a house or a remodelling job, either of his own or for a friend. In 1952, he built six houses and an addition to our little restaurant on our farm.

A. B. was born on a farm in New Hampshire, where his family had lived for generations since coming to America on the English ship *Increase*, in 1635. When he was grown, he moved to Michigan, then came west, where he thought there was more opportunity for young men.

He likes to tell a story on himself, about a man he worked with in Michigan who was, as he puts it, "The durndest tinkerer I ever saw." One time A. B.'s watch had quit running, and the "tinkerer" took it home to his hotel room overnight. The next morning he brought it back to A. B., and it was running perfectly.

"No use throwing that watch away," he told A.
B. "It'll run for twenty years yet." It did, too,
though A. B. maintains he should have pensioned it
off long before he did. Its persistent and steady
ticking reminded him of an error in judgment which
he has often regretted.

That same "tinkerer" kept urging A. B. to invest in his new venture, that of building a new-
fangled machine called an automobile. A. B. per-
sistently declined with thanks. Some years later, one
of the original investors awoke one morning to find
himself richer by some twenty million dollars. The
"tinkerer" was Henry Ford.

As in all logging camps, discussions often run
warm and noisy. Ours was no exception.

Chuck loved a good argument, and could present
very logical arguments on either side if he chose.
He had been baiting Chub for some time, and one
night he exploded a bombshell by saying offhandedly,
"Well, money isn't everything."

"Hah!" Chub retorted instantly. "I'd sure as hell
settle for everything it would buy!"

That particular argument went on all evening.
The celloglass windows of the bunkhouse bulged outward with all the hot wind expended as everybody
joined in, pro and con. I dropped in several times,
to add fresh fuel whenever it looked like it was
running down. Sonny chipped in his share, too, and
away they'd go again. It was midnight before they
finally settled down and everyone went to sleep.

But there was one argument that was never settled;
one that older loggers discuss at great length: Which

are the ghosts of dead loggers, the squirrels or the camp robbers?

Toward the end of our seventh and last season for the Big Company, we had dinner at the local restaurant-tavern, and we found out just how well this logging family of ours stuck together.

Handlebars' seat was usurped by an outsider, and before long the discussion developed into something of an argument. I was getting such a kick out of the entire affair that I wasn't much help, and just watched how forces gathered on each side to take care of the situation.

Swede finally removed his glasses, and that seemed to be the signal. One logger quietly picked up a beer bottle and just as quietly joined Swede at the head of the table. Another came up the same way from the other side. Handlebars stood ready to defend his rights.

Suddenly Amy, Swede's wife, let go with her able tongue. There wasn't a blow struck, but the outsider finally gave up, looked toward the ceiling, and then grinned at the grim crowd of loggers encircling him right and left. The pals he had brought along to "clean up" our crowd were sitting down at our end of the table, talking with Sonny and me. They were old schoolmates of the Felt brothers, and hadn't wanted to fight anyway. I was laughing so hard I could hardly eat my steak. We all credited Amy with preventing an out-and-out brawl.

All our loggers, especially Chub, loved Kim. One season, when she was three years old, Kim and Chub carried on a pint-size feud that ran like this: Kim would make a positive statement about something, and Chub would say, "Oh, I wouldn't say that." And much to his delight, Kim would retort, "Well, *I* would!"

One day, one of the cat drivers brought her a wild bunny in his lunch pail. It quickly escaped, but Kim had enjoyed the rare privilege of holding a little wild animal in her own two dimpled hands.

When the logger is laid off in the woods, he usually returns to his stump ranch to eke out his living. In 1950, we bought The Farm, about five miles from Graham, the nearest post office, and about halfway from our North Lake home to the logging woods. The gracious two-story white house is of 1928 vintage, with eight rooms, and since we installed a modern furnace, a very comfortable home. The tall poplar trees behind the house are nice any time of the year, from the stark graceful branches of winter through the early green leaves of spring to the golden autumn colors. (And since there is no present demand for poplar for peelers or other lumber uses, they still stand, safe from the axes and falling saws of my gyppo husband.)

So far, we haven't farmed, outside of raising a short crop of hay and two breachy steers who wouldn't stay inside the pasture fences. I chased them all over the neighborhood one summer and fall, and breathed a sigh of relief when we delivered them to the slaughterhouse.

Sonny had often made the remark (on Monday morning, when we had to start the day short-handed

or with a hung-over crew) that he should own a
beer parlor, so he could pay his loggers with one
hand and take it back with the other, come payday weekends. The idea took hold and stayed with
me, and finally evolved into a plan to turn a small
produce shack on the corner of the farm into a
hamburger joint. No beer parlor, we agreed, but
being on the main road back to camp, we could
provide a convenient stopover for the loggers (both
ours and others) returning from town on Sunday
night. Also, with a hired cook and Vicki's help,
there was tourist trade we could catch during the
summer; hunters, fishermen, and skiers the rest of
the year, and an income of sorts for ourselves during the winter months when snow shut us out of
the woods.

The place was a quick success, with loggers dropping in for black coffee and staying to eat when
they felt more like it. We still have that little
restaurant, and it is still going strong.

Vicki has become my right-hand waitress and she
can cashier like a little veteran. Arithmetic has
always been difficult for her in school, but recently
she was the only one in her class who could explain
how to make change. Grown-ups have often stood
watching her admiringly while she counted out
change for a twenty-dollar bill with never a penny
error. She also mastered all the details of how to
operate the cash register and change the tape before
I did. She can remember orders and keep them
straight, too, but I still have trouble in getting her
to greet customers with a smile.

Kim might be called my hostess. She enters into

conversation with total strangers, and carries on for a half hour at a time if they will talk to her. She explains about the latest batch of puppies, and if I don't watch her, she might even go into detail as to exactly how they got themselves born. She takes such things so matter-of-factly that at times it is hard to keep her from talking too much. It isn't always Kim who gets the education. Sometimes it's the customers—and sometimes it's the mother!

Last winter, I'm sure we had the only snowman in the Northwest that had three heads. I think we also have the only "mama" doll that has cried in the gallery of the State Legislature during session. (Kim got so interested in the proceedings that she let the doll slip into crying position.) She is also an interested follower of the children's programs on television, with sometimes surprising results.

"Do you know there are *two* kinds of flying saucers?" she asked us one day. Then she went on to explain, making circles with her dimpled hands, "There's the saucer type, and the two-ring type."

Sonny reminded her that we have no television at camp, so he hadn't seen the program; then he asked, "How do you account for flying saucers? Have you found out where they come from?"

Kim shook her head.

"No-o-o," she said seriously, "but I think Jesus has something to do with them."

Truly, Kim has her own delightful little place in our list of "characters!"

Of Fires and Firebugs

IT WILL LIKELY DISAPPOINT SOME FOLKS WHO THINK of the deep woods as a cool place to spend a summer vacation to find that this isn't always so. The only cool place I've found in the woods was near a running creek, under the tall sword ferns, on a moist sandy bank. Out where the trees grow thick, it's like a hot street on a busy shopping day. The air is still, and heat presses down on you, and the humidity is stifling. You stand still and listen to the sounds of the deep woods. The birds are stilled by the hot sun; a limb cracks, alarmingly loud, as the sap retreats from the heat; and the sky above is clear and brilliant. The loneliness can be oppressive, and not a little frightening. You wish for just a little breeze to set the fir needles to waving in their old friendly way, and for the rubbing of the branches against each other to let you know the trees are still alive and not lost in some alien limbo far removed from the snow-capped Cascade Mountains.

It is a welcome sound when you hear the cats start up again after the noon hour, and the far-off sound of an angry buzzing power saw eating its way into a reluctant hemlock tree.

The most dreaded danger in the logging woods is fire. During the hot dry season, tension mounts as the humidity drops. Loggers, company officials, and fire wardens are equally concerned over the fire danger. Here in western Washington the heavy undergrowth, combined with logging debris, presents a great fire hazard. Ferns, moss, fireweed, and brush gradually build up a deep matted bed of vegetation beneath the trees, in which a fire cannot only be easily enkindled but can be extremely difficult to extinguish. You can understand our feeling of sitting on a tinderbox, and see that it doesn't stem entirely from our imaginations.

The forest associations, and the state forester, send out dry-weather warnings, and the local companies' fire wardens cooperate to see that the warnings are heeded and fire regulations are followed. Some insurance companies add their weight to the argument by refusing to pay loss when the logger insists upon logging after the humidity has fallen to 28 or 30 degrees.

At the beginning of every season, the first thing to be attended to is the fire equipment. Fire tools are checked by the logging outfits, and replaced if found missing. Fire extinguishers are refilled, and are carried on every cat, donkey, truck, and loading rig. Tiny hip-pocket-size extinguishers are carried by the power-saw faller, for a power saw can set sudden and devastating fires.

The advent of this tiny hip-pocket-size fire extinguisher caused a long remembered episode, involving Chub and Swede.

"I'm already carrying two wedges, a fifty-foot steel tape, a falling ax, a fifty-pound power saw, a gasoline can with two gallons of gas, and my grub bucket," Chub complained. "Where in the hell am I going to put that son of a gun of a fire extinguisher?"

Swede surveyed Chub, arrayed in all his logging equipment, wedges strung on a buckskin string and hanging over his brawny shoulders, his lunch bucket hanging from the other, ax fastened to his belt, power saw in one huge hand and gas can in the other. Swede shook his head sadly at Chub's problem. Even his pockets were bulging with snoose, tape, gloves, and various other items.

Swede scratched his head. "Well," he drawled, with that deadpan look on his cherubic face, "I don't think Felt cares *where* you *put* the damn'd thing, but keep it close to you when you're falling timber."

Chub roared at Swede's implication as to where he could carry the fire extinguisher, then took the disputed piece of equipment and climbed into the crew truck for his ride to the falling area.

The district fire warden checks every requirement to see that it is fulfilled, and puts a seal upon the big red fire box so it cannot be opened, or the tools used, except in case of fire.

Felt and Company got into trouble the second year, over the fire tool box. Since we were so under-financed in that second logging season, we couldn't afford enough extra saws for both falling and the fire tool box. Sonny and the fire warden were walking along the track one day when one of the buckers came along, went to the apparently locked fire tool box, reached in, and extracted a falling saw.

"Hey—what goes?" the warden asked. "That box is supposed to be locked up. It's got the state seal on it."

Sonny had to grin at being caught red-handed. The box was a makeshift affair from which the back could be removed without disturbing the seal put on the hasp by the state fire warden. The warden practically stood over Sonny while he had a new box made.

The new fire box looked like a coffin, with two projecting handles on either end. It was absolutely legal this time, made out of waterproof plywood, lined with tar paper, and with hinges on the inside so it couldn't be opened except by breaking the seal. Then it had to be completely outfitted with six axes, six shovels, six grub hoes, and two bucking saws with handles.

To keep it out of harm's way (and temptation), Sonny securely bolted the fire box on the very top of the shovel; even drilled holes through the roof of the shovel to give it firm attachment. There was one disadvantage, however; it couldn't easily be seen, and had to be pointed out occasionally.

One day a Big Company representative came up and told Felt he was there to close him down for not complying with fire regulations.

"What the hell makes you think I'm not complying with fire regulations?" he asked the pompous little messenger.

"The Supe says you haven't got a fire tool box," was the answer.

"Just raise your sights, my friend," Sonny said. "See—up there on top of the shovel. I've got a fire tool box, completely outfitted, sealed by the state fire warden a month or so ago, and *painted red!*" Sonny was just a trifle put out about the whole thing. He couldn't understand why the Supe should suddenly decide we didn't have a fire tool box.

During fire season, the sale of snuff soars, for the cigarette and match are a dangerous combination for the logger. With snuff, he's sure.

Somehow we escaped any serious forest fires, although there was an occasional small one. Sometimes they were accidental, and sometimes they were just darn foolishness—like a noon fire built to toast sandwiches.

Our first camp, however, was a natural fire trap. The ancient railroad cars, with their rotting wood and insulation, were linked solidly to each other by couplings and by built-in porches and steps. The location was an old landing, where trash and debris from loading countless thousands of logs was spread five hundred feet down the slope, almost to the swamp. We tried to keep our newer buildings away from the main camp, but for some reason the place chosen for the washhouse was within a couple of feet of the west side of the caboose, close to our own sleeping and office quarters. We had had several small fires that caused little damage. We would be eating breakfast, and someone would shout, "The washhouse is on fire!" and we'd all go running, buckets in hand. Sometimes it was a coat hung too near the heater, and sometimes the oil burner had exploded.

One weekend in September of our second season, I brought my family up to camp: baby Kim, now nine months old; Vicki Anne; and Auntie Jewel Morrison, who took care of them in my absence. I had also dragged along a batch of eight pups just a month old, and their black cocker mother. She was running out of milk for so many babies, so they had to have supplemental feeding, and we couldn't leave them at home.

Early Sunday morning, Sonny built a fire in the washhouse, as usual. It was one of those rare September days when the mornings were just the least bit crisp, the pale shafts of sunlight filtered down through the trees, and all was right with the world.

After building the fire, Sonny placed the puppies in a box on a bench just inside the washhouse door, to get warm and stay quiet until I could warm up their milk; then he came back to the kitchen to help me.

Suddenly, a scream from Auntie Jewel brought us to the back steps with a rush. She brushed me aside and rushed into the first compartment of the caboose, which we were using for a nursery. Naturally, I thought something was wrong with the baby, and rushed right after her. The moment we opened the door, I found the reason for the excitement. The reflected color from a fire in the washhouse bathed the baby in a rosy glow as she lay peacefully sleeping in the middle of the bed.

Auntie Jewel wasted no time. She grabbed up baby, sheets, pillow and all, and left by the same way she had come. Vicki was standing uncertainly at the foot of the steps, and Auntie Jewel grabbed

her hand and dragged her off up the hillside, to the
protection of the tall timber. She had one eye on
the collection of gasoline and diesel oil barrels standing near the end of the caboose.

By this time the alarm had spread, and everyone
started tumbling out of tents and bunkhouses. I
manned the faucet in true "heroine at the dyke"
fashion and filled pots, pans and buckets with water
until both the three-hundred-gallon pressure tank
and the hundred-gallon hot-water tank ran dry. Two
of the fire fighters were taking the containers from
me, climbing the iron ladder of the caboose, and
throwing the water down into the blazing inferno.
The side of the old caboose was beginning to flame,
and the big spar tree at the end of the cookhouse
was beginning to smoulder.

There were perhaps a half dozen of the crew in
camp that weekend, and they all tried frantically
to help save the camp. It looked as if the fire would
take it all, from the washhouse straight through the
length of the cars to the bunkhouse.

Right in the midst of the hectic activity, Sonny's
brother Wayne and his wife Wilma arrived to spend
the day with us. Wayne left his car several hundred feet away and ran to help Sonny, while Wilma
coaxed Auntie Jewel and the children down off the
hill and into the car. From there, they had a ring-
side seat.

When the caboose caught fire, and it looked as
if the entire camp would go, Sonny decided to try
to pull the railroad cars apart and save the cook
car and bunkhouse at least. But in their excitement,
he and Wayne couldn't start either one of the two

smaller cats, and the large one had the motor out of it. (Just before that, they had driven the new flatbed truck up on the hillside to park it out of the danger zone. Why it took two of them to park it I never found out.) Then both of them jumped out of it at once to return to the scene of the fire —without setting the brake! Luckily, Wayne caught the truck before it smashed into the cat sitting at the foot of the hill. When the cats wouldn't start, they brought the truck back down and hooked a line from the channel iron on the rear of the bed of the truck and around the rear trucks of the caboose. Nothing happened—except the channel iron came off the truck. (It took some remembering, later on, to figure out the reason. They had blocked the cars up high and rigid off the springs when they built the camp. Only the big tractor could have pulled the caboose loose from its mooring.)

By this time it didn't matter too much anyway. The washhouse had burned to the ground, and only the caboose was still burning. Wayne ran in from one side to throw a pan of water on the blaze, and Freddy came in from the other side and got the full benefit of the water. By that time the water tanks were empty, and I began throwing bedding and clothing out of the caboose. All the rest of the crew were still at their self-allotted tasks; all except one old bucker, who contented himself with throwing a desultory shovelful of dirt once in a while, in the general direction of the fire. And there was Harlan, who shared the caboose with our family when the bunkhouses were full. He was wandering about in his shorts, only half aware that his

bed had been a scant two feet away from the raging
fire. He was still not much more than dressed when
I started throwing things out of the caboose, but
when I threw his good suit into the garbage can,
he did come to long enough to retrieve it.

The caboose survived, charred and weakened, but
still standing. The huge spar tree, which had saved
the storeroom and cook car, smouldered for days.

I checked up on the children, and found them
safe in Wayne and Wilma's car, with no more serious involvements than Kim's wet pants and cold
bottle. After taking care of Kim, Auntie Jewel reported that her own lower plate was missing. She
usually put them under her pillow at night, so we
began looking through the bedding I had so uncere-
moniously dumped in the yard. Freddy came by to
ask what we were looking for, but Auntie Jewel
wouldn't tell him. After some time spent in fruitless
search, we retraced our steps and found the missing
denture beneath the false floor of the porch, where
it had fallen through a crack to the old steps beneath.

"You know, Margaret," Auntie Jewel confided,
when we were alone, "Mr. Felt didn't accomplish
a thing. Now don't you tell him this, but he just
ran around like a wild man, and didn't do anything
worth while until it was all over." We giggled over
that for days. Later, when we razzed him for his
erratic behavior, he only answered that it was quite
a different matter when his own camp was about to
burn down.

There were tears in Sonny's eyes when he told
me he hadn't been able to save the puppies. The
heat of the fire wouldn't even permit him to reach

in his hand for them. We tried to console ourselves with the thought that they must have smothered to death before the fire reached them.

Later, in the ashes, I found a strange lily-like flower growing just where that little box of puppies had stood. We all mourned those baby puppies for some time.

That was our first fire, but it wasn't our last. The next season, when we had built New Camp, we had the second fire—and again it was the washhouse.

We had two types of architecture at New Camp —the modernistic shed type, and the commercial or boxcar type. The new washhouse was of the latter (boxcar) type. The center roof beam was placed higher than the walls, and inch-thick boards were nailed across to form the rounded-effect roof. Then it was covered with tar paper.

About the end of the fourth season, Sonny was sitting in the cookshack one day, trying to decide whether to take the roof off the washhouse for the approaching heavy snows of winter, or prop up the roof with car stakes. Lee, the speeder operator for the Big Company, was drinking his noon coffee with us that day.

Suddenly we heard a peculiar crackling noise. I looked out to see if a truck was coming up from the creek, over the frozen ice and snow. Instead, I saw fire gushing from all the cracks, the windows, and the door of the washhouse at the rear of the cookshack. It had too good a start to stop it, so I grabbed my new camera, loaded with color film, and while Felt and Lee posed proudly before the

flaming edifice, I snapped their pictures for posterity. Lee had just recovered from a bout with
pneumonia, and claimed it was the first time he had
been warm in three weeks.

"Well, don't think I set fire to the washhouse
just to warm you up!" Sonny retorted.

When the crew got in that night, Sonny and I
stood in the kitchen window, watching the different
expressions that went over their faces as the loggers
rounded the corner of the cookshack on their way
to the washhouse that was no longer there. Sticking
out of several inches of freshly fallen snow were the
two blackened water pipes, starkly marking the spot.

Swede and Chet remembered the other washhouse.
"Aha! Firebug Felt has been busy again!" they said.

When Earl first came to work for us as truck
driver and bull cook, he had an experience that would
have discouraged most young fellows on the spot.
The very first week he stayed in camp to watch
camp during the dry season, he set the cookshack
on fire.

It was really a dumb trick, all right. He admitted it himself, but said he was following the example
of "Diesel Oil Felt"—only he thought it was gasoline Sonny used to start fires in the cookstove. He
began to pour the gasoline into the wood, and the
gasoline promptly caught fire, can and all. Carefully he set the gallon can down on a kitchen chair
and considered what he should do. Deciding at last,
and thinking he was acting calmly, he picked up
the chair with the flaming can on it and started
toward the door. It was ten feet or so, and he spilled
the can, and the flames shot ceiling high. The soft

inflammable streamers of cedar that hung from the rafters caught the fire and spread it further. Earl was never certain just how he put out that fire. He hurled water fast and furiously, and beat at it with his jacket, and finally it died out. Except for some burned oilcloth on the counters and table, and a blackened ceiling, there wasn't much damage except to Earl's pride. To have such a thing happen on the first week of a new job! We had to laugh at his chagrin, but never after that did I drive down that last hill to New Camp without wondering if the camp was still standing.

It was interesting to watch a slashing fire being set, even though they got out of control occasionally and threatened our outfit. When the superintendent of the logging company down the creek from us decided the weather was just right (rain being in prospect within a couple of days, and little or no wind), he would give the signal to set the torch to the logged-off area to be burned. A half-dozen men, with torches made from diesel-soaked bits of waste or old mattresses, run from place to place, setting fires in likely brush piles. Tiny blazes soon begin to spread, and within an hour an entire hillside can be afire.

It is an awesome thing to watch a controlled fire start, let alone one out of control. It is such a ticklish business to decide the best time to burn slashing, for if it is too dry, or the humidity is too low, it endangers the entire countryside. Even the fire wardens sometimes make mistakes, however, and issue permits for slashing fires that never should have been lit. But if it rains too hard they can't get a good burn—so mistakes are bound to occur one way or the other.

A slashing fire out of control can give everyone within miles a bad time. It happened several times to us.

The first time, my mother-in-law and her father, our Grandpa Woodruff, had been visiting us, and I was about to drive them back home. We had been watching the smoke billowing up from the fire down the creek all forenoon. It became more apparent, as we started the trip back to civilization, that this fire was much nearer the main logging road than was earlier thought. We found out for sure when we rounded a curve and came into a rocky cut behind a lineup of trucks—logging trucks, tie trucks, and dump trucks—their drivers clustered in a knot waiting for the superintendent. Not knowing just what the situation ahead might be, I stopped, too.

After a few minutes, the superintendent came, appearing ghostlike in his four-wheel rig, through the gray curtains of smoke. His eyes were reddened by the acrid smoke, his temper short, and suddenly my reasons for wanting to get to civilization were quite unimportant. After he had told the drivers to roll their windows up tightly and take it easy, he came to me.

"What kind of a load have you got, Mrs. Felt, and how necessary is it that you get down below?" he asked.

I told him I had a load of fifteen empty gas and oil barrels, and I swear his face turned from red to green.

"Don't you know that the fumes in an empty gasoline barrel make them far more dangerous than full ones?" he fairly roared at me. I hadn't known, but I nodded dumbly in agreement with his decision that I should turn right around and head back to camp. I meekly and quickly obeyed.

By the next morning the fire had died down, and we went out again. That time, we made it. There was little smoke, but the road was full of smouldering chunks and debris. What I couldn't remove or go around, I had to jump. We made it down in good order—but it was my return trip alone, late that night, that I shall never forget.

It was a moonless night, and at every turn the ink-black canyon walls were filled with the blinking ruby eyes of fire in the logs and chunks on both sides of the road. The road never seemed so long, or did it ever have as many curves as it had that night, when I wheeled that flatbed truck home alone through the dying slashing fire. Camp never looked so good to me as it did that night, its mellow lights welcoming me back from that eerie world where the fire devil held sway. My imagination, as usual, was working overtime.

Another time, Sonny and I went to see a fire that had burned up into some green timber. We couldn't get much nearer than a quarter of a mile, but we had a good view. As the big old-growth trees fell before the terrible onslaught of the fire demon, they exploded, the very vitality twisting and shattering in protest as it left the doomed wood. There was a good draft uphill, toward the draw in which we were standing, so we left in a hurry. A shift in the wind could have brought it to our own dooryard. We went home, crossing our fingers.

Fires are caused by various things, some of them most curious. A four-thousand-acre fire in the eastern part of the county, a couple of years later, was caused by a farmer who put his hay into his barn too green, which resulted in spontaneous combustion and a fire which spread to the nearby brush and forest. Many small fires are caused by the sun's rays on a glass jug, or piece of glass, which can set fire to dry leaves and brush. There was also a bad practice of blasting the heavy bark off big, old-growth trees with dynamite. After it caused a bad fire in some virgin timber, this practice was discontinued. Lightning, carelessly tossed cigarettes, and carelessly doused campfires are also prime offenders during the tinder-dry fire season in the woods.

The company we worked for considered their logging the selective kind, and of course they could not burn without destroying the younger growth coming up. Consequently, every time they went through the timber, taking out certain types of trees, they left more debris to pile up on the ground and create more fire hazards.

The companies who burned their slashing behind them usually would clear-cut log a certain block of timber, skip a block to leave standing for a firebreak, and clear-cut again. They didn't always reseed, but expected seed trees in the area to accomplish this.

The method seemed to be governed mainly by the type of logging being done. I saw very little actual reforestation in our years of salvage logging. Some twenty-year trees, a few miles en route to our camp, was one of the few examples of reforestation, although I'm not sure if they were planted or if they are natural growth.

Everyone in the logging business, from the highest mogul of the biggest Big Company to the lowliest gyppo, recognizes his common enemy — fire. Nothing else can devastate an area so fast or so ruthlessly, or strike so unexpectedly. Within bounds, it has its uses and its purposes. Out of bounds, it is a rampaging enemy of all who make their living in the woods.

Cooks and More Cooks

THE COOK WHO FOLLOWED COOKIE WAS ALSO A baker. In fact, he was more baker than cook. Although there would be plenty of homemade bread and doughnuts and cakes, there would be little of anything else on the table. The loggers didn't think much of his doughnuts after they got cold, either.

"You should have seen what happened to a camp robber today," Chub told me. "He picked up a doughnut and took off with it. It was heavier than he thought, and he couldn't gain altitude. Flew right into an oil barrel."

"Ha! That's nothin'," Sonny put in. "We had a real optimistic camp robber up where we had lunch today. He threw two doughnuts around his neck, picked up one in each claw, and when he tried to take off, he fell into a mudhole."

But all the jokers fell silent the night they came in and found no cook, a cold kitchen, and no supper. I was at the fire gate, twenty miles away on my return trip to town, at four o'clock in the afternoon, when the watchman told me our cook had departed for parts unknown in the middle of the afternoon. I made a record run in, to find a crew of hungry loggers and nothing on the cold range but a pot of overcooked beans.

Hastily we all pitched in and cooked supper; then we all sat around discussing the baffling disappearance of the cook. Scotty told us he had seen the cook imbibing from a bottle on occasion. That explained everything, as far as I was concerned. I threw out the balance of his stale pastries and took over again until the head loader's wife (a different head loader than the first) came for the rest of the season.

The third season there was another new cook. Me.

By this time it was becoming increasingly obvious that the Big Company was not going to keep its promise to board our men, even though our logging operations were steadily moving farther back into the woods with every landing. Accordingly, the kitchen and dining room were counted in when we built New Camp. While the men salvaged windows, water pipe, electric wiring, plywood, and other building materials from Old Camp, Amy and I gathered up cooking utensils, beds, bedding, dishes and other domestic paraphernalia, to be moved to New Camp along with the refrigerator and light plant. Scotty even tore off the "civilized" toilet seat from the little john.

"Might as well be comfortable," was the way he put it.

I ran a nail in my foot, which didn't help matters any, but with Amy's help I managed to keep the building crew fed and happy. We agreed on all points of the care and feeding of loggers. They must be as well fed to take the weather as they are to get out the logs that gave us our living, we agreed.

Amy and I are about the same height, five foot eight, big-boned, and on the husky side, and we seldom hide from work behind a shield of femininity. In coloring, though, we are entirely different. Her eyes are green (mine a rather light brown) and her hair is darker than mine and shows a glint of red in the sun. We have often laughed at the preconceived idea she had of me. Someone had told her about my dislike for keeping house, and how I never was seen without a book or magazine in my hand. (They had also mentioned that I preferred being out of doors, but she overlooked that bit of information.) She promptly imagined me to be the type who smoked cigarettes in a long holder, read confession stories, and ate chocolate creams as I undulated about my ill-kept house in satin lounging pajamas. The day Swede brought her over to meet me, I couldn't read the curiously disappointed look on her face, and thought it was because of my blue jeans, T-shirt, red hands from hot soapsuds, and the wet spots on my knees resulting from scrubbing the kitchen floor in my usual fashion. My dishes were still in the sink and my beds unmade, but stacked beside the garage door was a load of dynamite just unloaded from my car. No wonder the poor woman was confused! It was a long time before she could bring herself to confess her first ideas about me.

Amy was a good sport about the discomforts and inconveniences of our wilderness logging camp. I've seen her more put out about something I forgot to write down on the grocery list than having to walk three miles through deep mud with a pack of groceries on her back. She could wield a mean scrub brush and accomplish a scrupulously clean kitchen as easily as she could drag a winch line up a long hill and anchor it firmly about a stump so that the stymied truck could be drawn upward. She worked for us three seasons after I "retired." It made a very convenient arrangement, for her husband, Swede, became Sonny's right-hand man in the logging outfit.

But during the seasons of 1949 and 1950, I reigned in the cookshack. The first year we had Earl for truck driver and bull cook. The following year, Scotty served again in the bull-cooking capacity.

Scotty and I had a few differences, more comic than serious. He loved to mix up the pancake dough in the mornings, but I asked him to let me do it for I had my own way. Reluctantly, he gave in, but seldom could he resist giving the dough a quick, secret beat or two as he passed it each morning. One time, he was supposed to prepare the potatoes for me if I didn't get back from town in time. When I arrived, he was industriously removing the skins, all right—by whittling! He held the knife as if he were making willow whistles, and the potatoes looked it, too.

My day as cook for a logging camp began early, at the bull cook's call at 5:30. (That is, unless the crew had to "hoot-owl," or work their shift early enough to be able to quit before the heat of the day. In that case, we arose at the indecent hour of 2:30 A.M.) I was unhappy on the cold mornings when

I had to shiver into my clothes while the big, husky loggers got babied with a hot fire to get up and dress by. Finally, after a hint of revolt, I got *my* fire built too.

Upon arriving at the cookshack, I would find the bull cook busily setting the table, and the big gray coffeepots steaming on the hot stove; so my first job would be to measure the coffee into the pots. The pancakes were next to be mixed and set aside to leaven a bit. Into the pancake batter I chucked a half-dozen egg yolks, then frothed up the whites to lighten them. (This was to ease my conscience. If the loggers *had* to have pancakes, at least they wouldn't lie like lumps of clay on their stomachs all morning.) Then I broke three or four dozen eggs into a couple of bowls, to fry at the same time as the sliced bacon Scotty had ready for me. The oven was a perfect place to cook the bacon slowly, in a large, deep cake pan.

Just before time to take up the bacon and eggs, I would start baking the pancakes. This made a bit of a scramble to get all of them off the stove and onto the table on time, but with a little practice I finally mastered it. I had to have at least eight pancakes baked ahead before the breakfast bell could be rung, but no more than that lest they become "sad," as my father expressed it. With two big griddles, it was fairly easy to keep up with the demand. Just as fast as I could pour them onto the griddle, take the baked ones to the tables, get back, flip them, take them off onto the platters, pour out more onto the griddles, take them to the tables and back again, my "customers" made them disappear and sat waiting for more. But nobody complained, because waiting that few seconds insured everybody hot ones. Then, after a while, I would find a cake or two left on the platter when I retrieved it from the table, and knew the saturation point was near. Then I could run a little slower.

Before breakfast, most of the loggers put up their lunches, from the "makings" the bull cook put out for them. I've seen eight or ten different kinds of meat, cheese, and jelly for sandwiches, and still someone wandering around wishing for something to make a sandwich of. In addition, they ate vast quantities of pies, cakes, cookies, apples, tomatoes, onions, and oranges, cantaloupes, bananas, and berries in season. It kept me hopping, not only to serve them the food but to buy the right kind and quantity in the first place. They used two huge pots of coffee for breakfast and their lunches, and if it was cold or rainy, even more.

We had long before discontinued the practice of putting up the loggers' lunches for them, and found it saved on food. They were less apt to throw the food to the camp robbers when they had prepared it themselves.

From the way some of the men did it, it was evident they enjoyed every minute. There was Chuck, the meticulous chokerman, for example. He wrapped each sandwich carefully, after considerable concentration on making each one, and placed it just so in his lunch box. Then he polished his apple, being certain to include a knife because of his "china clippers." Then the pie must be placed in its entirety (not a crumb less than was coming to him) in another piece of waxed paper. He tested all the coffeepots for the hottest coffee, and neatly filled his thermos bottle. For good measure, he tossed in a piece of celery, or a fresh tomato or peach if they were on the lunch table, and then closed the lid on his lunch box. It took a good man to heft it, let alone carry it out to the tractor where he hooked a ride with the cat skinner up into the woods.

On the other side of the book was Chet. He would have been happy if someone would have built his lunch for him. One afternoon Swede noticed him sitting on the end of the logging flat, looking dejected.

"What's the matter, Chet?" Swede asked him.

"Oh, nothin' much — except I'm hungry," was Chet's reply. "If I make my lunch after breakfast I'm not hungry enough to make enough lunch." Then he stopped and sniffed in the direction of camp, a half mile away. "By golly, I think Margaret's frying onions and spuds for supper," he said. "Let's get goin'."

Sure enough, we did have fried potatoes and onions for supper that night. Chet's nose was accurate.

After the loggers had left, I made my pies. Here, my idea of efficiency didn't jibe with either Cookie's or Amy's. They couldn't possibly make their pies until their breakfast dishes were done. I could and did make my pies first, and while they were baking I'd do up the dishes and get the roast ready for the oven. None of this la-de-da housekeeping for me. My object was to get it done as quickly as possible and get out of the so-and-so place!

When I made pies, I usually had company. Bright-eyed little chipmunks slid in noiselessly through the crack in the corner above the sink. They loved pie trimmings, and swiped them as fast as the opportunity to do so presented itself. They also loved cookie dough, and when I made cookies I didn't dare turn my back on the spicy dough for a minute. Usually, however, I took pity on their open begging and set the trimmings from the cookies upon the sills, where they vanished immediately. This didn't keep them from hopping into the very center of a freshly baked applesauce cake when I set it out to cool on the counter. They hopped right off again —but quickly! They were such cute little rascals I couldn't trap or poison them, so I learned to take precautions, like covering my cakes and putting the pies in the screened-in pie case. But later, when Amy replaced me as cook, she settled the chipmunk problem with a cat—much to my dismay. Of course I couldn't expect her to put up with my pets—or pests, as they came to be.

While the pies were in the oven I cleared the table and washed the dishes. By the time the last pie was out, the roast would be ready to go in. When we had fry meat planned for supper, my time in the kitchen during the morning was cut considerably.

On Monday mornings the beds were changed, the bunkhouses swept out, the porches cleaned off, and the garbage disposed of. A can of chlorinated lime was sprinkled wherever it could do the most good to keep the camp free from odors. It was a job in itself to keep a primitive camp like ours fit for human habitation, but we accomplished it after a fashion.

When the new camp was established, there were still numerous conveniences to be put into the kitchen, especially counters and cupboards. I put up with a couple of low benches in lieu of work counters, which almost broke me in two in the middle, bending so low to my work. Sonny had a stock answer to all complaints: "You hired out for a tough job, didn't you?" This, and his unrelenting attitude toward nagging, had taught me in the early years of our marriage to keep my mouth firmly closed. But when two days went by, and they kept building onto the bunkhouses and shop and made no move to finish the kitchen, I put my foot down, but definitely!

"This kitchen is to be completed immediately, or you can get your own meals," I told them.

It worked. Sonny was inclined to treat my temper humorously, but he recognized a really mad Dutchwoman when he saw one. Scotty moved his tools into the cookshack, and within a day or two my kitchen was completed.

I loved the early-morning sounds of our camp: the log trucks roaring up the hill road beyond camp; the lonesome whistle of the locie far down the canyon; the coarse voice of a bluejay sassing a crow; the solitary ringing of a falling ax far up the hillside, as some faller put in an undercut; the quick chuffing of the duplex machine over at the reload; the welcome voice of the speeder operator at the door, "Got any hot coffee this morning?"

Usually, the speeder came in about two o'clock in the afternoon. If I were napping or wandering, his whistle at the reload half a mile away would give me time to set the coffeepot on over a quick diesel and paper fire, and get out the latest pie. The operator was my official sampler of bakery goods, especially pies, though he approved of everything. An astonishing effect it had on my ego, too. Me, of the poor cooking reputation!

When my morning's work was done, there would be from one to three hours of leisure time for me, depending upon what was on the dinner menu and how much time it took to prepare it. I spent these hours in many ways: reading, writing, fishing in the creek, wandering about in the woods, digging up ferns and little pine trees for transplanting at home. The creek formed a deep pool back of camp which served me as a delightfully icy bathing place when I was all alone in the middle of the day. Or the faint warmth of a late September sun might find me leaning against a stump, near enough to the landing to watch the cats yarding and the shovel loading logs, but far enough away to be out of danger. Here I met some delightful animal friends whose natural curiosity and taste for the moss from the tips of the newly felled trees led them to almost within arm's reach of me. Up until just a day or two before hunting season, the deer were quite tame. They would come noiselessly down the soft pumice-stone cat road to stare wide-eyed at the logging operations, sniff gently in my direction, and walk by unafraid.

If I felt ambitious enough, or the need was apparent, I would grab a roll of the black annealed wire and a marlinspike and go to the top of the loaded cars and wire across, back and forth, doing what we called "wiring the loads." Each car was wired three times on either end of the load as it was built up. The third and last time around, they were twisted securely with the marlinspike, and the log ends were branded, the car numbers copied down, and they were ready to go. It was quite a thrill to watch four or six big loads of logs go swaying off down the track, and to know you had a minor part in producing them. I didn't care whether it was the pie in the logger's lunch pail that I had contributed, or the top wire on the loads; I had a share in every one of those loads.

Sometimes Sonny took me with him up the steepest of cat roads in his four-wheel-drive rig. I was always reaching forward for the horns of the mountain goat, which is what I often thought the four-wheel rig resembled on those climbs. We would visit the logging operation, or look over a new landing, or perhaps we would visit the operation of one of our neighboring gyppos, or the Big Company. Once or twice we went over the ridge and down to the very depths of the canyon where the Big Company had their modern logging camp. Its neat gray-painted buildings and grounds made ours look pretty sick. It was comforting, though, to know that many loggers preferred our camp because it was more "homelike," as they expressed it. Most of them were from small towns and the larger cities, and they didn't *have* to live in shake-covered shacks, but I guess they meant the big camps had a colder, more impersonal atmosphere in which few of them felt at home.

From the top of the ridge we could see perhaps a hundred thousand acres of forests, like a great green mat spreading out to the east and south. Here and there could be seen evidence of man's creeping assault on the native timber. Where the creek had cut the canyon walls to find its bed, the blue mists of distance settled even during the day. Southeast, there was a glimpse of Mount Adams, and by stopping on another curve, we could see Mount St. Helens; again, an abrupt switchback would throw us face to face with majestic old Mount Rainier.

They hauled logs up out of this canyon, to be loaded upon log flats near where we loaded ours. We waved at the truck drivers, and sometimes Sonny would stop and pass the time of day with some old friend we saw. Down at the camp, we visited with the cook for a minute, admired some catches of trout recently taken from the rushing creek behind the camp, then started back. It would take longer to get out of that canyon than it had to drive in—and after all, I, the Felt & Co. cook, was out gallivanting with the boss! It was time I was thinking about getting the rest of supper ready for the loggers by quitting time.

After the dishes were done, then came the quiet time of day when each person in the camp pursued his own interests—unless, as was sometimes the case, there was some overtime work to be done. Some of the boys went fishing, some would play cards or shoot dice, and some just lie on their bunks and

read lurid literature (as I called their taste in reading material). One or two might come over to the
cookshack to visit with me, finish up the balance
of the coffee, have a finger rebandaged, or just sit
around. The long evenings during the summer are
grand times just to sit around listening to the noisy
little creek beyond the little bunkhouse, and do
nothing. We got a lot of it done, too.

The job of a woman cook at an isolated logging
camp covers far more than just filling the stomachs
of hungry loggers. She is first-aid man, mother con-
fessor, good-will representative (in my case), labor
arbitrator occasionally, house mother, and generally
an uplifting influence. (Wait until Sonny and his
crew read this!) It was Herman, the Indian faller,
who told me I was an uplifting influence. He claimed
that the minute I stepped into the bunkhouse whenever the boys were playing cards, their language immediately ceased to be profane. So there.

Whenever I retrieved pieces of steel with pincers
or pliers from calloused fingers, or bandaged saw
gashes, or bathed eyes with condensed cream for
welding flashes, or treated upset stomachs with my
mother's remedy of hot ginger tea, or doctored tooth-
aches or chronic appendicitis sufferers, Chub and
Chet would accuse me of practicing medicine without a license. Unfortunately, I never got to practice
my home-remedy medicine upon either one of those
tough guys. If they sneezed I was johnny-on-the-
spot with the Mentholatum or Vicks, hopeful that
I might rub their chests. They wouldn't have suffered such indignity even if they had pneumonia,

for they knew how roughly and thoroughly I rubbed chests, ears, necks, and temples. Swede had reported on my tactics, although he said I saved his life a time or two.

Chuck, the hook tender, said he'd just as soon die of the ailment as the cure. I had rubbed grease even on his bald head. However, we didn't have a single mortality in the pneumonia department. Sonny gave me my worst scare, during the third summer. His pneumonia sneaked up on him, and I didn't suspect it in time to rub his chest—much to his relief!

Four days a week I cooked—through breakfast on Friday morning—and then I'd leave for town to get the weekly check, make out the payroll (if it was payday), pick up supplies, and generally take care of the company's business. It was a treadmill, but a rather interesting treadmill. It would have been fun to cook in Felt's logging camp without having to worry about all the other aspects of Felt's logging outfit.

And then, of course, there were the children. They were being well cared for, but that wasn't the same as being with them myself. I was missing too much.

By the third year Kim was old enough to be brought to camp occasionally. There were times when I was too busy to take care of her, but with Vicki's help we managed a day or two now and then.

Vicki was seven years older than Kim, and would play house with her, wheeling her around in the big doll buggy, feeding her, and cleaning her up when she got dirty. It wasn't a bad idea, having a baby sitter half raised by the time the second one came along. Both of them are pretty strong-minded, however, so as time went by they quarreled a good deal.

They both became quite immune to the rigors of camp life, the trips to and from, and doing without many of the things they desired because a new tire had to be purchased before the new doll, or a roller for the cat before a new dress or pair of shoes. They often went with me to buy groceries, vegetables, parts, and wire. At the fruit and vegetable wholesale house they soon made friends with the white-haired, kindly man, Mr. Barber, who always supplied a willing little hand with a banana. They soon knew most of the salesmen; the laundryman who always brought them a sucker, and could always answer nicely when someone asked about their health. Kim sometimes would get disgusted with me, waiting here and there, and would heave a big sigh when I was ready to go home.

"Do you *haveta* be so long?" she'd ask plaintively. Her expressive little face could register impatience, disgust, anger one moment, then it would light up with a broad smile. I saw tiny milk-white teeth set in a wide bridge, a round, pink-cheeked face, large lustrous brown eyes set slightly slanted beneath straight brown bangs. We kept her hair cut in a Dutch bob until she was old enough to take an interest in it and express dissatisfaction; but it grew every which way and was hard to manage in any other fashion.

Vicki was more on the delicate side; in fact, a spindly little creature for her first ten years of life. Mother Morris used to say her little legs resembled two toothpicks stuck into a couple of punkin seeds.

Vicki's eyes are also dark, with that same tipped-up setting beneath flyaway brows, a tiny nose, small mouth, and a slightly cleft chin.

Both children adjusted themselves with veteran's ease, no matter where we took them. First thing after breakfast at camp, they would gather up the spare coffee cans and lids and old pie tins, and begin Operation Mud Pie; an operation which had moved from our comfortable home on North Lake to our later home on the farm, and now to camp. They also spent considerable time trying to trap chipmunks with figure-four traps, but if they did catch any, the little rascals dug themselves out before the girls could lay hands on them.

Kim loved the stories about the little animals in the woods. There was one I used to tell her about the Crooked Tail Chipmunk and the Kangaroo Mouse, taken from the little stub-tailed chipmunk I called Tony, which came to New Camp that first year. However, I discovered I was away off on the kind of mouse I called a "Kangaroo" mouse. The little white-vested fellow turned out to be a white-footed mouse, so I had to make up another story called Willie the White-footed Mouse. We also had a story about the pack rat who didn't know he was stealing when he picked up things, and about the twin bear cubs, Tillie and Billie Bear, who got into all kinds of troubles. Another was about the flying squirrel family. Nature was most prolific in providing material for stories, and we kept enlarging on them, while Kim kept asking why I had to plot the stories until they were complete.

One day, when the two girls and I were alone

in camp, Kim got lost. One minute she was dab-
bling in the pumice stone near the overflow, and
the next she was gone. I sent Vicki to look in the
outhouses while I looked under the cookshack and
the bunkhouses. We called and called, and ran up
every road a short distance. Just as panic was beginning to catch up with me, I looked down toward
the creek and saw the flutter of the little magazine she had been playing with earlier. The creek
was five hundred feet east of camp, and its noise
drowned out the crying of the little girl lying on
a soft pumice-stone ledge a few feet above its rushing waters. She was lying there on her back, like
a little stinkbug that can't get its footing. If she
had been able to turn, she might have fallen into
the creek. We picked her up and loved her until
she stopped crying.

"My baby—my baby," she sobbed, as we started
back toward camp; so Vicki had to give her her
doll. After that, we kept darned close watch on
my baby!

Vicki loved to ride the cats. Whenever Sonny
would take her, she would go out with him when
he built road, and stay with him a half day at a
time. One time, when he was dragging in planking for building the new camp, she slept for an hour
on the way, relaxed as a pound of warm butter, over
rough, rutted roads, the noise of the cat ignored.

Vicki was in the seventh grade by the time Kim
got to go to kindergarten. She came home the first
day quite disgusted—and she was still disgusted as
the year wore on.

"We just don't learn nothin'," she claimed. "We

just draw and color and slide down slides. Oh, I like it all right—but sometimes I'd sure like to learn how to read and write!"

Then, because she was still young, she didn't get to go to school the next year. Being born in November has its disadvantages!

By the time she was fourteen, Vicki had grown tall, with a promise of a lovely figure. My worries about her health dissolved in pride. But Kimmie was my chunky one. We worried more about her getting too fat than we had about Vicki's being too thin.

Before I get too far away from the cookshack, I must tell the history of our four kitchen ranges, and how they came to play such important roles in our lives.

The first was that big army range, in which we installed an oil burner and electric fan. It served us well for the first two years, but when we decided to move to New Camp, Sonny was inclined to think we should get another stove. The old one wouldn't stand the move, and besides, it looked as if that second winter had rusted it quite badly. So, for ten dollars, we purchased the "Little Gem" from Scotty.

The Little Gem was a small home-size kitchen range, but we thought it would serve us until we could find something better in a month or two. It lasted the better part of two seasons. It gobbled up wood by the cord (cut at overtime pay, to the tune of about twenty-two dollars per cord) and gave forth as little heat as it could manage. When I complained about the Little Gem's faults, Sonny decided that perhaps the old oil burner could be moved after all. We could take out the oil burner and convert it to wood. So one night he took several men down to Old Camp, and with might and main and block and tackle, and no little leverage, they managed to get it aboard the flatbed truck and haul it to New Camp. Then they proceeded to move it just inside the cookshack door, and there their strength and enthusiasm deserted them. And there the stove sat for a week.

In order to get to the farthest table, we had to crawl over it; so that got old quick. Then one night they decided to install it where it belonged, and get it out of the way; a matter of their convenience more than mine, I suspected, though I was in no position to question motives. Several times Sonny raised his sledgehammer to bust the Little Gem into many pieces, confident that the old range would work; but he didn't. And it was a good thing he refrained, too.

After they had the stovepipe heightened on top of the shack for better draught, and the range was set in place, hot-water pipes connected, and everything in order, they lit a fire. In less time than it takes to tell, the smoke was so dense they couldn't see each other across the shack. It was the consensus that the "Goddurn thing was no Goddurn good," and they began hammering it to pieces and throwing the pieces out the doors and windows. Sonny even brought in his cutting torch to make a better job of destroying the old range. Then they reinstalled the Little Gem, and I cooked on it until the bottom began falling out of it, bit by bit, asbestos and all.

My next purchase in the kitchen-range department was made at a railroad car rebuilding shop, where they had some ranges taken from army dining cars. I paid twenty-five dollars for a big old iron range, had them load it on the flatbed truck, and merrily took off for the woods.

This one had a firebox big enough to sleep a five-year-old child, and the oven was a bit uneven, but it did the work I had paid my money for. Scotty kept the woodbox full, and I shoveled pumice stone into the oven so that my cakes would set level.

Sonny's diesel-oil method of starting a fire was a little hard on fireboxes. Sometimes he had a fire in the firebox, sometimes on top of the stove, and sometimes down below, in the ash container. We got one good season out of this range before it burned through the bottom of the firebox and set fire to the planking of the kitchen floor. We patched it, and began planning on a bottled-gas range.

After a week or two in the 1952 season, we accomplished this dream. The new range and gas equipment was installed with hilarity and minor incidents —such as Sonny getting his eyebrows and lashes burned off when he lit the gas heater beneath the hot-water tank and was blown back against the refrigerator. Chub walked around up on the roof in his "corks," declaring that this modernization program was all foolishness; that he'd have to put a few new holes in the roof so the cook would have enough drips down her neck in rainy weather to keep from getting uppity. They threw the now useless smokestack off with a great clatter and banging on the ground. There was much free advice, laughter, and joking. Swede hooked up the gauges and gas tank. Amy and I cleaned up the mess and made coffee, then we all gathered about the big oilcloth-covered table with that feeling of a job well done. Now we had a modern kitchen!

But not for *this* cook. I had done most of my cooking on stoves one and two, and partly on three. Then Amy took over—and it was she who cooked on the new gas stove. And I "retired" to full-time duties as wife and partner of the gyppo boss man.

CHAPTER ELEVEN

Life of a Wife of a Gyppo

AH, FOR THE LIFE OF A WIFE OF A GYPPO LOGGER! Be it truck driver, cook, flunky, nurse, supply sergeant—name the job and I've held it, during the more than nine years we have been in business. Let's take a single day in the life of a gyppo logger's wife.

Let's take Monday. This is usually supply-purchasing day for camp. The grocery list that couldn't be completely filled on Saturday, when the cook made it out, can now be finished. It is amazing the miscellany of things it takes to run a logging camp for a dozen or so people back in the woods. Besides staple groceries, vegetables, fruits and meat, milk, bread and eggs, there must be such things as light globes, bottled gas for the kitchen range, magazines for the bunkhouse library shelf (made from a discarded orange crate), mousetraps, a case of beer for that hot weather nip after work, a length of stovepipe, oilcloth, a dozen cups, a couple gallons of ice cream. It's usually a list that sends me from one end of Pierce County to the other to fill, and occasionally over into King County; then I take it all back to Lewis County to be consumed or used in our wilderness logging camp.

To keep the logging operation itself running

smoothly, there was another list to run me ragged
and gray my hair. The weekly supply of four-by-
five-by-ten-foot wooden car stakes; that half ton
of black annealed wire that cost more each time I
bought it; power saw parts; a tire for the pickup;
gasoline and oil and diesel and grease and ether for
starting the cats; white paint for marking the car
stakes, so we can reclaim our own at the dock after
the cars are unloaded; cat parts; bearings; muriatic
acid and babbit for making chokers; choker bells
and knobs; a bull hook; axes, shovels for the fire
box, and handles for axes, sledges, and hammers.

The business end of the logging company often
sent me even farther afield; to Olympia, to see about
a piece of state timber, or to check up on an industrial insurance claim; to Chehalis, or to Longview,
or perhaps even to Portland to investigate a second-
hand set of arch wheels, or some second-hand car
stakes, or a flatbed truck. I've entered every kind
of place from a tavern on Skid Road in Seattle to
employ loggers to a small-town hotel where I borrowed a room when a broken-down truck stranded
me overnight. I suppose I've spent more time waiting for loggers to show up in their favorite taverns,
and drank less beer in the process, than bartenders
would care to talk about. They soon got to know
me, and knew well the men for whom I had come
looking. They would throw up their hands and
start pointing down the street when they saw me
coming.

"Chub was just in here a few minutes ago. He
was with so-and-so and they were going across to
the Mecca." At the Mecca, the bartender said he

thought they had gone down to another tavern just down the street. From there, I found they had gone up the valley five miles. So with Sonny's orders in my hot little fist, I'd wait until Chub came back within grabbing distance. Then I'd hie him up to his apartment, wait while he threw his shaving kit and a few clothes into his turkey and grabbed up his "corks," and we'd be on our way.

Chub and I used to draw the tough assignments like walking into camp three miles, from the spot where all the equipment was broken down, through slushy, extremely hard-to-navigate snow, with packs on our backs in order that hot meals would be ready for the crew when they finally made it in. Chub, the inexhaustible, usually ended up with all the packs, but we were pals from such journeys. And back in civilization, all the bartenders were happy when I had rounded up Chub and the rest of the loggers —not just because they could begin anticipating a few months of regular paydays from the loggers, but because they no longer had to put up with my determined chasing of loggers in and out of all the taverns in town!

We had our favorite supply houses at which to trade. We found that generally those easiest to deal with were the smaller business houses that had come up the hard way, like ourselves. At one logging supply house in Tacoma, I liked the friendly air of welcome whenever I appeared on the scene. They soon grew used to my rough logging attire and seldom did more than give me a quick surprised grin when I drove up with a well-loaded truck and a couple of half-loaded loggers, waving a fist full of

orders from my gyppo boss. Certainly I never had
the feeling they raised an eyebrow at me in dis-
approval. The senior member of the firm would
pull his glasses far down on his nose, look at me in
mock disbelief, and proceed to give me a bad time
about gyppo loggers and their truck-driving wives.
Then we'd go into a deep discussion on how I was
going to pay my bill, and on the advisability of
taking this kind of bull hook or that, to fill the
boss's order.

"Now looka here, Mrs. Felt—you ought to tell
your husband used line for chokers isn't a good
deal." Just then a salesman would go by with a
gallon jug of muriatic acid. "Be sure you pack that
well in vermiculite. Mrs. Felt's got a rough trip
ahead of her. . . . And you tell that gyppo this
chipper chain is the best you can get for power
saws, Mrs. Felt. Lasts longer. They got your wire
out there to load on your truck. Now, now, don't
you try liftin' it. They weigh a hundred pounds
apiece. . . . That's good, boys. Now, you take it
easy, young woman."

He would follow me out to the curb to wave
good-bye. Billy and I had that special feeling about
one another that made me certain we were "good
tillicum."

Another place I loved to go was to a big wholesale
grocery house on Puyallup Avenue, where row upon
row of cases of canned goods stood ready and labeled
for shipment to the most interesting sounding places;
Anchorage, Juneau, various logging outfits up on
Vancouver Island, Spokane, Walla Walla, and the
many institutions and logging camps within Wash-

ington State. In their big warehouse was the dry, dusty odor of tens of tons of staples, ground spices, and coffee. Many times I loaded my automobile with several hundred pounds of groceries, until the fenders rubbed on the tires. Here again was that kind of friendly interest in loggers and logging.

The fresh-produce house down on the tideflats, with its high arched roof, its well-filled refrigerator rooms, fascinated me too. Such a wealth of green vegetables, onions, cabbage, lettuce, carrots, asparagus, radishes, and citrus fruits; bright red cherries and berries and soft fruits in season, yellow bananas and striped watermelons in their crates as large as calf pens. There was always a humming activity of unloading some fresh produce cars from faraway places.

At the big hardware store in the tideflats I would order bolts, hard to get anywhere else, and pick up wire; and since they, too, were well versed in logging trends, I also picked up the latest scuttlebut on the logging industry. Mr. Hardy, a tall man with the gray-touched hair, never missed an opportunity to come out, shake hands with me, and ask how we were making it. Along with a keg of nails I'd always get the best wishes of the people who waited on me. Somehow they always gave me the feeling that someone cared what happened to a little gyppo's logging outfit.

In that high-ceilinged building was housed every kind of hardware article you could ask for, from wheelbarrows to hydraulic jacks; from thirty-penny spikes to rope core cable; from hard hats to canvas water bags; from splitting maul handles to choker bells. In the rear of the building there were heavily laden shelves that fairly groaned beneath the weight of the dozens of kinds of bolts, nuts, and screws. Here I learned the difference between a lag screw and a carriage bolt, the difference between a bull hook and a shackle. I learned the hard way, by buying the wrong thing, lugging it seventy miles into the woods—to be met by a hard-eyed young gyppo who promptly sent me back to town to get the right article.

I also learned to know the different surplus stores and their owners quite well. However, I was never much of a trader. I just took what price they asked and didn't bother to bargain. There was the manager of one of our favorite surplus places who said he'd rather sell to me than to that gyppo of mine because, although he (Sonny) used to be a pretty good guy, he was getting so he wanted new stuff at a second-hand price. We had a standing joke for some time: He would buy a small cat we were offering for sale if Sonny would toss me in with the deal. He said that any time I would get rid of the gyppo, he wanted to be at the top of my list. It was harmless enough chitchat for laughs, but I think we shocked the nice lady who kept books for him.

Out in the yard and storage building of this surplus and junk business there were literally mountains of junk that must have represented every branch of the military service. There were all kinds of metal, machinery, canvas, rope, old cat tracks and used oil line. I doubt if they could possibly have made a list of every item they had in that place. If I needed some used line for chokers, we would go out into the yard, cross over the low water-filled spots on old pieces of boiler plate or linked mats from flying fields, and dig around in the huge pile of coiled line of all sizes and descriptions. Sonny was a firm believer that used oil line made as good a choker as any new line he could buy at a high price. "Now this should do it. How much do you want? Two hundred feet? Hmmmm, I wonder—— No, here, here, this is better. Hey, come here," he would say, calling a couple of his men. One of them was as large a Negro as I had ever seen and his slightly-built partner was of Scandinavian extraction and name. They would come and dig the stuff out and load it for me. Then we'd argue about price, just to keep in practice, although I always paid more than Sonny would have—and then I'd get heck for it when I got back to camp. No wonder the guy liked to do business with me!

We purchased most of the tires for our several vehicles in a shop in Tacoma, and I swear the owner-manager could tell when I had money in my pocket. I told him he must be able to smell money, or had an electric eye to pick up the information whenever I came within a block of his shop. He would come galloping up, mockingly rub his hands together, and say, "Got any dough for me today?" If I had, I paid him. If I didn't have, the shoe was on the other foot. I'd try to hornswoggle a tire for the pickup for a week or two or three, and we'd go around and around. In mock anger I'd tell him that the only time I was in his favor was when I had money. He'd agree, then tell one of his boys to "put a new tire on Mrs. Felt's pickup."

With all these delightful characters to deal with,

I rather liked my job as supply sergeant, although I would spend hours gathering the numerous items together in one vehicle and come home tired unto death. There were many rough spots in those trips. Take the many times I loaded from a hundred to a hundred and seventy-five car stakes by hand. They weighed from sixty pounds, dry, to a hundred or more when wet, and were a handful for me to lift, especially when the load built up high.

New car stakes were an item with an initial cost of at least a dollar and thirty cents apiece, so reclaiming them was a matter of financial necessity. We wore some of them down almost to nubbins. In order to quickly dump each load of logs into the bay, the dock crew at the mill would burn the wire where it was wrapped around the stakes on a loaded car—to the detriment of the stake, of course. They knew, however, that saving every stake possible for us was greatly appreciated, so they did their best.

If the dock crew with the crane was down on the dock, unloading the long strings of logging flats, they would always take the time to load my pile of stakes for me. Charley, the dock boss, was one of my favorite people. He was never too busy to help a gyppo or his wife. Guess he figured they needed all the help they could get.

But there were times when I had to load a hundred car stakes down on that dock all by myself in the dark. The day wasn't long enough, usually, to get them before the sun went down.

One time I was busily transferring from pile to truck when a watchman came down, swinging his little flash lamp. I chattered away to him, thinking

him the watchman I knew, but when I climbed up
on the seat to drive off, I got a good look at his face.
He was a total stranger! He didn't let on that he
thought perhaps gyppo's wives were slightly nuts
to be down on the tideflats alone after dark, loading a truck, but I'll bet he thought it.

Several times help came from an unexpected
quarter. Neither Charley nor any of his dock hands
would be around, and a Big Company official would
see me and send down a couple of men. One scolded
me roundly.

"Mrs. Felt, any time you're alone and need help
to load a truck, you just give me a ring," he said.
"We've got a lot of men around here who can give
you a hand." But I was stiffnecked about asking
for help. If a tire was low, I'd ask the mechanics
for air from their air compressor up at the mill
shop, but I never went out of my way to ask for
help to load a truck.

Many times, when I had trouble along the road,
I had a chance to study the general cooperation of
motorists. Few stopped, but those who did would
go all out to help. Possibly they were folks who
had had trouble themselves, and received—or needed
and didn't get—help from passersby.

One day I hit the pan of my automobile with a
rock, coming down on the logging road from camp.
The leak was so slow that I was far down on the
state highway before I noticed that my oil pressure
was gone. It was two miles out of Elbe, near the
Lewis County line, and I had Kim with me.

After stopping a car and sending a message to the
garageman at Elbe, we sat and waited—and waited.

When it became obvious that he wasn't coming to our rescue, I had Kim lock the doors of the car and promise to stay in it until I got back, and I started to walk. (Kim was five at the time, and a very self-reliant young lady.) After walking for a mile with no offer of a ride, our gas distributor came along, picked me up, heard my story, and took me back to my car, where he but in five quarts of outboard motor oil and followed me to the next garage. Then he took us into Eatonville, where I caught a ride with the local laundry truck, and we finally got home.

The first flat tire I had on the new pickup occurred two miles up the logging road from the fire gate, and for an hour I struggled vainly to get the wing nut off the spare tire so I could change the flat. Finally a couple of loggers came by in a pickup, and it took the might and main of both of them to get that wing nut loose. (I really should have written a letter to that company for using such a silly contraption for holding a spare tire in place.) Then the loggers changed the tire for me, although I could have done it—having had vast experience in such jobs.

Another time I hit an icy spot at the top of the cutoff hill above Eatonville and skidded all over the road, coming at last to rest against some big log guardrails. I got out, patted the logs fondly for having saved me from a quick trip down an almost vertical bank of five to six hundred feet, then surveyed the damage and the loss of my cargo. There were several blankets hanging on the alder branches, a number of cans of rhubarb scattered down the hillside, lodged in the rocks, and my brand-new spare tire was entirely missing. (Some little boys later found it and claimed the reward.) The tie rod was badly bent, making it almost impossible to move the pickup in any but a spraddle-legged fashion down the road, and the front fender was badly dented.

I sent word for the wrecker by a passing motorist. The eyes of the "helping hand" widened a bit at what he thought was blood on the dashboard of the pickup. It was cocktail sauce, I hastily explained, and I was unhurt. It was left over from Thanksgiving, and I was taking it home.

Sonny had heard about the accident from Swede, so he stopped on his way home from camp to peek into the window of the garage to see how badly the pickup had fared. Later, when I accused him of thinking first of his pickup, he grinned and said he had the wife paid for, but he'd likely have a hell of a time paying for the pickup, let alone getting the front fenders straightened out again.

"Oh, for goodness' sakes," I said disgustedly.

One time I got stranded in one of the small towns, and had to camp out in a "borrowed" room. It was either that or sit outside in the rain all night, or on the stairway of the hotel—and I *did* try to rent the room first!

It happened this way. The flatbed truck developed a bad cough in its innards on the way home from camp one night. Swede came along, and I had him give a listen. He diagnosed it as a blown head gasket, and advised me to have it fixed at the nearest garage before going on home. I had pulled in at our favorite restaurant, which had a tavern in connection and was a sort of stopping-off place for loggers, and was having my dinner. As soon as I had finished, I contacted a recommended mechanic and got his promise to work on the truck that night. Our friend who owned the restaurant then drove me into the nearest town, two miles away, and left me in front of the main hotel on the main street, about one thirty in the morning.

Not until after he had driven away, and I had walked up to the door of the hotel, did I discover that it was closed for the season.

I didn't know a soul in town; at least not one I could find at that hour of the night; so I wandered down the street, somewhat at a loss as to what to do. At the telephone office, the thought crossed my mind that I could call my friend to come back and rescue me, but they had such a tiny house that I hated to impose on them. Down the street, I saw a couple getting out of a car, so I asked them if they knew of a motel in the town. They didn't, but pointed out an old hotel three blocks down the street.

I set out briskly, for it was beginning to rain. By the time I reached the place, the rain was coming down hard. The front door was open, and on the door to my right a blue and white enameled sign said "Manager." I knocked lightly. No answer. I knocked harder. Still no answer. Finally I pounded, but still no response.

I crossed the narrow entryway at the foot of the stairs and tried the door on the other side, but with no better results. Finally I sat down on the bottom step and reviewed my situation. I was thirty-five miles from home and forty miles from camp, and I might as well have been in the middle of the Sahara Desert for all the fellow human beings I could arouse. I got up and took another look out the door. The rain was coming down on the wide porch roof in torrents, and splashing up from the sidewalk as high as my knees. I pounded on the doors again—the right, then the left—but still no response.

When looking out the door, I had been aware of a gleam of light from an upstairs window. Maybe the manager had moved to the second floor for some reason or another, I thought. I tiptoed up the stairs and along the hallway to the room with the streak of light shining under the door. My knock brought a sleepy grunt from a man inside that both startled me and changed my mind about wanting to talk to him. It sounded most assuredly as if he were under the influence of more than the rain. I quickly tiptoed back down the hall, afraid he would answer his door before I could get out of sight.

As I rounded the corner, high white curtains covering a doorway leading to the third floor suddenly whooshed out against me like ghosts, giving me further fright. I stopped at the head of the stairs leading down, fighting panic. What was I going to do? I couldn't sit at the foot of those stairs all night, and outside the storm was getting worse by the minute.

Then common sense came to my rescue. Where there's a hotel, there are rooms with beds in them. If I couldn't rouse the manager now, I could see

him in the morning. If I couldn't check in in the
orthodox way, at least I could check out after he
got up—or had slept it off, as the case might be.

So off I went again, tiptoeing along the uneven
floor of the dimly lit halls. A room with the door
partly open proved to be an empty one. To make
certain no one else was planning to sleep in it later,
I looked into the dresser drawers and peeked in the
closet, and then pulled back the spread on the bed.
The room was vacant, all right, and the sheets were
obviously fresh, the pillow slip clean, and the pillow
plumped up invitingly. Quickly I snapped the Yale
lock on the frail-looking door and put a chair beneath the knob. Then I got into bed for some much-
needed shut-eye.

My sleep was light, of the half-conscious kind I
often am bedevilled with, but at least I was snug
for the rest of the night. I felt safe from the rest
of the occupants, and was warm and sheltered from
the raging storm outside.

About five o'clock in the morning, I was awakened
by the sound of footsteps passing back and forth
beyond my door. Obviously my fellow roomers were
making their morning trips to the bathroom down
the hall. There was much grunting, hucking, and
an occasional deep-voiced swear word or two.

All at once realization struck, and I stuffed the
sheet in my mouth so my giggling wouldn't be heard.
This was a man's hotel I had invaded! Railroad
men lived here, I suddenly remembered. It was un-
likely that there was another woman in the whole
place!

To get out of there without being seen would

take some doing. When everything had quieted down in the hall, I got up and dressed. Then I opened the door and peered up and down the hall. Stealthily I crept to the top of the stairway. Not a soul was in sight.

At the bottom of the stairs, my conscience overtook me long enough to make me stop and pound once more on the manager's door, hoping he wouldn't respond. He didn't, so I hurried out and walked back to the middle of town.

I've often thought of stopping in to pay for the hotel room I borrowed, but sober second thought knocks my good intentions into a cocked hat, for how could I possibly explain? So, to save my dignity, I've carried that unpaid room rent on my conscience all these years. I slept so lightly, and smoothed the sheets so smoothly, I doubt very much if they ever knew a woman had spent the night in that men's sanctuary anyway!

In June, 1948, we traded the 1941 family automobile in on a new ton-and-a-half truck, in which we trundled about for some time, until we got the second new four-wheel rig. Finally, after more than three years of patient waiting, we purchased a family automobile—*after* the company trucks were paid for.

For some time the rule against hauling anything in that car that even hinted of a heavy, greasy load for camp was enforced. But it was bound to happen that it had to be used for camp transportation as well as loggers occasionally. But while the feeling of pride of ownership was still with me, I made

myself obnoxious by looking meaningly at the sharp
caulks on the boots of the loggers whenever they
got into my car. I had them trained to step on
pieces of thick cedar shakes when they had to come
into the house, but somehow they couldn't be convinced that the car could be just as easily disfigured
as the floors of a house.

Before many months had passed, the new car was
pressed into service for transporting groceries, an
occasional barrel of grease, line, and a few rolls of
black wire. Thank goodness there was no way that
car stakes could be loaded upon its smooth, dark
green top!

I grumbled about this hauling at first, but it did
no good. Logging came first, Sonny told me, much
in the same manner we had both reminded the girls
upon occasion. But the night we lost a barrel of
grease out of the turtle of the car on a hill, in the
dead of night, I made up my mind that our next
automobile would be some kind of combination passenger and pickup; a suburban, or station-wagon type
of thing. No use trying to keep a nice-looking car
around a logging outfit!

Some of it was my own fault, I suppose, or at
least a matter of expediency. When I became truck
driver and jack-of-all-trades, it was no longer necessary for me to stay at camp so much. In fact, it
was even possible to get in a little writing now and
then, and spend more time with my girls, and to
pretend that I was a housewife—until down would
come a messenger with a note, or there'd be a phone
call, and I was the gyppo's partner again.

When it came to business, my gyppo was never

sentimental. The letters or notes he wrote to me during the week, or the notes he sent me by a truck driver, went something like this:

MARGARET [not "Dear" Margaret!]:
Here is John's time for this week. He had 28 hours straight time, two cartons of cigarettes, 1 week bed and 4 days board. In last month's time he thinks he has an hour's overtime, but I don't think he has. The dirty bastard isn't worth five dollars a day. I've got more troubles this morning than Carter's got pills. Loads shipped this week 16, maybe 4 or 5 more today somehow. To top all my troubles that marker is around checking on my falling. Can't cut green trees and can't get decent logs to ship from snags, so what the hell? Everyone is coming down tonight but Swede and I and we'll be down Saturday afternoon sometime. Send this truck driver down to Tacoma to get these tires fixed then he can pick up the diesel and gas on his way back. Also get me a piece of 1 and ¾ inch hose 12 inches long, three gallons of anti-freeze and a can of starting fluid, a tank of oxygen and a tank of acetylene. SONNY.

End of love letter, scribbled on the back of an old envelope with blunt pencil—as private as a pawn-shop window!

Things weren't going so good on that particular day, but another time he'd gotten a break, and the jubilance broke through. The note went like this:

MARGARET: If you have not got those bolts for the cat tracks, don't get them. Babe gave me a damn near new set of tracks complete. I have to get him two boxes of Red Dot cigars, the long slender type. He says he doesn't like those flat bastards, so bring up two boxes of the right kind because I want to get the tracks Tuesday night and put them on. Sure as hell need them. Don't forget those two hoses for the light plant. Be sure to pick up all the damned tractor books that you can find in the desk and around the house, also that one on the shovel. Get me two cans of good radiator stop leak. You can get them at any service station and two rolls of tar paper. The wash house is leaking so bad you don't need to turn the faucet on to get the back of your neck washed.

See you soon as you can get up

SONNY

When it came to phone calls, Sonny didn't actually need a phone. He shouted into the transmitter and it came out my receiver like a bolt of lightning. Then, when he got absorbed in telling me something, his voice would fade to a mere murmur, and I'd have to shout "I can't hear you!"

The conversation might go something like this:

"Hey, Marg, that you? This is me. Say, I want you to go down to the dock in Tacoma and load up a hundred car stakes—I can't get down myself and got no one to send."

"What'll I do with the baby?" Sometimes I had no one to leave Kim with when he called.

"Why, wrap her up in a blanket and bring her along! And say, while you're down there, go to the logging supply house and get me a 110-foot tong line, six choker knobs, and twenty pounds of babbit. Oh yes, I need some wire until I can buy another ton."

If I demurred or beefed at all, I was sternly reminded that if we expected to have five or six carloads a day to meet the coming payroll, I'd have to turn truck driver again. So sadly I'd hang up the phone, turn off my washer or my oven, or put down my typewriter, bundle up Kim, and turn truck driver and supply sergeant again.

"Mine not to question why, mine but to do or

die——" I often paraphrased that old poem as I bumped along on some errand, or started out on the boss man's orders.

One time I courted disaster by driving Swede's little red coupé a good fifteen miles after dark with not much more than a flashlight with which to see where I was going. Company delayed my leaving home on that particular Sunday evening until everyone else had left for camp. Sonny was a bit on the cross side because someone was keeping me from his side in the logging business. When he left, he bade me sternly, "Now, you had better leave within the hour, Margaret. The lights on that coupé aren't dependable, and you don't want to be driving in the dark up that canyon road."

I agreed, and kept on trying to be polite to my company, while worrying about the approaching twilight. An hour and fifteen minutes later, I finally got started, and drove for some time before darkness caught up with me.

At first the lights worked fine, then they suddenly dimmed and went out. I pulled over to the side of the highway and stopped, letting long strings of returning Sunday drivers from Mount Rainier go by; then I crept out and made a run for it until I met another string of powerfully headlighted cars. There was a service station just before we turned toward our camp, and I planned to have a mechanic friend of ours look for the trouble.

When I arrived, he wasn't home, his garage was closed, and I sat tapping my fingers on the steering wheel, wondering what to do. Finally I decided to look for the trouble myself, so I raised the hood and shook the wiring harness. The lights came on full and bright. So I hopped in and drove off merrily, thinking I knew what to do now in case they blinked out again.

Two miles farther on, while climbing up the steep switchback road, they went out again. I kept on in the sudden blackness for a few feet, then stopped and set my brake. This was going to be a bad night.

I lifted the hood and gave the wiring harness a shake, and the lights came on again. Hurriedly I jumped back in, to drive on as far as possible before they went out again.

This happened a half-dozen times during the next three miles. The road became more crooked as I traveled along the canyon rim, sometimes four hundred feet above the creek below. Whenever the lights went out, the darkness would be so intense I'd be blind. So I'd stop, open the hood, shake the wiring harness, and again get lights—for a little ways farther.

Then either my touch failed, or the short in the wiring became more serious, for I had to shake harder and got dimmer lights for my pains. At last the method failed altogether, and there I was, still almost fifteen miles from camp, and no headlights.

I rummaged around for a flashlight, and finally located one beneath the seat. Holding it in my left hand, I drove slowly and carefully with my right, hunched up tensely while trying to stay in the middle of the road. When I reached the turnoff to camp, I stopped and said a grateful little prayer that I had made it through the canyon safely. That rough old pumice-stone road looked pretty good to me after traveling along that dark void of a canyon for ten miles or so.

Rough as it was, the road was easier to negotiate, for the tall trees and old stumps marked either side, and the pumice-stone surfacing showed a white trail toward camp and Sonny. An occasional bump would bring the lights back on for minutes at a time.

Finally, I arrived at camp. Sonny was having coffee in the cookshack, and when I walked in he raised those black eyebrows at me in surprise.

"Well, I didn't expect you——" he began.

"Not expect me!" I blazed at him. "Why, you told me positively to be up here tonight; that I had to drive the truck out tomorrow for supplies!"

He shrugged his shoulders. "Oh, I didn't really think you'd leave your guests tonight," he said. "You could just as easily have come up in the morning, in daylight."

I could have killed him.

It was a cat radiator that led me to one of my most delightful encounters on my truck-driving trips to Tacoma. Every season, one or two radiators have to be taken off one cat or another, and sent to a radiator shop to have its pipes looked into.

Taking a radiator to a recommended shop one day led me into a dim little place where no one seemed to be around, working or otherwise. Then from the door to the rear of the shop came a weird sound, like bagpipes without the bags. And that was exactly what I found when I peeked into the cluttered little office. A man with his feet on the desk, a crisp head of white hair, and a wholly contented look on his benign countenance, was blowing into a peculiar-looking mouthpiece. He finished his sad little tune, wiped his mouth with the back of his hand, and grinned at me.

"What on earth is that?" I asked him, in some amazement.

"This? Oh, this is the mouthpiece to my bag-pipes," he told me. "I belong to a bagpipes band, and I'm practicing."

I immediately sat down and we began talking like old friends. I'd never seen the man before in my life, but there is nothing more thrilling to me than bagpipes. (Must be that dash of Scotch blood from my paternal grandmother.) I saw and heard a bag-pipes band once in Canada, and it remained one of my brightest memories.

This Scotsman was mighty hospitable. He began hunting for a bottle of Scotch he had had just a short time before. He looked in the desk drawers; no, not there. In a file case—behind the wastepaper basket—no, but, oh, yes, he had put it up above the door inside the closet. Aha, we would drink to the Scotch. I sipped a very short one just to keep him company, because I had a trip ahead of me that needed a drink at the end of it rather than at the beginning. But I've often thought of that happy man who would rather play the bagpipes than re-pair a cat radiator—and did! I envied him. I wished I were able to do the same.

Gyppos' wives fall into three general classes. There are those who take no interest in their husbands' business, except to know that he is logging, or land clearing, or building road for some logging company. Perhaps if you were to ask one of them where her husband is on a certain day, she might drag out a map and tell you where he *said* he *would* be. They are by far the smartest of the lot, for their world stays within the confines of their homes—and so do their worries. How many times I have wished I had stayed out of my husband's business; sat on that proverbial cushion and sewed a fine seam!

Then there is that group of wives who would be the same if they were married to any other man in any other occupation. They spend all their time spending their husband's hard-earned money with never a thought of how the employees will get paid, or the taxes, or the bills. A new car is a necessity; fine clothes, parties, general big-shot ideas far beyond her husband's income become essential. Perhaps, eventually, all this is the cause of his bankruptcy. This may sound overdrawn, but it is not exaggerated. Such women *do* sometimes marry loggers—though I'll never know why.

The last group contains many of the hard-working women of my acquaintance who (and I think they will agree with me) are probably the dumbest and the most helpful type of gyppos' wives known. Dumb because we undertake to be full partners to our husbands in business, usually putting the business before the home. Helpful because we can always be depended on to answer the gyppo's call for aid.

One outstanding example is Hattie Gustafson, wife of Sonny's old friend Helmar. She drove truck to town for parts, cooked for the road construction crew, raised two children, and lived in out-of-the-way places, wherever her husband's operations had to be.

I know from my own experience that such hard work as gyppo and road contractors' wives are called upon to do often breaks a woman's health. One I know, Mabel by name, paid for her truck driving experience with her health, but when she was needed during World War II as a dump-truck driver in her husband's road graveling outfit, she was right in there pitching. She taught her sixteen-year-old son to drive, and a good one he became, too, under his mother's tutelage. She was pace setter for the rest of the crew, and usually ended up with more loads of gravel to her credit than any of them at quitting time. Then, though the men were through for the day, she went home and cooked a big dinner for several members of the crew.

Another Margaret, mother of our young cat driver Don, and wife of a land-clearing contractor, had her troubles too. Her duties were like mine, involving driving pilot car when the cat was being moved, bookkeeping, collecting bills, and washing for three greasy men instead of just one. When her now-grown sons were just nine and eleven, they were paid so much a day to grease the cat. Margaret then found her diesel-soaked laundry tripled, even at that early date. (That was when I was happy that my children were both girls.) She was the only one who didn't marvel at those two youngsters loading a huge cat on the big moving truck and taking off down the road with it to a new job.

Later, Margaret operated the loading rig for their smaller logging shows. When a log lodged behind a stump, her husband's temper sometimes misdirected itself toward her. She would set the brake, get off the rig and start off, hopping mad, toward the car, to return to the housework she had been neglecting to help her husband earn a living. Then he would realize how much he needed her, and would dash after her to persuade her to return to the job. She always came back, but she quit often enough to make certain she was appreciated.

Tillie was another gyppo's wife. Hers was the first fan letter I received from a sister of the logging racket after my article on gyppo logging appeared in the *Post*. She wrote me how she and her husband earned their living by gyppo logging up Packwood way, in far-eastern Lewis County. We came up with the idea of organizing a gyppo loggers' wives club, with dues consisting of the worn-out tire or broken roller off a cat that had to be replaced before the gyppo's wife got a new dress or a pair of shoes.

My own mother-in-law, Dorothy Felt, spent many years living back in the foothills of the Cascades, near the logging woods where her husband made his living—and where her sons learned to follow in their father's footsteps. No doubt she, like me, often wished her husband followed another line of business than logging, with its ups and downs, its uncertainties, its heartbreaks.

There are many more, those known to me and those I've never met; but whether they drove truck or stayed home and raised the future generation of loggers, I think they must be a particular type of woman.

When the gyppo makes his stake, then the wife

may find her life a little easier; but I doubt if any of us ever forgets the old days when we had to be ever ready to come a-running at the gyppo's call.

Stormy Thanksgiving

UNTIL WE ACTUALLY LIVED THROUGH ONE, WE
didn't realize the effect a post-election year would
have on our business. We didn't even begin to log
until a week after July 4, and on the twenty-fifth
of September we had a snowfall which gave us a
scare. Altogether it was a nervous kind of year,
with worry dogging our every foot forward. On
Thanksgiving weekend we were finally stormed out,
so that made only four and a half months of logging
that season. We could hardly blame the post-election
year for the weather, but we weren't too happy
about it. (We had an even shorter year in 1953,
four years later, when we worked only three months.)

On the morning of that September snow, we had
a visitor, in the person of Supe. He came in out
of the cold for a cup of coffee, and stayed to drink
the fifth of snakebite remedy I set out in a mistaken impulse of hospitality. I had one mixed drink
with him, but it didn't help to lift my spirits. The
steadily falling white snow just kept on making me
blue.

"Looka here, Mrs. Felt," the Supe said, "don'tcha
look so downhearted. The snow'll go away bye 'n'
bye."

But I wouldn't be cheered. It looked like the end of the season to me, and with only seven weeks of logging for the season, it could easily be the end of Felt & Co. Period.

Finally the whiskey was all gone, so the Supe staggered out. I tried to submerge my worry in turning out some good pies. The chipmunks swiped my pie crust every time I turned my back. Then, when I decided to make some cookies too, they decided it was their favorite kind, and were right back sniffing and craning their necks over the edge of the bowl. So I got real mean, and covered the bowl between bakings. I'd rather hurt their feelings than have to retrieve a doughy chipmunk from the cookie dough.

Happily, the day turned out much better than I expected. Winter changed its mind and waited another two months to close in on us.

At Thanksgiving time we were still logging, and our hopes and spirits were considerably higher. We planned Thanksgiving in camp, and sent Earl, the truck driver, out with the flatbed truck to bring in our small daughters for Thanksgiving dinner with us.

He was due back about eleven, and when he hadn't arrived by quarter to twelve, I began to get worried. I was having troubles enough without that, too. We were still cooking on the Little Gem range at the time, so I had quite a bit of trouble fitting a thirty-one-pound turkey into the oven. I had it turned "kitty-corner" with a cup set beneath the overhanging pope's nose to catch the drips. Finally I basted the turkey well, banked the fire, and dashed off a half mile to the landing to see if my special guests had arrived there. They hadn't. There wasn't a sign of them.

"Could you send someone out to meet Earl, and see if he's stuck in a mudhole somewhere?" I asked my gyppo.

"I've got half the crew out there now," he snapped at me, and then I knew he was as worried as I was. I just stood there, not even caring that my fire was going out in the cookshack, my mind completely engrossed with all kinds of pictures of what could happen to two little girls in a big, drafty truck, riding over rough mountain roads.

Then suddenly, there they were, coming down the abandoned railroad track. First I saw Earl, with two-year-old Kim riding piggy-back on his shoulders, and then Vicki, daintily picking her way over and under the logs strewn across the tracks.

"Hi, Mommie," Kim's tiny voice cried out across the stillness of the logged-off mountainside. My eyes filled with tears as I ran to meet them. We had asked so much of these little tykes to come on so rough a journey just to be with us over the holiday. I hugged and kissed them as if I hadn't seen them for a month, though I had been home just the weekend before.

After learning that the little cat was coming in with their suitcases and more supplies for dinner, we went on down to camp. I rebuilt the fire (with Earl's generous helping of diesel oil), basted the turkey with butter and onion juice (not with the diesel oil, as Chub suggested), and it began to brown beautifully.

Then Sonny came in to inform us that a storm

was coming, and he was having the fallers cut all
the trees around the camp that might be dangerous
to leave over the winter. At this time of year, it
was a day to day question as to when we'd have to
shut down because of the weather, and falling those
trees had to be part of the protection for the camp
when we had to abandon it for the season.

Right now, it was for our protection as well. So
for the next two hours, we had to leave the cookshack every few minutes at the fallers' shout of
"Tim-ber-r-r!" and see another potential menace
crash to the ground. Between times, Vicki and I
managed to set the table, peel the vegetables, and
generally get the balance of the Thanksgiving dinner.
Then Chub sounded the "all clear," and things returned to normal.

"What was all that yelling we heard once?" I
asked Sonny, when he came in. "We looked out,
but couldn't see anything to get upset about."

"Oh, Chub felled a tree across Swede's tent," was
the casual reply. "He didn't exactly appreciate it,
I guess."

It wasn't funny to Swede, of course, but I had
to laugh just the same. Swede was—and is—our outdoor man, who never sleeps in a bunkhouse or inside
anywhere when he can help it. He always has a
tent of some kind—and something is always happening to it.

The turkey was a big success. Sonny brought out
a couple of bottles of bourbon. We had shrimp
cocktails to start, and the whole dinner went off
without a hitch. The refrigerator rolls were just
right, light and fluffy, with lightly browned crusts.

Everyone was happy, especially the gyppo, who likes to see his men eat and be gay. And the crew was happy because, in honor of the holiday, they had worked only seven hours.

That afternoon the wind increased, and all during the night we could hear the dull boom, boom, boom of falling trees. The younger white firs, left unprotected as the larger timber was logged off, would snap off forty or fifty feet up in the air as the fury of the wind increased. The old snags, held together with heaven knows what, would meet their maker at last; the old hemlocks, loosening in the light pumice-stone ground and rearing huge network fans of widespread roots as the heavy trunks crashed to the ground.

The booming sounds went on all night, the rain came down in torrents, and by morning we could see that our chances for getting the crew, equipment, and ourselves out of this isolated area were getting slimmer all the time. We couldn't work with such a high wind anyway, so we sent the crew out on the speeder. Shortly after they got out, the high waters of the rushing creek, in several places, took out the railroad track over which they had just passed. Trees were falling all around them, but they got out all right.

We stayed until Saturday to finish the work on the shovel loader, but then we could see it was wise to be getting out while the getting was good. Sonny took the small mattress from one of the bunk beds and placed it on the fuel tank of the cat for Kim and me to sit on. She sat between my knees, all wrapped warm and snugly. Vicki sat beside her

father on the cat seat, and we took off for Old
Camp, three miles away, where Earl had left the
truck the day before. Swede was with us, but declined to ride on the tractor; said he'd rather walk,
thank you.

Swede walked the railroad tracks which paralleled
the logging road in places. Our little clattertrac
went along steadily, although the trees were still
being laid like matchsticks around us by the high
winds. Later, Swede told us he would see a tree
falling, and would wait fearfully for it to hit the
cat; but a breathless moment later he'd see the little
cat still moving, unscathed, along the muddy road.
The roof of the cat was too low to permit us to
see our peril, and ignorance was indeed bliss! When
we reached the truck, and climbed into it, a snag
fell directly in front of the front wheels. We stopped,
all took a deep breath—and held it until we were
safely out of the heavily timbered area.

Our real feeling of Thanksgiving came when we
reached our warm and welcoming home, safe and
sound.

CHAPTER THIRTEEN

The Gyppo's Ingenuity and the Gyppo's Wife

I ONCE READ SOMEWHERE THAT THE AMERICAN GI'S
were the most ingenious fellows in the world when
it came to making something out of nothing in the
mechanical line. They tinkered with, and repaired
machinery, using the remembered methods of work
on the old Model T and Model A Fords of their
boyhood days. Likely some of those same GI's had
occasion to apply such ingenuity to difficulties they
encountered in the logging woods, for a gyppo logger is past master in the field of resourcefulness and
"make do."

And somehow, my gyppo was always a genius
when it came to getting work out of *me*.

Take the time, for instance, when a cat broke
down in the middle of crossing the creek, and the
motor had to be hauled to town for repairs.

Most logging operations employ up-to-date methods
of removing a motor from a cat. They have the
machinery on hand, the big shop to repair, and
the know-how of siderods, superintendents, and mechanics, whenever they encounter any such difficulty. But when the gyppo removed a motor from
a cat, he used methods that almost defy description,
to say nothing of all the laws of gravity.

Lacking a hoist truck, and too far from the loading rig for help, he went out into the woods and cut down three poles, ten inches through and twenty feet long, from which he rigged up a tripod. Then he anchored a chain hoist firmly from the apex (which he had placed directly over the dead motor) and set about lifting same from its place of business.

The metallic clink of that hoist, as it inched the motor up and up, sounded vaguely like the clinking of dollars running through my bank account. As Teeney said, this was one of the days when the loading crew had their hands in my pocketbook. With only one cat dragging in logs, they didn't have much to do.

After the motor was inched up as high as it would go, it had to be transferred to the bed of the flatbed truck. To swing it from above the motor cavity to the truck presented a problem. It was a dangerous-looking deal, and Chet promptly took off, saying he had no desire to get himself killed off.

But first, the still alive cat backed into the injured one, picked up its turn of logs, and took them to the landing. The skinner kept the extra chokers, to bring in larger turns to try to compensate somewhat for the crippled cat's layoff. Then the skinner came back with his cat to drag the now motorless cat from beneath the tripod, so that the flatbed truck could be backed beneath the motor dangling from the chain hoist. Then the dead motor was lowered to the flatbed and propped up with pieces of car stakes—and the gyppo called his wife to take over.

"Are you sure it won't fall off?" I asked nervously. Everyone laughed.

"What are you talking about? It weighs two tons," I was told. It didn't look it, measuring only about four feet in length by three feet wide and three and a half feet in depth. It was only a small part of the total twenty-four tons of cat it came out of, but, nevertheless, I was certain I'd be very happy to get it safely delivered to Seattle.

I took it as far as home that night, and when I went out to get into the truck the next morning, I discovered the motor had moved ahead to the point where it was gouging a hole in the cab of the truck. There was nothing to move it back with. I could hardly move two tons of cat motor back by myself, so I took it to a garage on the main highway. There the boys pulled it back with the wrecker, and I continued on my way with a much better feeling about the whole thing. I had begun to regard that motor as some sort of monster trying to get into the seat with me.

When I picked it up a couple of weeks later, I made certain they nailed the car stakes to the bed of the truck, to prevent a similar happening.

A slack puller is a power unit that reverses the main line drum so that it will play out line, instead of having the second loader pull the line off the unbraked drum by hand. (That's what they told me, anyway.) Such a bit of apparatus would speed up loading and save the second loader's strength so he would be a good *old* man—if he lived that long.

A slack puller was far beyond the purse of the

gyppo's outfit, so Sonny decided to build one of his own. First he looked around, getting ideas from the commercially built slack pullers on the market, from those other gyppos dreamed up, and from one his own brother Wayne had built. Then he proceeded to haunt the junkyards and surplus houses, where he purchased used shafting, sprockets, gears, chain, and a surplus clutch; then he and Swede, taking their precious armload of stuff (about eighty dollars' worth) and the welder down to the landing where the shovel loader was sitting, proceeded to improve upon all the slack pullers they had seen in the building of their own.

It took about a day to put together this prize bit of ingenuity, and although it wouldn't have won any award for beauty (lacking the usual camouflage of a bright coat of paint, which they both considered unnecessary to the efficiency of its operation), both inventors claimed their product to be a vast improvement upon any slack puller then on the market.

Perhaps it is because a logger carries on his operations so far from the nearest convenience of machine shop or garage that he learns to be resourceful. He finds that a piece of bacon rind will temporarily take the place of some bearings; that a fence post or a rock can be used in place of the tire jack he left in some other vehicle; that pliers will do nicely instead of tweezers to remove a jagger of steel from a calloused finger. Pliers can also serve as a wrench with which to twist lugs off a wheel, too.

I have seen my gyppo drive a pickup that had its

steering apparatus tied together with a piece of rope.
We would be going down a steep hill, the steering
wheel would suddenly go loose in his hands, and
he'd run the pickup into a pumice-stone bank to
stop it. Then he'd get out and crawl underneath,
whistling that tuneless little tune he always whistles
when he's gay and carefree, tie up the rope, and
get back into the pickup, quite unconcerned.

"The tie rod fell off," he'd say casually.

"Sonny, why don't you get this blamed thing
fixed right?" I'd ask.

"Can't spare the pickup, and besides, it's really
not dangerous."

Oh, no, I'd mutter to myself, and shiver as I
looked over a steep bank on my side of the road.
Oh, no—it's not really dangerous.

One time we were caught out five miles from
the nearest garage with a front wheel bearing completely shot. The fault was mine, he said; couldn't
I hear the front wheel squeaking all day? Yes, I'd
heard the wheel squeaking, but had been in such a
hurry all day I hadn't paid much attention to it.
Besides, my education about wheel bearings had been
more or less neglected.

That omission was remedied, then and there. The
front wheel was about to fall off the automobile.
I've been very squeaky-wheel conscious ever since.

First, Sonny wrapped some electric wiring around
the wheel where the bearing should have been but
wasn't. That lasted only half a mile. Then we
stopped again, and I could see his agile mind working out a solution as he walked around and surveyed
the sedan from all angles. I wasn't sure but what

he planned to use the box of dynamite we were carrying to blow up the car or me, but after a few moments he evidently decided against such drastic measures and set to work removing the right front wheel; the healthy one. Then he robbed it of half its vital parts, to put in enough washers and other things to get us to the garage. That worked until we pulled into the garage, and I let out the deep breath I'd been holding.

Somehow I always got a share of the blame for not knowing how heavy machinery should be loaded. In May of 1952, for example, I was delegated to bring out a set of arch tracks from Seattle. Upon investigation, I found that each track weighed 3,675 pounds, which meant that one alone was more than the proper load for the three-fourths-ton pickup, so I decided to haul them one at a time.

I watched dubiously as they loaded it. They were dangling it from the line of an old winch truck that looked as if it might give up the ghost at any moment, and they insisted that the rolling thing be set squarely upon its tracks inside the pickup bed.

"Wouldn't it ride better if you lay it on its side?" I ventured to suggest.

"Oh, no," they assured me; so I shut up, figuring they knew their business better than I did.

When they had finished, I redistributed the groceries and other supplies around the arch track, which they *thought* they had propped up correctly, and took off for the woods, a hundred miles away. Before I had gone very far, it was apparent that I was going to have a most worrisome trip, if not actual trouble. Every curve, every bump set those arch wheels to tossing back and forth, just enough to send my heart up into the region of my tonsils and keep it there.

Finally I got to the woods, over that first eighteen miles of road, and finally to our own rough logging road. Around every curve, at the top of every hill, I looked for my husband to be waiting for me. He would be worried, perhaps, about how I was making it. He must know I was overloaded, and might have trouble. Just around this next corner he'd be waiting; just over this next hill. Hope springs eternal in the woman's breast—even if she's a gyppo's wife!

Then, just beyond Old Camp, on a steep little pitch, the tracks fell over against the side of the pickup body and bulged it outward. I stopped, got out, and surveyed the situation—and the damage. The right rear tire was low because of the great weight which now rested directly over it. I picked up an old car stake and tried vainly to move the arch track into a better position, but I might just as well have tried to budge old Mount Rainier three inches off its base with a toothpick. So I said a few words that neither my daughters nor my mother would have approved of, crossed my fingers, dashed the frustrated tears from my eyes with a grimy hand, and started off toward camp once more. I was still confident that my gyppo might send some help out for me. He was surely expecting me, and I was already late. He'd know I was in trouble somewhere along the way.

Another half hour of driving at a snail's pace found me coming down the slight grade between massive stumps into camp. By this time I was just plain *mad*. A dozen or two loggers in camp, two trucks, three cats—and I had to make it in all by myself! It wasn't the first time it had happened, and I should have been used to it, but I was so mad I wasn't thinking straight.

Then I saw why I hadn't been met. I had made the mistake of leaving my new car in camp, and it had a radio in it; and at this moment it was fairly overflowing with loggers. Front seat, back seat, fenders, both doors open and loggers sitting wherever they could find space to squeeze in. They were listening excitedly to the Jersey Joe Walcott fight. My hands were on my hips as I walked up to the car and confronted my husband. Everyone said "Sh!" and motioned for silence, but I ignored them all.

"Didya get the tracks, dear?" Sonny asked, attempting to head off the storm.

"I got *one* track, and where in hell were you?" I demanded. "I thought surely you'd meet me on Nemesis Hill." But he had turned back to the radio. A knockout was imminent. So I stood there, fuming and biting my tongue until the fight was over, heartily wishing for a scatter-gun loaded with rock salt. With a single shot, I could have gotten one gyppo, one head loader, a shovel operator, a couple of chokermen, a faller, two cat drivers, and one *Saturday Evening Post* photographer!

I didn't hear how the fight turned out, but after some loud-mouthed recapitulation by the announcer, Sonny decided to have a look at the track. Someone murmured that the boss might have a fight of his own to settle, by the looks of the old lady.

"Why'n hell didn't you have them lay it on its side?" Sonny exploded, when he saw the side of the pickup body.

"I told them to, but they seemed to know more about loading junk than a woman did," was my nasty reply. Then he said a few things about the intelligence of machinery dealers, and got in a crack about women—and I up and quit.

It was possibly the eleven hundred and sixtieth time I had quit, but this time I meant it! I stalked off to the washhouse to wash up for dinner and comb that gyppo right out of my hair. I'd had enough! This gyppo logging life wasn't for me. I'd worked my fingers to the bone. I took a look at said fingers; looked at the callouses, the griminess around the broken nails. Fine hands for a woman! And my jeans were stained from mud and grease, and my shinbone ached where I'd slipped and bumped it against the bumper of the pickup.

And while I was in the mood to feel sorry for myself, I took a good look in the mirror. Good Lord, I was getting to be a regular old crow! Me, who had been about halfway good looking once upon a time. My hair showed three gray hairs at once at the temple, my brows were furrowed from worry, tiny crow's-feet at the corners of my eyes—and my face was as grimy as an urchin's.

I heard footsteps coming down the walk, so I busied myself with washing the offending face. It was the man I married, but I acted as if I couldn't see him. After a while, he began talking softly.

Aha—the same old trick! Don't think you can trap
me again with *that* line, Felt!

"Gee, it's good to have a wife who can drive
truck and cook for loggers as easy as she can lift a
gas barrel or have kids, and carry on the business
on top of all that, and look like a million bucks
when she's dressed up."

Do you know what happened then? It had happened before—and each time I swore "Never again!"
But there I stood, staring into that cracked washhouse mirror over the dented wash pans, and watching my traitorous female self fall for that line, hook,
line, and sinker! The feminine self of me was always
a sucker for that sweet talk, even while the sensible self ("Margaret, you're *so sensible*," my mother
always told me) was frantically reminding me that
it would happen all over again.

"Look, Dopey," Sensible Margaret told Feminine
Margaret, "you'll be right back in the thick of it,
sticking out your neck again, putting your pride
in your jeans pocket, asking the creditors to extend
your credit to the breaking point, lifting gas barrels
and sloshing through knee-deep mud and snow to
bring food three miles to feed a batch of hungry
loggers—and what do you get out of it? Sure, sure,
I know—you get to sleep with the boss; but have
you taken a look at your wilderness boudoir? How
many times have you stubbed your toe on a cat
roller on your way to bed, or dodged the transmission grease cans just inside the door? And how many
mornings have you shivered in a stoveless shack because the bunkhouse stove went haywire and yours
had to be borrowed—and was never returned? And

what about those chilly mornings when you shivered your way to the little john, threading your way around mud puddles and heavy equipment? How about washing your face in that icy water, or bathing in the creek when you could stay home with your daughters and enjoy all the modern conveniences like hot showers and furnace heat? How many other women would put up with this?" But even while Sensible Self was still sneering, the Feminine Self went toward the gyppo, wiping the dampness from her face with a towel, and wound up sitting on his lap, laughing and smoothing the black patch over his right eye.

Mmmmfffh! The Sensible Self snorted, and gave up.

We had a cheerful supper with a crew, a fast game of dice (during which I lost two weeks' gambling allowance all at one time) and went to bed in that same primitive little bedroom I had been despising such a short time before. Next morning, the gyppo had a list of orders as long as his arm for his favorite errand-doer—and you guessed it. She was right there again, sticking out her neck, lifting gas barrels, filling that list of orders, fighting for her gyppo even though she knew he was still conniving to keep the gyppo's wife on his payless payroll and, at the same time, wondering how he was going to solve the next difficulty that confronted him.

Whenever our logging operations were moved from one location to another, the situation was pregnant with problems. Perhaps that is where Sonny got his favorite expression for when he finds an apparent solution to some problem: "That's a pregnant idea!"

Building a new landing is an operation that must be done as quickly as possible, so production won't be held up. Losing time for any reason at all during the short logging season was to be avoided at all cost, for it was only for the loads of logs that we were paid.

I liked to watch the humming activity that went on when a new landing was being built. Each logger had an important part in the project. Early in the morning, the fallers and buckers would begin felling the smaller white firs in a wide circle at the site. Sometimes there were older stumps still standing, when this had been the site of another landing years before, when they had logged out the big peeler logs. Some of these stumps would have to go, as well as the stumps of some of the smaller trees; so the bulldozer moves in, on the heels of the arch cat, which is dragging the small logs to one pile near where the shovel will set.

Having nothing else to do at the moment, I rested comfortably, out of the way of falling trees and dirt-pushing tractors, against a sun-warmed pumice-stone bank, and watched the proceedings. Sonny is doing the bulldozing, pushing fallen trees and brush out of the way, the snorting of the cat deepening as the load ahead of the blade becomes heavier, and lessening as he pushes the gearshift into reverse. He wears his businesslike air of seeming to have no thought for anything but the matter at hand—that of running one of his beloved tractors—and I had to put my hand over my mouth to hide a small grin. It always surprises me to find this man of mine donning this mantle of the gyppo, withdrawing into that small world that seems to surround a man on top of one of those big machines. Of course this *was* serious business. You can't be irresponsible when running one of those monsters. I found that out when he made me drive one occasionally to help him in his mechanical work. Still, I can never resist a bit of a grin when that gyppo climbs upon his throne of a cat seat and becomes an entirely different person.

A branch of salal brush touches my head in a friendly way, and a tiny green forest vine trails over my shoulder. Such a delicious feeling to be just lazy for a change! The earth Sonny is pushing before his cat now is chocolate color, showing enough pumice stone to give hope that this landing wouldn't "mud up" too badly. (A false hope, as we learned when the rains came.)

Chet has a partner over at the other side of the landing, where they are weaving the ends of a large piece of cable in and out to form an eye in the end of a main line for a cat. They're using a marlin-spike and mallet, with surprising ease and rhythm.

The fallers are close, and occasionally the ground beneath me shudders as a tree falls. I suppose I never will get over the feeling of sadness when I see a tree begin to quiver, then come down groaning to the ground. That vacant space on the skyline, the scores of years it took to grow, and the terribly few short minutes it required to fell it, all combine to make tears come to my sentimental eyes. It's almost like seeing some dear friend die and leave this world forever.

But there's the other side of logging I'm beginning to understand. Much of the salvage logs go
to pulp, then to paper; and paper is a most useful
product, needed by practically everyone—even for
writing books on gyppo logging—and the lumber and
veneer went to build many homes for American
families in this broad land of ours. Timber was
evidently put here on earth for our use, and when
I began to widen my viewpoint on the subject of
logging, I began to appreciate the worth of the industry. Without becoming too commercial (for I
still love a beautiful stand of timber), I find myself
growing much more sensible about the entire business of logging. I don't hate it quite so much. I
admire the loggers as a special breed of men, and
that hardheaded little old gyppo captured my heart
and imagination—and my respect most of all.

The other cats are already seeking a turn or two,
down some of the logging roads that fortunately
are still useable from the former logging operations
in this area. The buckers cut the windfalls from
across the roads, Sonny grades the roads, and things
begin to shape up.

Scotty begins building a bench upon which the
barrels of gasoline, diesel, hoist oil, transmission grease,
and cases of ether and power-saw oil will be placed
when the driver of the whoopee truck arrives and
begins dumping the cases and fifty-gallon barrels.

Nearby is the four-wheel-drive rig with the welder
behind it, brought in by the truck driver. It always
pays to keep the welding machine near the cats
when they're working.

Lunchtime, and I mosey down to get in on the

story Chet is telling the men, about the green logging crew he worked with shortly after the end of
World War II. Seems this young gyppo had learned
to drive cat during the war, and decided that the
life of the logger was for him when he got out of
the service. So he bought himself a surplus cat and
a small batch of timber, and hired half a dozen men
to help him log. First, they were all fallers. It took
the whole crew to fell a tree and get it bucked up
into log lengths. Then they all had a hand in putting chokers on the logs. Then, when the cat had
a turn of logs ready for the landing, all six members
of the crew jumped up on the arch and cat, and
rode to the landing. They had a merry time. I
doubted if they had a paying proposition, but the
situation of the "green gyppo" convulsed me.

By two o'clock the shovel is being unloaded and
set upon the platform of logs. Oh, oh! I *thought*
this was all going too well to last. The train can't
push the load of empties past the end of the shovel
platform. They're sawing the ends off the logs, as
much as they dare—but it still isn't enough. Are
they going to have to move that whole shovel platform?

The brakie has an idea. Why not move the railroad tracks instead? No sooner said than done. With
hooks, lines, and gyppo ingenuity, they move the
entire railroad track over a few inches, and lo, the
entire Milwaukee Railroad passenger train could have
gone by with ease!

It was on this landing that the entire crew pitched
in one day and built the little shack called "heaven,"
which they have tenderly moved from landing to

landing ever since. It's always the first on a flatcar when a new landing is to be located. Mud, cold hands, cold, wet feet and chilled bodies are the accepted lot of the logger who gets the logs out of the brush and sends them on their way to the mill, so this little shack is a haven from the elements whenever they had a chance to use it.

It wasn't long before this new landing was in full production, and the train crew was leaving the regular quota of log flats. It was a good landing. Lots of logs. Now, where did *I* get that commercial viewpoint?

"An Eye for an Eye"

I'VE OFTEN WONDERED JUST HOW MUCH OLD MOTHER
Nature has to do with accidents in the logging woods.
Could it possibly be that she resents puny man's
robbing her natural resources? It seems that way
when a limb falls out of a tree—a "widow-maker"
—and strikes a logger a death blow. The wind can
weaken a snag and send it crashing to the ground,
or whip the top out of a tall tree, to threaten the
lives of the men working below. A rockslide into
a cat or logging road; a washout where, before that
sudden rain, there had been a solid roadbed; a rolling
log. All these things can be caused by the elements
—the forces of old Mother Nature—called in to
obstruct or defeat man's logging attempts.

There's the human element, too. Carelessness can
cause injury or death to a man in the woods. Statis-
tics prove that carelessness is the prime cause of
accidents, both in the woods and elsewhere. Carelessness around heavy woods equipment, or with an
ax or saw; carelessness in hooking up a turn of logs,
or in setting the caulks of logging boots well into a
slippery-barked log. Logging companies constantly
preach safety rules and regulations to their employees,
and it's a state law that all loggers wear "hard hats."

A hard hat can save a life, as evidenced by many stories (with pictures to prove them) of the instances where a hard hat saved a man from injury or death. Sonny has several times found a hard hat a lifesaver. In fact, he has had his hat jammed so hard upon his head by a falling limb or crashing vine maple tree that he had to pry the hat from around his ears.

But actually the gyppo's first serious accident could not have been prevented by wearing a hard hat.

It happened the first day of our fourth season, in 1950. We had just shipped our first day's quota of logs. The camp was in order, the crew settled down, the machinery as good as could be expected, except for a broken track on the little tractor. I was busily doing up the supper dishes, humming happily, quite content that at last we were getting an earlier start than we had expected. Outside, across the yard, I could see several of the men at work around the track of the small cat. Someone was pounding, the ringing of steel sledge hammering on steel tracks sounding and resounding in the still mountain air. Just as I began drying the knives and forks, Sonny came in and asked for a mirror.

"I just put my eye out," he said calmly, peering into the small rectangle of mirror I handed him.

"Just a piece of dirt, maybe," I said, just as calmly.

"Nope—all I can see is a lot of little red and black commas floating around," he said. "Piece of steel from off those damned cat tracks." He kept on examining his eye in the mirror for a few minutes, then went back outside. Since he hadn't asked me to look at it, or said any more about it, I assumed it was just a scratch of some kind, and wasn't particularly concerned at the time.

By ten o'clock that night, it was really paining. I doctored him with everything in the kitchen—tea-leaf pack, cold cloths, aspirin, and everything I could think of and everything he would consent to. It was a rough job, trying to doctor a bullheaded logger like my husband. It took a whole night of pain for him to agree to a speeder ride to civilization and the doctor.

I walked with him over to the speeder at the reload, where we met the Supe. He was genuinely sympathetic and concerned, and called the dispatcher for emergency track clearance, and instructed the speeder operator to get Sonny down in a big but safe hurry.

I walked back up the railroad track to our spur, and then to camp. I was worried, of course, but I really had no idea how badly he had been injured. I think what bothered me most was the fact that my stubborn little gyppo had had to admit pain. All his life he had been a toughie. I remembered a story I'd been told about when he and Wayne were small, and an uncle was asked to baby-sit with them while their parents went visiting one weekend.

"What?" he yelped. "Leave me alone with those kids—and no gun?"

As the day wore on, in spite of my getting the baking and cooking done for the crew a hard core of fear began to form in my mind. The first day of what had looked like a good logging season, and this had to happen! Or, what was more to the point, *what* had happened? How seriously had his eye been

injured? Sonny, the little toughie, the little old
roughneck who brushed aside all thoughts of danger
in logging; who wouldn't even admit to a limp.

When he was just a baby, Sonny was a victim
of polio, and the first eight or nine years of his life
were largely spent in hospitals, in casts, in braces
and on crutches; but his was the shining spirit that
didn't allow a thing like physical lameness to down
him. He was still as active as his younger brother,
despite what, in some boys, might be termed a crip-
pling condition. No one could be around him for
long and remember that he limped. That limp had
come about when, after he became twelve or so, it
was discovered that one of his legs wasn't growing
like the other. Even after extensive treatment, the
difference could not be entirely corrected. There is
still an inch or so difference in the length of his legs.

One old friend tells of the first time he ever saw
Sonny. He was walking along the street of the
small town where the Felt family lived at that time,
and he saw a dark-eyed, snub-nosed kid crossing the
street. About the time he reached the far side and
started to step up on the sidewalk, he stumbled and
fell, smashing his face into the boardwalk. Then he
noticed that the boy was wearing braces on his legs,
and started across the street to help him up. He
was too late. The boy picked himself up and, with
a great and fluent outpouring of all the cuss words
in the English language, betook himself on into the
store. That boardwalk likely smouldered for days
afterward from the cussing it got for tripping a boy
that nothing could down.

I thought of all these things about my husband

on that long, long day, and the feeling deepened that this thing that had happened to his eye was much more serious than he had led me to believe.

Several fruitless trips to and from the telephone a half mile away gave me plenty of time to remember other things about the man who had been such a good husband to me and a good father to his little daughters. His wonderful sense of humor; his infinite patience with his logging outfit; his logging ability; all these things I thought about as I trudged along the unevenly spaced ties, back to camp, and automatically took up my duties of feeding the loggers. The logging business must go on. Sonny was depending on us.

Finally, late in the afternoon, I got an answer to my question to the dispatcher, "Have you heard from my husband yet?"

"Yes." The dispatcher's voice hesitated, then, "Mr. Felt has three pieces of steel in his right eye, and must be operated on at once. Your father is on his way to get you."

By the time the crew came in from work, I was practically a nervous wreck. I called in Chet and Swede and turned over the responsibility of running the logging outfit to them. They were our oldest men. A smoothly running operation was now especially important. They readily agreed to do all they could, then Swede called Gene, the cat skinner, to take me out three miles to where my father would meet me with the flatbed truck.

I rode on the winch of that spine-jarring tractor through the tall timber, over winding pumice-stone roads, up hills and down, my mind on my husband's plight every moment of the way. Past Old Camp and across the railroad track to where we met my dad and my brother with the truck. I hastily gave Dad instructions for cooking for the men until I could get back, and climbed into the truck for a record run to our home seventy miles away.

By the time I arrived, Sonny was in the hospital, and I was brought up to date on his trip home by my mother. He had driven my father's car from Mineral, about fourteen miles, to a doctor in another small mill town. This doctor had removed a super-ficial piece of steel and sent him on to Tacoma to a specialist. He also warned my bullheaded logger that if he persisted in driving himself, the pain and strain might blind his uninjured eye.

Perhaps it was because he is just plain stubborn, or maybe it was because his friend Jay, who drove the local ambulance, had always promised him a fast ride some day, that Sonny persisted in trying to drive himself to town. About six miles down the road, the doctor's warning became a reality, so he stopped at a roadside tavern and fumbled his way to the telephone booth to phone for help. My mother answered his call to our home (she was taking care of our little girls at the time) and dispatched aid in the person of my sister Midge's husband, Arnie.

After a few minutes, Sonny figured he could make it farther, so he returned to the car and drove for another four miles, to the end of Alder Lake, where he was compelled to pull over and park. Arnie, making like Barney Oldfield, almost missed him, but slammed on his brakes when he saw Sonny slumped over the wheel of Dad's car. Then Sonny insisted upon being taken home to wait for my arrival before going on to Tacoma, so Arnie drove him there.

Said brother-in-law, Arnie, came in handy more than once when this branch of the family was in trouble. A year later, when I became violently ill, Arnie came in time to summon a doctor, who ordered me to the hospital immediately. Arnie lifted me (who made darn near two of him) into his fast automobile and rushed me to the hospital. His only remark was that he should go in for more petite sisters-in-law. Even before I knew what a close brush I'd had, I was sincerely thankful to have had a quick-thinking, quick-acting brother-in-law on the job, believe me.

Fortunately, Sonny's mother and sister arrived at our home about the same time he did, and they made him go to the hospital. By the time I arrived, he had already been taken to surgery.

It was a very difficult and painful operation, without anaesthetic (as he had to be able to move his eye at the doctor's request during the operation), and one more piece of steel was removed. The specialist was most unhappy, however. A smaller bit of steel was lodged against the optic nerve, bowing it like a bowstring, and would have to be removed before any sight could be assured. After exhaustive X-rays, they decided to try to remove it with magnets.

During this, the third operation (although the first one had been minor) I sat with the assembled family in the waiting room. Pure agony was the only word to describe the tension, the waiting, the sympathetic pain we all felt for Sonny. We knew that this was another operation without anaesthesia, to enable the doctor to remove that last treacherous bit of steel with a powerful magnet.

It was very rough on Sonny, he told us later. For a while he had been able to watch the operation in the mirror in the ceiling of the operating room; then the doctor noticed it and covered the good eye. He could hear the tense voices of the skilled doctor and his attending nurses, and knew when the magnet touched the unyielding piece of steel. He knew the frustration of their failure. It was the same desolate feeling we all knew when the doctor came into the waiting room and told us he hadn't been able to accomplish his purpose. The remaining piece of steel was evidently a bit of burnt slag that would not magnetize. He further said that he was reluctant to try to remove it by surgery, for if the optic nerve should be cut in the exceedingly delicate operation, the chance of sight would be forever lost.

Sonny still carries that souvenir of that particular set of cat tracks in his right eye.

The nine days that he stayed at the small hospital in Tacoma must have been nine days of wonder for the nurses. They likely wondered what would happen next with that irascible patient from the logging woods, for as soon as the pain lessened a bit, he began to regain his interest in the world once more.

For several nights he had been given hypos so he could sleep. He loved the sensation he described as "sleeping on bubbles," so when the hypos were withdrawn, he raised an awful fuss. I scolded him, telling him that narcotics weren't to be taken in fun, but he just cocked his unbandaged eye at me and grinned.

"Don't worry about me, Ma," he said. "I ain't about to become a dope addict."

But he got the extra hypo or two just the same.

He had been there for three or four days when the doctor told him he could get up and go to the bathroom. Sonny asked in all innocence, "What's the matter, Doc, the can been out of order?"

"No," the doctor answered, in some puzzlement. "I meant you're well enough to get up and walk about a bit now, so you can go to the bathroom instead of using the bedpan."

"Hell, who uses the bedpan?" Sonny countered. "I've been walking to the bathroom every day since I got in this joint."

This brought him a sound scolding from the doctor, and the nurses came in for one, too. For some time he was in the doghouse with the nurses.

One evening he sent me out with a list of groceries. He wanted olives, potato chips, bananas, cookies and tangerines; all the things he dearly loves when he's well. So I dutifully went over to a store and brought back all he had ordered. By the time I got back it was late, so I gave the big sack to the nurse— along with a tip on how to get even with that logger.

After that, I thought I detected a subtle change in the relationship between my husband and that nurse, so evidently she had put the tip to good use. He always claimed that when Commencement Bay went completely dry he *might* have trouble with his bowels, but not before! What is there about an enema can that makes strong men quail at sight of it?

But outside the hospital, all was not peaches and cream, by any means. The gyppo's wife was having more trouble than Carter had pills. Sonny was very proud of what a smart wife he had, and enjoyed bragging about me to his fellow patients. One of the other fellows in the ward said he couldn't even trust *his* wife to fill out a check correctly, or pay a bill, much less run a logging company or drive a truck. So I was *really* on the spot, from all directions.

Every time I went in, he had a list of orders for me to take, and he questioned at length every report I had for him. It wasn't easy to keep anything from him, but I managed to leave out those things I knew would worry him. Like how tough the hungry creditors were after a long winter. About how the tax departments were wanting to clamp down and sell our outfit out from under us. About how very little money I had been able to get from the mill until more logs were shipped.

At the end of our first week of logging, I went to the office of the Big Company to ask for an advance. It was growing warm, and the light wind from the bay brought with its mixed odor of salt water and tideflats the warm, sulphuric breath of the pulp mill. I glanced off toward Mount Rainier as I went up the steps to the office. No clouds, no hint of a rain cap over the peak of the mountain. I hoped that the humidity wouldn't go too low to log.

As I entered the lobby and asked for the head accountant, I noted the twinkle in the eye of the pretty receptionist and telephone girl as she looked me over. I was used to being looked over by impeccably dressed office girls. Once I had been one of them, before I went into partnership with a gyppo logger as a career.

As I sat down to wait, my eye turned to the broken shoe lace in my knee-high rubber boot. It was symbolic; just the sort of knotty, broken shoe-string this logging outfit was being run on. No wonder I had to wear such rough clothing as jeans, knee-high boots for negotiating the knee-deep mud, wool socks, wool shirt and jacket, and hunting cap. Oh, well, I sighed to myself, there may come a day when I won't have to cook and drive and worry and beg and borrow.

When the accountant told me to come in, I still had that broken shoelace on my mind; also that husband of mine lying up on the hill in a hospital bed. It was just the end of our first week's logging, and we didn't actually have much money coming—but I had to have enough to cover the payroll and buy food.

The head accountant of the Big Company came to be one of my favorite people in time, and he in turn called me his favorite headache. He was always fair and understanding. He could go only so far, according to his own instructions from higher authorities, but seldom did he turn aside my problems with a cold word. My respect for him increased as the years went by, and finally he remained the one man of the Big Company for whom I could retain respect.

Perhaps that day my exhortations were more desperate than usual. After all, I told him, we had to feed ten men, buy gas and diesel, cat parts, wire and stakes, until that necessary two weeks could elapse until we were to be paid. My usual burden was doubled by my husband being unable to run his own logging operations, and, in addition, I couldn't sleep at night for worrying about Sonny's suffering.

Finally, the head accountant got special permission to advance money on several carloads of logs, and the pressure was relieved. I had been to see him twice before, with no success, so the tears I shed that day on the turnout on the hill above Hylbos Bridge were tears of relief. For a few days I could manage, although I couldn't meet any of the pressing obligations. I had to put my pride in my pocket once again, write more letters to creditors, and keep the outfit together until Sonny could get about once again.

I couldn't do anything else. My husband is well known up in that part of the country, having been raised up there, in and around the several small mill towns. Many of the people watching him grow up may have had misgivings as to his future. They knew the love of logging he had inherited from his father, but when he became a gyppo with an outfit of his own, more than one eyebrow lifted. Some of them were only waiting for him to go broke. They had watched for "big shot" tendencies, but when nothing of the sort happened, they had begun to think he might make a go of it after all. I couldn't let him down.

Many of the folks in our part of the country took a keen interest in his accident. For a week after it happened, we had to reassure more and more people that he hadn't been killed. The train crew was going to take up a collection for flowers. When Chet and

Swede visited Sonny at the hospital and told him this, he sent back word for them to save their money; that he was going to be around to give them a bad time for quite a while yet. The exaggerated reports of his death delighted that sense of humor of his.

Until a capsule of gristle could be formed around the piece of steel, the doctor warned Sonny he would be in almost constant pain. After his release from the hospital we stayed home for ten days, then he could stand it no longer.

"I can't run a logging outfit by long distance," he declared. "Let's get the hell out of here and back to the woods. I can take it." So we did, with me dancing attendance.

Our trip was far from being uneventful. It was almost as if everything combined to give him a dubious welcome. First, we were whirring along at pretty good speed when an oncoming car turned directly in front of our big flatbed truck. The driver goosed his motor, or I'd have flattened that sedan all over the pavement. Then, out near the fire gate a couple of miles farther on, a big deer jumped out in front of the truck, and we slowed down and swerved to miss him. Dusk was just filling in the hollows, and I turned on the lights, just as a doe with twin fawns came bouncing down into the right front tire of the truck. I couldn't stop fast enough, and struck one of the little blinded fawns. Sonny opened the door and took a closer look at the dazed infant. The little thing sat back on his haunches for a moment, shook his head, and at last got up and walked off the road to his waiting mother and sister—or maybe it was a brother. With a big sigh of relief, we continued on our way.

For the next ten miles we had little trouble, but with that rough three miles of pumice-stone road, with its mudholes and slick hills to come, the worst was still ahead. We made bets with each other, and crossed our fingers that we wouldn't have to walk in. I drove hard, gritting my teeth against each shuddering bump of the truck, knowing how it was hurting his eye, but trying to get it over with as fast as possible. It took all my strength to keep the truck in the road at the speed I had to maintain in order to sustain my momentum.

The first real trouble came on the steep pitch just beyond Old Camp. We backed up and tried it again and again. Finally Sonny took the wheel, and I got out and pitched pumice stone on the slick spots while he backed down the hill and took another run at it. We finally made it.

Then we got through several mudholes, over a small washout or two, and came to the foot of Nemesis Hill, which had earned its name from the trouble it had given us so many times. Here we met more trouble, with a capital *T*. I pitched pumice stone from a dry bank while Sonny put the truck in compound, then low, and tried a dozen times to make the hill. My hands became so sore I thought they must be raw and bleeding, but when I looked at them in front of the headlights they were only red from the harsh soil. Sonny tossed me a hard hat to dig with and we tried some more, but finally decided it was no use trying to get up the hill and on into camp that night.

It was raining, and I didn't want Sonny exposed to the danger of taking cold in his eye, so instead of walking in we stayed in the truck all night. There was a window missing, and we had only my flannel nightie out of the clean clothes bag for covering, but we huddled together for warmth and slept fitfully until dawn.

"Let's try it again, huh?" he suggested. I knew his eye must be giving him fits, but he gave no sign. With the hard hat I again made like a sanding crew, scooping pumice out of the deposit in the bank at the side of the road and spreading it thickly in the ruts for several feet up and down the hill. Then I stood to one side and waved him on. He made it the first try, and I ran happily after him, slogging along in shoes heavy with mud, to catch him at the top of the hill. I never did figure out how and why daylight often seems to solve problems we couldn't lick the night before.

Thus it happened that the boss who had been reported dead less than three weeks before came driving back into camp just as the crew was sitting down to breakfast. In the usual way of men who show little emotion, they greeted him with joshing, a few slaps on the back, and with open admiration for his big white bandage—and with advice on how to get even with the wife who bopped him in the eye. They called him "the one-eyed gyppo," and reported at length on the reports of his death, to his great pleasure.

After breakfast, he insisted upon taking a few

of his pain pills and starting out to recapture control of his logging outfit from the forces of nature.
I shivered with old-country superstition when I
heard him say to someone, "Couldn't kill me with
a broadax."

"Tempting the gods," I thought to myself, and
breathed an earnest, silent prayer for his recovery
and future safety.

For the next few weeks I was his veritable shadow.
I bandaged his eye, carried out his orders, ran his
errands, drove his truck, and held his hand. It was
six weeks before the prophesied capsule of gristle
began to form to the extent that the pain lessened
in his eye, and we could leave off the bandage in
favor of a black patch.

One day we were sitting in the waiting room of
the doctor's office when a small boy came in, took
one look at the black eye patch, and yelped, "Look,
Mama—there's a pirate!" He began circling around
him, eyeing him with obvious admiration. Sonny
grinned at the little fellow, which gave him the
courage to ask, "Say, Mister, are you really a pirate?"

"Yep, that's what I am—a pirate," Sonny replied
not being one to ruin a small boy's illusion.

Sonny's left eye had always been the weakest, but
now it had to do the work of both. Miraculously,
it strengthened, so that was something we could be
grateful for, although he had a dreadful time adjust-
ing his lost sense of judging distance. He took many
tumbles in the brush for that reason, and in jump-
ing from one log to another he sometimes missed
by several feet. All of which made him pretty "put
out" about the deal. He tried wearing dark glasses,

but had a couple of accidents on account of them, so gave them up.

But despite all this, and my pleadings, he wouldn't stay away from his beloved machinery.

There was the time he undertook to start the cats so they would be warming up for the drivers while they ate breakfast. He was several hundred feet up the road from camp. The cats were roaring nicely, and he used the welder to start the motor on the four-wheel-drive pickup. In doing so, he misjudged, and cut the gas line with the welding arc and set the motor afire. Then in his haste to get at the key inside the cab, he struck his glasses on a jutting door hinge. The shattered glass stuck in his eyelid and blinded him with blood. For an awful few minutes he was alone and blind, with a fire raging in his pickup. With all the noise of the cats and the welding machine, he might as well have been in the Arctic for all the help he could summon in a hurry. With great presence of mind he wiped the glass and blood away, reached again to the dashboard, and turned the key off. This stopped the flow of gasoline through the electric fuel pump; then he scooped pumice stone on the fire until it was smothered.

When he came down to the washhouse to clean up, I saw him, and was scared stiff.

"Nothing serious—just broke my glasses," he said casually.

Another morning he started the little cat, and did something he had always warned his cat skinners about: he left the cat in gear, and when it started, it rolled forward, throwing him to the ground (he

was standing on the tracks) and coming very close
to running over one foot. He came in baffled, trying to reason out the loss of his old instincts about
being cautious with his cats.

But as the season wore on he became more accus-
tomed to doing with just one eye. With a gay grin
he would tell me he could still see the good-looking
girls on both sides of the street, and the good logging shows he would know by instinct, so why worry?

On May 29, 1951, a year to the day, he lost his
right eye, Sonny took the place of his head loader,
who had failed to show up after a weekend. It had
snowed slightly the night before, and the morning
sun melted the snow water, which ran down upon
the brake in the loading shovel drums. Swede had
a log aimed for the middle of the car they were
loading when suddenly he found he couldn't make
the brake work properly. At the same time, Sonny
looked up to see the log coming at him with un-
diminishing speed. He ran from it, feeling the mon-
strous thing almost at his neck—and then it was.
It hit him a hard jolt, knocking him down between
the cars, ten feet below.

Swede released the log. He climbed down from
the shovel, his face dead white. He was certain he
had killed the boss. Chub sprinted around the end
of the loads and came to where Sonny was lying
beneath the drawbars of the connecting flatcars.
Sonny raised up abruptly, hit his head on the iron
drawbar above him, and fell back heavily into the
mud.

"What the hell you doin' down there?" Chub asked roughly.

Swede dragged him out from between the cars and got him to his feet. He didn't seem broken up. His head ached, but he could stand. Then they noticed he wasn't quite straight in the shoulders. One arm was dislocated. He couldn't lift it.

"Jesus, Felt, your shoulder's crooked," Swede said.

"Yeah, but I seem to be okay otherwise, except for a headache," Sonny said, feeling himself all over. "I'll go up to camp. See if you can get the rest of the cars loaded out, and if I don't feel better pretty quick I'll get one of the fellows to drive me out to the doctor."

About five that afternoon, when I came home after a day-long business trip to Tacoma, Vicki met me at the gate.

"Daddy is hurt, Momie," she told me, and at the alarm in my face she went on quickly, "But not too bad, honest. Don't get excited. He's in the living room."

I rushed in. Sonny was on the davenport, sitting carefully and nursing the dislocated shoulder, which had been put back in place by the doctor.

"Oh, it's nothing much," he said, when I confronted him. "Just a dislocated shoulder or arm or something—got knocked off a load of logs. Wish you'd go down and look up that damned loader and get him up to the woods."

"Logging, always logging," I grumbled, both relieved and angry at his thinking of logging before his own injury.

"Well," he grinned, a bit painfully, "the loggin'

show must go on, even if I do get knocked off. If I ever do get it, I hope to Christ you don't get any silly notions, like laying off the crew just to come to my funeral."

At that moment I couldn't see any humor in the remark. I went to the phone to call the loader.

I couldn't locate him.

"Then I've got to get back to the woods," Sonny said. "Get somebody to take care of the kids."

After more futile phone calls, trying to locate the loader, we went back to the woods. The next day I came back down and found the loader, and took him to camp. He felt pretty bad about the whole thing, and blamed himself for Sonny's accident.

"Well, I don't think Sonny will blame you too much—but don't let him down like this again," I told him.

Thursday morning we were still at camp. Sonny seemed to be suffering much more pain than was normal for just a dislocation, but the doctor had claimed the X-rays showed no breaks. We couldn't understand why he should be having so much pain.

But the worst was yet to come. In spite of the pain, he asked me to drive the four-wheel rig over to the landing so he could check up on operations. As he stepped back into the pickup, he said "Ouch!" in such a breathless way I was alarmed all over again. What could have happened? I had driven carefully (as carefully as possible, anyway) and he had walked carefully, without jarring his shoulder. Yet there he sat, unable to move.

We sat for an hour, waiting for the pain to diminish so we could get back to camp, then de-

cided it was no use. When we did get back to camp,
he was in agony. He had to rest for three hours
before we dared to start the trip down to the doctor. Then we crept out, and I could feel along with
him the bump and hurt of each chunk, each rut,
each root as the truck passed over them.

The journey seemed endless, but at last we got out
to the highway and down to the doctor. Another
X-ray showed a broken collar bone, with the jagged
broken ends overlapping each other and gouging into
the flesh. Evidently that step into the pickup had
been the last straw that had snapped those broken
ends apart and started them jabbing into the flesh.

The doctor taped him up and we went home,
but Sonny still had no relief from the pain. Then
we changed doctors. We went to the young doctor
who had saved my life earlier in the year. He bound
Sonny tightly with elastic bandage and turned him
loose.

We hadn't gotten two miles away from the doctor's office until Sonny made me pull over to the
side of the road. We got out, and I had to untie
him and re-wrap the bandage less tightly. Again,
we had a sleepless night, and Sonny had no relief
from pain.

So back we went—and that next visit brought
an appointment with the hospital, where they put
him under an anaesthetic and forced the broken ends
back into place with pressure and sandbags. If that
didn't do the trick, they'd have to operate and remove some of the bone.

"Hell, I haven't got time for that," Sonny said.
"Put on that devilish contraption you got fixed up,

and let me go back to logging. I'm tired of messin'
around."

The "contraption" was a couple of pieces of birch
plywood which the doctor fashioned into a cross,
padded with cotton and adhesive tape. Then he
bound Sonny to the cross with more elastic bandage,
with sponge rubber where it rubbed under his arms,
and I took him home. I think they were glad to
be rid of him.

He wore his cross for four weeks. I danced attendance, driving him about, dressing and undressing
him, running his errands—all but spoon-feeding him.
When I had to be absent on a business trip, Amy,
who was cooking then, would look after him for
me. Swede helped him dress, and Amy would re-
bandage him and douse his chafed back and arms
liberally with cornstarch. Sonny said he felt like a
well-tended pudding!

The gyppo wasn't absent from the logging job
very long, but his aching bones made him grouchy.
Everyone took his injury into consideration, though,
and tried to overlook his tempers.

About the time he had knitted well, we spent the
Fourth-of-July afternoon with some friends near
Tacoma. He was walking across the yard with a
bottle of beer in one hand, looking with yearning
at the swimming pool, when he stepped into a hole,
spilled his beer, and tore his shoulder loose once
more. It wasn't too serious, fortunately, but back
on went that cross for several days again. His language was something to hear—but definitely not
for children.

The following year, on the twenty-ninth of May,

we threatened to wrap him in cotton batting, but nothing happened. Apparently the curse was broken.

There were many times in my life as a gyppo logger's wife when I suffered all the jitters that any jet pilot's wife could suffer. Between those monster cats and those unpredictable trees that are such ideal widow-makers, my worries were ever with me. Whenever Sonny was late getting home, or meeting me somewhere up in the woods, my mind conjured up all sorts of terrible accidents. Could he be lying beneath a cat track, horribly mutilated by those heavy cleats? Or crushed beneath a log, or struck on the head by the quick backlash of a vine maple?

One thing I seldom watched was the loading of a tractor upon a low-bed truck and trailer—or even on a railroad car, for that matter. This was because Sonny didn't believe in completely blocking up the plank ramp leading up to them, and sometimes, at a crucial moment, the planking would slide and the cat would go sideways. Naturally, he was always at the wheel of the cat himself at such times. Where his men were concerned, safety rules were as strictly enforced as was possible; but whether it was haste, or just a streak of perversity, he had no qualms about taking such chances himself.

One day, Vicki and I both held our stomachs against that dreadful sinking pain while we watched him load the small cat onto a low-bed trailer, off a steep roadway. For several breathless minutes he fought that machine to keep it from turning turtle with him, but finally brought it to safe landing on the trailer.

"Oil got on the clutch," he explained later.

But whatever the reason for that performance, Vicki and I solemnly promised not to watch again.

Of Death and Taxes

ALTHOUGH THE FIRE SEASON BEGINS FEBRUARY 15 and ends on October 15 in Washington State, it is between June 15 and the end of the season that the forestry department really takes its duties seriously. Upon every habitable lookout, they try to establish some person, or couple of persons, for the duration of the season. The big slabbed-off rock above our camp was about 4,300 feet elevation, with a fifty-foot quite inaccessible peak above that. According to the map, it had always been known as Harrington Rock. But of course the map meant nothing to us after Amy, through a misunderstanding of Chub's butchered English, thought it was "Halibut Rock." So Halibut Rock it became.

The fire season of 1949 found a lookout inhabitant there, by name Milt, who was a friendly sort of cuss. He often stopped at the camp on his way to pick up groceries from the speeder, and soon became another sampler of my pies and coffee. When his fire lookout job for the season was finished, he came to work for us as carpenter and bull cook.

He was from southern California, and before that Arkansas, and by coincidence he and Chub found that Milt's brother Sam was a bosom buddy of Chub's, so they got along famously. The two of them often stayed in camp over a weekend, and went fishing and hunting that fall. One Sunday night we came back to find the two of them at the table, behind an enormous pile of fishbones. Between them they had eaten fifty fish; thirty-five for Chub and fifteen for Milt! They also had a plate of cleaned grouse for me, and a long tale to tell of their adventures over the weekend.

Milt had often told us how good a shot he was, having had some police experience in California, but nobody quite believed him. Then one Sunday he and Chub took the dogs along with them when they went fishing. There was Corky, the big parti-color male, his little black mate Beauty, and another female, Babs. The dogs would go anywhere Chub coaxed them.

Just in case they saw a grouse on the fishing expedition, Milt took his .22 pistol along. Around mudholes and through the brush they went, until they were over a mile from camp and halfway out into the swamp. Then Milt sighted some grouse, but just as he was ready to fire, he fell into one of those treacherous mudholes the big swamp is noted for. He came up splashing, his eyeglasses smeared with mud, and while Chub and the dogs stood with mouths open, he shot the heads off of five grouse. He missed the sixth—the mud smeared his glasses, he said later.

Then several things happened all at once. The cockers, who had begotten some wonderful hunting progeny, took off yelping for camp as if all the furies were after them. Grouse started dropping out

of the trees and brush, and Chub started laughing
so hard he almost let Milt drown in the swamp hole.

"By Gawd," Chub reported later, "if Milt ever
yells 'Halt or I'll fire' at me, I'll tear up the ground
for a block, sliding to a stop." He no longer doubted
Milt's shooting claims.

Once while Milt was still fire watching, he invited us to take the trip up the hill with him. Earl
and I went along, and it was one of the most thrilling trips I ever took, for the view from the top of
the lookout was magnificent. It was fairly easy going until we reached the foot of the fifty-foot-high
"haystack" of rock which stood between the lovely
little log cabin and the actual lookout point. From
there, the lookout was reached by a rocky path a
bit scary in its narrowness.

Below us spread the panorama of eastern Lewis
County, of great forested ridges spread off in every
direction. Blue spruce trees and scarlet vine maple
grew rampant in the steep gullies that led to the
base of the cliff a thousand feet below. Even the
rock haystack wore a crown of evergreens on its top.
To the southeast was Mount Adams, a big-shouldered
white mountain; to the southwest was the neat ice-
cream-cone peak of Mount St. Helens; and from
the cabin itself we looked directly north at the majestic king of the Cascades, Mount Rainier.

It was a thrilling sight; three mountains, untold
acres of forest land, ruggedly beautiful and altogether capable of reducing man's ego to proper proportions. We looked down at our camp below, lying
so quiet, so doll-like, in the afternoon sun. One of
our cats was toiling up the mountainside for its turn

of logs, and there were the white puffs of smoke from the duplex loading rig at the reload. The sounds of roaring logging trucks up and down the distant canyon road to the Big Company's logging operations came clear and true across the stillness of the mountain air. An occasional human voice could be heard, even from this distance, raised in a shouted command.

To the west were several completely denuded hills, where man had barbered off the trees and burned the debris. I could see the selectively logged area below me, with its mounting accumulation of brush and dead treetops and dead snags, a tinderbox for any fire that might get out of control. Our little camp, reposing helplessly at the foot of this old rock, was in a bad position between these two conflicting methods of logging.

With a sigh I raised my eyes from the successful debauch man was making of the forest below, and looked again over the wide stretches of untouched timberland. Sonny had told me about a solid township, thirty-six sections of timber he knew of that had never so much as had an ax in it. But sooner or later man will begin his insidious operations— tree by tree, acre by acre, section by section—and the land will be robbed of its precious forest cover. If they would only replace what they take with reforestation!

Milt went part way down with us, to fill his buckets at the cool spring at the base of the cliff. He actually enjoyed his stay there, he told us, and I know the forestry officials were happy to have someone who would remain as he did. They didn't have

anyone to replace him for the four years following, while we were there. No one liked the loneliness or the hard climb for groceries each week. I
often thought it would be a wonderful place to write
a book.

The trip down was much tougher on the leg
muscles than the climb up had been. My legs ached
for a week afterward.

Milt's brother Sam worked for us on a land-
clearing job we had that fall. We sub-contracted
it to a friend of ours, and Sam was one of the men
hired to pick up chunks and put them on the great
roaring fire that was consuming the stumps and debris off this six acres of land. He worked from noon
until four, then disappeared. Everyone thought he
had gone home with the plumbers who were working on the house which was being built on the same
land.

It was about daylight the next morning when the
mystery was solved. The cat skinner came over to
punch up the fires. He made a swathe around the
pile with his cat and squared away to push his blade
into the blazing inferno; then, right in front of his
cat he saw a man's blue jean clothed legs sticking up.

It was one scared driver who climbed down from
his seat, took a look at the dead man in the stump
pile, and ran for his pickup. White-faced, he reported to the contractor that there was a dead man
on the job, and they called the sheriff and the coroner.

It was Sam. After thorough examination of his
body, and some reconstruction of events, they came
to the conclusion that he had been instantly killed

the afternoon before, probably while pushing a chunk into the fire at the same time the cat came in from the opposite side. A piece of stump had fallen over him, crushing and suffocating him.

It was our industrial insurance which covered the job, so we had visitors.

The man's family had been alienated from him for many years, and according to our own accountant, who had made out Sam's income tax in previous years, he had not claimed his wife as a dependent all during the war. Since that time he hadn't made enough to support her—but the family claimed he had, to the tune of $75 a month.

The department of industrial insurance set up an $11,000 claim against us, and began paying Sam's widow $75 a month for life. Legally she had it coming, I suppose, as she was still his wife; but, technically, I thought it an imposition that a small company like ours should have to bear the increase of insurance rate to the extent of an $11,000 claim being held against us for our business lifetime, just because a man worked for us for four hours.

Ordinarily, however, industrial insurance is a wonderful thing. It saves costly lawsuits that a small business could not otherwise stand. We have never killed a logger on our logging operations, and our accidents have never been more serious than a broken ankle or a wrenched back or a jagger-infected finger. (Curiously enough, that infected finger cost us more than any other injury that season.) We don't approve of a man deliberately taking advantage of the state fund, any more than the state department does. When that fund gets low, then our hourly rates are increased. Once our cost was down as low as ten cents per hour, including medical aid; but now we pay more than twice that amount. We don't mind paying it too much, knowing that the fund is well administered, although we have to point out to the loggers now and then that the money comes out of the employer's pocket entirely.

The tax we *do* mind paying is the Employment Security, or Unemployment Compensation Tax. We resent it a great deal, as each winter finds us limping along, barely managing to keep our business together and live, while our employees collect their "rockin' chair" money for several months without turning a finger. Most employees seem to have the attitude that since they pay for it, they should collect it. Instead of considering it Employment Security, as it was intended to be, they refuse to look for work until they absolutely have to. I've known some of them to stay on it for six months, until we were ready to resume logging in the spring. Of course that sends the reserve fund low, and we don't get back as much experience rating credit as we should. (We had to work for four years before we were even eligible for experience rating credit.) It also works a hardship on those businesses that work the year around.

There has been considerable agitation about raising the 2.7 per cent tax the part-time employers pay, and lowering the tax paid by the full-time employers. My own idea would be to tax the employees who benefit from this tax; not the overburdened small business.

Social Security I approve of. At least it is more

fair than the industrial insurance and employment security, which we shoulder entirely, for in Social Security the employee pays half of it.

Then there is income tax. Our loggers are taxed as if they worked for the entire year, which they seldom do—and they always have a refund coming.

My sympathies have always been with Vivien Kellems, back in Connecticut, with her forthright brave opposition to being a tax collector and getting no credit for the job. I take on the responsibility of withholding those taxes and paying them to the government, which for a small company is a devilish chore. I do believe that it would be much easier for us to pay the full wages to the men, and let them pay their own taxes.

My last big gripe about taxes in this, one of the highest taxed states in the Union, is the State Business Tax we have to pay. The 3 per cent sales tax we all pay, so that's all right. (In our own case, we collect it on commissary and meals, and remit to the state.) But we have a little joker called the Business and Occupational Tax, which actually amounts to an income tax on our gross business. If we were to operate all the year around, we would pay twelve hundred dollars per year; so what must the big businesses have to pay? And for two years we had to pay a surtax—a tax upon tax—until the legislature finally repealed it.

There are tax collectors and there are tax collectors, we have learned, in our ten years in business. Down through the years we have had occasion to get well acquainted with many of the field representatives of the various tax departments—state, county, and federal. You don't often meet these men unless you get delinquent, or they decide to audit your books. Some of them are the cold, brutal type who act as though the taxpayers are there for them to practice all the bad manners they can dream up, while others are definitely "good joes." There were a few outstanding representatives who always showed us every consideration. We always managed to come through, so their cooperation paid off. At almost any time during those difficult years, any one of the departments could have put us out of business; but the field representatives retained their faith in the guts of this little gyppo logging outfit, and they always held off lowering the boom.

It was curious that the department to whom we always owed the least was the one that gave us the most trouble. We disliked cooperating with them, on the subject of a direct assignment at the mill, for that reason. A couple of times I had to call down the wrath of the gods upon their heads to keep their gestapo agent from wreaking havoc with our business. I was always ready, willing, and able to fight for the little business we had nurtured for so many years, and often had to. For every business sold out by a tax department, there were that many more men to be absorbed by some other business, homes lost, hearts broken—and with a little cooperation on the part of the department, plus intelligent direction, it could have been avoided.

But the nice people I know in the departments far overshadow the nasty ones. I can gossip over a cup of coffee with Fred, when he comes out to see me about a report for the period of last winter's layoff. Cecil goes to the trouble of giving me regular reports on how my assignment sheet on account from the mill each week is being applied. Dan makes a special trip just to see that the annual government report isn't giving me trouble. These men are the warm, understanding kind that a small business firm like ours will go all out to work with. They know and understand the problems of an underfinanced gyppo logger. They remember that, after all, the taxpayer is also the tax collector's employer.

CHAPTER SIXTEEN

The Gyppo Photographer

SELLING AN ARTICLE TO THE *Saturday Evening Post*
brought a great deal of excitement to our family.
The day the letter arrived, I had been in town all
day, and came home to find Sonny so excited, and
the girls too, that they could hardly stand still.
Sonny made me comfortable in a chair in the breakfast nook before telling me the big news.

"You'd better sit, Hon," he said. "You've got
a letter from the *Saturday Evening Post*."

"Oh," I said wearily, not knowing that he had
already opened it, "they don't want my article."
That was nothing new; nothing to get excited about.

"Well, now, take it easy!" Sonny soothed, un-
necessarily. "They *bought* the article!"

I stared at him wordlessly for a few seconds, then
burst into tears. It couldn't be true, after so many
disappointments; it couldn't be true! But it was
true. It was! Sonny was waving the check under
my nose like a bottle of smelling salts, and the girls
were capering around like wild colts.

In June, 1949, I had written to the *Post,* asking
if they would be interested in an article on gyppo
logging. Their reply was that if they could have
more information, they could better tell me.

Every time I tried to answer that letter, I came out with four thousand words, so I put it off until January, 1952, when my instructor in an evening class in writing at Auburn High School advised me to write again. (By this time I had a 5,500-word article written, which had been read in class and had been well received.) So acting upon her advice, I queried once more. This time they said that as long as the article was complete, I should send it along. This I did, along with eight color transparencies of the country and characters mentioned in the article. So they bought it, but sent back my pictures, saying they would send their own photographer to take the pictures to illustrate it. The gyppo's wife had taken her own pictures, and didn't appear in any of them.

I promptly wrote back, telling them to send the photographer in May, when we would be back in camp and logging again.

For a comparatively little traveled person like myself, International Airport was an exciting place. The strange foreign gifts in the little shops, the wonderfully fascinating maps upon the walls, the deep intoning of the arrivals and departures of the various flights, all were thrilling to me. My mission there that day was the big event of my life. I was meeting the *Saturday Evening Post* photographer!

I knew Gus Pasquarella only by his letters and his very hoarse voice on the telephone. (He had contracted a cold on his assignment covering a story of Richard Neuberger's in Portland a few days before.) When his flight came in, and the big silver-winged plane began disgorging passengers. I looked them over to try to pick out the right man. I finally decided that the rather slightly built, dark-complexioned man with the bright tan carrying case over his shoulder must be the right one. As he came through the door, I greeted him by name.

"And you're Mrs. Felt." His greeting was grave, a trifle tired-sounding and (I thought) bored with it all.

"Oh, oh," I thought. "This isn't going to be easy." We picked up his several pieces of baggage, which included ample supplies of film and flashbulbs, and drove to Tacoma, where I took him on a brief trip around Commencement Bay so he could see the many mills, log booms, and the skyline of Tacoma. He looked even more bored, if possible, and I finally asked him if he wasn't interested in the little jaunt.

"Well, we've got mills back East," he told me. "In fact, Curtis Publishing Company has its own pulp mill. I'm just not interested in the big companies on this assignment. This is strictly gyppo."

Those words stuck in my mind, and eventually became a suggested title for my book on the subject. Thank you, Gus Pasquarella!

My impression of him was of a man of the world who had seen all, conquered all, and cared less. Later, when we had gotten better acquainted and he had recovered somewhat from his cold, he confessed that his first impression of me—as a phoney—was even less flattering. He had taken one look at me, dressed in my new orange coat, tan linen dress—my very best Sunday-go-to-meetin' clothes—and thought to himself, "*She*—drive a truck? A gyppo logger's wife?

Who's kidding who?" We were both to change our
minds about the other within a few days.

Gus's first project, after getting settled in his room
at our farmhouse, was becoming acquainted with
our daughters, then aged four and eleven. It wasn't
a difficult task, for both of them were friendly little
monkeys. Kim entertained him with showing off her
puppies and her dolls, and with tales of riding on
Daddy's cat when she went to camp with us. Vicki
was working in the little restaurant with me, and
intrigued him with her ability to make change. She
would get failing marks in arithmetic in school, but
could still beat many high-school girls at making
change in the restaurant.

We readily accepted Gus into our family circle,
and soon found out how easily he could fit into the
logging family too. He had no more difficulty in
talking with the rough and ready loggers than with
a white-collared businessman out in the restaurant.
Chub was soon calling him "Easy-money Pasquarella,"
and trying to coax him into a dice game. Gus would
rather take pictures of the gambling activities than
take part in them. He took several in the bunkhouse, of me losing my weekly gambling allowance
to Chub.

While waiting for blue skies, he drove truck,
baby-sat, and enjoyed himself generally. He even
found himself taking fewer ulcer pills for the threatened ailment which hypertension and civilization had
brought him.

The first night we went to camp was the event-
ful one, previously mentioned, when we exchanged
the old army range in the cookshack for the new,

gleaming white gas range. Like most such projects, the entire crew was in on it. Gus came to stand by me where I was leaning against a counter, watching the proceedings. We could hear Chub tramping around on the roof with his corks, making certain Amy would have a few drips through the ceiling to keep her from becoming spoiled by such new and modern "fixin's." Then he threw the now unneeded stovepipe to the ground with an awful clatter—and Sonny almost blew himself up trying to light the heater.

Gus turned to me with a grin.

"Why, I could write an article about this outfit that would put yours in the shade for sure," he said.

"Maybe, Gus," I said, laughing, "but I'd charge you a royalty on my characters!"

Since the pumice-stone soil was about the same color as the streaked brown shakes on the sides of the buildings, it was difficult to get a picture with any kind of contrast. We had a carpenter build a high perch on the side of a hollow snag, several hundred feet from camp, in the direction of Harrington Rock. This perch had steps in the form of cleats leading up to the little platform, and a railing around it, and Gus spent considerable time up there trying to get pictures in every possible kind of light. (The picture finally published in the *Post*, with my article, made our primitive little camp look much grander than it really was.)

During the twelve days he was with us, we had only two really good days with enough blue sky and sunshine to get color pictures. One day, he

came crashing up the road in the pickup, slammed
on the brakes, ran into the bunkhouse, and came
out again almost immediately, carrying camera, light
meter, and flashbulbs. I asked him what on earth
was wrong.

"Oh, nothing's wrong. Everything's fine. The
cats are broke down. Nothing running but the
creek, Felt says, and it's darn near dry!"

In the face of that contradictory information, I
scrambled aboard the truck to investigate—and a
wild ride it was. Across the creek, up the hill,
around curves, to the Big Company's main truck
road we went rocketing along. Past the reload, and
bumping across the railroad track toward our own
logging operation. The sun was shining intermit-
tently, with many undependable scudding clouds ob-
scuring the light from time to time, and the late
afternoon was a difficult time to get pictures. Whatever it was he wanted to photograph, it was something that couldn't be staged for him. It was now
or never!

Riding along with this madman, I finally ascer-
tained that all, or at least most, of the gyppo's outfit was broken down—and in one spot! Ideal for a
long-desired picture. No wonder he was in a hurry!

I took one look at the scene when we arrived,
and sat down on a car stake beside my disconsolate-
looking gyppo. "Nothin' runnin' but the creek"
kind of situation it was, indeed. The little cat was
lying at a twenty-five degree angle, propped up on
one side while its right-hand-side track was being
removed. Handlebars was under it, his white teeth
showing through his black mustaches as he struggled

to loosen a bolt. Les, the long-legged cat skinner, was sprawled alongside the track, and Chub was doing something that kept his rump up in the air, so Gus had to yell at him to keep it down so he could get his picture. Beyond the smaller cat, Swede had the big cat backed in close to the welder, so the arch gooseneck could be repaired. Everybody was much more interested in getting things going again than in having his picture taken, so everybody was moving, the welder threw arcs and sparks, Chub waved his rump in the air—and Gus hopped around like a camp robber on a hot griddle, snapping pictures, cussing the inconstant light, and making like a photographer at a high pitch of excitement. If I hadn't been so concerned about the broken-down equipment and the lost time, it would really have been funny.

The next day, when everything was running smoothly again, Gus approached Sonny with "Say, Felt, I'm not sure those pictures I took yesterday are good enough. Do you suppose you could stage that little scene for me again?"

Needless to say, the suggestion was not well taken by the gyppo.

The one picture Gus had visualized all the way from Portland was of our logging against a main backdrop of Mount Rainier. What he hadn't known was that between us and that mighty mountain there was a three-thousand-foot ridge that occasionally reached four-thousand-foot levels. Sonny didn't want to haul a cat fifteen miles to the other side of the ridge for such a picture, nor could we very well relocate Mount Rainier; but if Gus wanted a picture of Mount Rainier, the gyppo would find a way.

On the far end of the landing we were working on at that time, an occasional glimpse of the mountain could be had; so the gyppo had a dozen or more trees cut out of the way so the white-capped peak could be seen. Then Chub and Lennart felled a tree for Gus, and Chub chopped off the limbs in the foreground, to become the "Internationally known limb-chopper," as he called himself after the article was published with Gus's captions on the pictures.

One Sunday, while Gus was still with us, Chet came over to the farm for dinner. During the afternoon our two good friends Dr. George and his wife Peggy dropped in to meet Gus. They soon found they had many mutual friends and acquaintances in Philadelphia in the medical profession. Doc had attended Temple Medical University, and Gus had illustrated many articles on medicine by people they both knew. Before long, Chet and Sonny left the living room to Doc and Gus.

"By Gawd, Felt," Chet said, "those two guys are using words longer than you could haul on a truck and trailer!"

We had cause to rejoice that day, for Doc had recently received a three-year fellowship to the Mayo Clinic in Rochester, Minnesota, to begin April 1, 1953.

The day Gus left us to return east, we took him to the same airport to catch a plane. Sonny had

him half worried about whether he had removed all
the cosmaline from the new lens of his camera (as
if the camera was a rifle) and the more than 150
pictures he had taken would be no good. But his
worries were without foundation, for he later wrote
us that the "pix" were all good.

We enjoyed learning to know such a man as Gus
Pasquarella, who in his way was as devoted to his
photography as Felt was to his logging. Gus went
back east calling himself a "gyppo photographer."

The article appeared in the August 31, 1952, issue
of the *Post*. Kim was in the lead picture, twirling
her baton, entertaining the loggers in the bunkhouse.
She immediately developed a sassy little reaction to
her new "fame." When I threatened to paddle her
for something, she put her hands on her fat little
hips and told me, "You can't paddle me. *I'm* in the
Saturday Evening Post!"

My immediate response to that was to roll up a
handy *Post* and spank her little bottom good. I
was somewhat relieved when things returned to normal—including Miss Kimberly Jane Felt!

For some time after the magazine came out, I
entertained some doubts about how the real loggers
would take such an article about the industry. The
magazine had sold like hotcakes in all the neighboring logging towns, and I knew that some of the
things I had said were controversial.

Mr. Cutting Rights didn't feel too good about my
words on selective logging, but the people I cared
most about thought the article was fine. The real

loggers were kind, and gave me not one word of adverse criticism. Perhaps I did the right thing in the beginning, when I admitted my ignorance and willingness to learn about the logging business.

There was one time when I thought I was going to get the real lowdown on what a logger thought about my article. Sonny and I had driven up to Selleck to get the latest dope on a raging forest fire in the mountains nearby, and happened into a tavern there to hear what was going on. I was listening raptly, as I often do, to the conversation of loggers just down the bar from us, when the subject of my article came up. One man said, "Oh, that woman didn't know——"

And just then his wife came in and made him come home.

I was so disappointed not to hear what he had to say, for he had no idea that I was "that woman" who "didn't know——"

At Christmas, Sonny gave me a wrist watch— buried in a seventy-five pound box of discarded cat parts!

The Last Season for Big Company

CONFUSION REIGNS WHEN WE RESUME OUR LOGGING operations each spring. We have to maintain a camp and boarding house for a dozen people, and the miscellany of groceries, cooking utensils, bedding, and logging supplies is almost beyond comprehension. For a couple of weeks ahead of time we are making and remaking lists of all the necessities, the names of the men we plan to hire, the routine in which the trucks must be loaded and driven to the logging camp. But there are always many things we forget —usually very important things, like all the sheets the pillowcases, all the bed linen and pillows—and for the first week or so we must be constantly filling in the missing items. There are never enough lunch buckets or tin hats or gas lanterns, and I get blamed for mislaying a marlinspike with which I had pounded a nail the week before.

Some day, I'd like to find that particular haven where rest all the lost lunch buckets, coffee bottles, choker knobs, and hard hats. I'm certain the value would keep my family in groceries for six months!

Everyone works twice as hard moving in or out of logging camp, but the air of jocularity prevails as usual. In the spring, the novice loggers are soon

singled out for initiation into the fraternity of logging knights of the dice table. If they are very
young, they may still fall for that old gag of being
sent for a left-handed monkey wrench, or some other
such errand. If they don't have a sense of humor, they
are soon out of the logging woods, for either they
quit or the boss lets them go.

The gyppo logger himself wears an expression that
varies from delight at going back to work to deep
concern over whether or not his equipment will hold
together long enough to get it moved back into the
woods, to say nothing of getting through the first
week's logging. He keeps his welder near at hand
so he can patch up the tracks on one cat, and he
prays the fuel pump he just installed on the other
one will produce enough power to drag in the logs.

The season of 1953 was no exception. The crew
showed up early one gray June morning; in fact,
they were overflowing the yard at the farm before
we had shaken the sleep from our eyes. There were
quick, joyful shouts of laughter here and there, a
handclasp between loggers who had not seen each
other since the fall before, the clink of hard hats
and caulked boots being taken from cars. It was
obvious they were all eager to return to work after
the long layoff.

I made breakfast and set out coffee for those who
were still hungry, while the gyppo organized the
day's trek back to camp. He was too excited to eat
much. There was a vast miscellany of the usual
junk he considered essential for his logging outfit
and the camp still to be loaded on the trucks. His
heavy equipment had all been moved back in a few

days previously by our good friend Jim Tonkin and his big moving truck.

Amy and I went into a huddle in the restaurant and in the farm kitchen, and I handed over the kettles and cooking utensils we had been using all winter. There were a dozen cans of spices, bottles of flavoring, and canned goods. There was the collection of laundry, sheets, pillowcases, tea towels and hand towels, blankets and mattresses. By the time these were all loaded in her little pickup truck, my house was slightly less bulging. I had already become philosophical about having only one pillow on my bed (instead of the three I liked for reading) and the two living-room couches dismantled because the extra mattresses on them were needed for camp bunks. We had enough pots and pans left in the restaurant to carry on there, but none to speak of in my house.

From the basement came considerable commotion, where Swede was putting a lame power saw back together. Presently blue smoke rolled out of the windows, and everyone coughed and laughed as the saw began putting in an orderly fashion once more.

"Now, if Chub were here, this saw wouldn't be running very long," I heard Swede say. "He'd have fir needles or sawdust in it, and then hammer hell out of it trying to make it run."

I stopped short and stared at Amy. Of course —*that* was what was wrong! Chub was missing.

Upon inquiry, we found that Chub was in Oregon or California somewhere, and wouldn't be back this season. There was a damage suit for an automobile accident hanging over his head in this state, so likely

we had seen the last of our old friend Chub. I
promptly became saddened indeed. Without Chub's
roaring laughter, his "sweet talkin' " the little dogs,
his teasing Kim, his hungry face at the dinner table
in the cookshack, this logging season just wasn't going to be the same.

At last everything was loaded down and battened
securely. Amy was driving the family pickup they
kindly lent us from time to time to haul light loads
up to camp. Erwin drove the company pickup
loaded with hundred-pound rolls of wire, tanks of
oxygen, acetylene and liquefied gas for the kitchen
range and hot-water heater, as well as tires, axes, saw
parts, and various other junk and apparatus. Sonny
took over the four-wheel-drive rig with the canopy
top, loaded with groceries and bedding. Swede drove
the big six-by-six truck loaded high with the wooden
car stakes. All the loggers rode in the various vehicles
in comparative comfort. (Later, they had to ride
to camp on Sunday nights in the rear ends of the
pickups that were going up; or they went to the
Big Company's headquarters and rode up on the
speeder.)

It was a thrilling sight to see our logging outfit
strung out for a mile up the road. Getting started
in the spring was a bit more orderly than coming
out in the fall. Perhaps it was because we had some
warning in time to plan for the resumption of logging season, while in the fall we always stayed as
long as possible and then let the snow run us out.

About half the trip from the farm to camp was
over county and state roads, but at National we
turned off the state highway onto the main logging

road. This road, which we had used through the courtesy of a big outfit for seven years, had been a lifesaver for us. If we had had to depend upon our Big Company's railroad, life in our logging camp would have been much less bearable.

We had to be on constant alert while traveling that road, for there were many big trucks using it too, hauling twenty to thirty thousand feet of logs —three or four times the load permitted on the state highway. Who wants to argue with a seventy-five or hundred-ton load of logs? Also, tie trucks and gravel trucks and pickups and crew trucks could be found on any turn, and although the road was a better than average logging road, in many places there were sharp turns and narrow stretches.

The first eighteen miles or so of road to camp was maintained by the company that owned it, but the four-mile length of pumice-stone road that led to our camp was our responsibility. As in all winters past, the road had suffered a good deal of havoc, what with fallen trees and snags, washouts on every little hill, and deep mudholes in every hollow or flat. This June, however, had brought weather warm enough to melt all the snow. Snow always brought complications with it, and left troubles in its wake. I had seen it take three days to get our men and machinery moved in over that four miles of rugged road. This trip was much smoother, not only because of no snow but because the gyppo and a man or two had cleared the road the week before, cutting out the fallen trees and pushing through one cat to camp. There were still places where the heavily laden trucks had to be winched up the steeper pitches, but fortunately there were always stumps and trees near enough at hand to aid in the process.

At the end of the journey the usual bleak sight of the deserted camp met the newcomers. (Remembering previous years, I didn't need the blow-by-blow account I received later.) In the kitchen, the orgies of the raccoon and chipmunk had left filth and destruction for Amy to clean up. Nothing much could be accomplished, however, until the water system was again in order, and the leak in the hot-water tank repaired so water could be heated for scrubbing. Then the light plant must again be coaxed —but this time it refused, because of a burnt valve. The refrigerator needed freeon gas in order to operate, and the little sheet-metal heaters in the smaller bunkhouse and washhouse were rusted almost beyond use. Besides the dankness of the bunkhouse walls, the bunks had gained a bit more rust from the winter's damp. The roof would have to be replaced on the washhouse because Sonny had expected heavy snow and had removed it the fall before. (He was right, for there had been about fourteen feet that winter.) The bears had become more brave and had thrust their hairy paws through the back-porch screening, to add to the general damage. And a detail like losing a bundle of blankets off one of the trucks didn't add to the general happiness, either.

Amy pitched in with broom and hot soapy water while the coffee was making. For lunch, the boys sat down briefly to beef sandwiches I had fixed at the farm that morning, and hot coffee. Then they all resumed their work of getting the camp in order. There were beds to be made, bunkhouses to be swept out, heaters to be patched and fired up so the buildings would be fit for occupancy by nightfall.

Some of the boys were delegated to go back for another load of equipment. On the way, near Old Camp, they found a crude arrow, made of sticks, in the middle of the road. It pointed to the side of the road where, under several pieces of bark set tepee fashion, they found the missing blankets. Beside it, under a smaller tepee, were several tomatoes in a neat pile, evidently lost at the same time. They learned later that some fire lookout repairmen had found the lost items. Good-neighbor policy in the deep woods.

As usual, it took a week or so to get everything running smoothly. Forgotten items had to be acquired, cat roads cleared of blowdowns and washouts graded, chokers made up, line spliced, new loggers tried out and replaced until enough of a satisfactory crew was found to settle into a routine.

Our first big problem was how to get any production with one big tractor that didn't work with the strength and vigor it should, one worn-out smaller tractor we hadn't even taken to the woods on that account, and a lonely, hard-working cat that never seemed to give up the ghost, although it was on the slow side. We had a chance to make a good buy on two large tractors of the make we usually owned, at a very good price. They had recently been overhauled and were in excellent condition. But getting the money to finance the deal was another proposition entirely. After three weeks of worrying, our local country banker came through for us.

Here should be the time and place to digress a bit, upon banks and bankers. Big city banks wouldn't even look twice at a gyppo logger or his logging show, or would any of the smaller town branch banks. We either did business with one of the big finance companies who charged twelve per cent interest, or with one of the outlying rural town banks. In our case, we found a man who thoroughly understood the problems of the gyppo logger and who, whenever he had the money available, would back him to the limit. George (Kelly) Hagen was that man, and in his years of banking at Morton, in Lewis County, and at Eatonville, in Pierce County, he helped many a gyppo get a start and stay in business when no one else would come to his rescue financially.

Kelly Hagen was from Seattle. He had reversed the rule of going to the city to make his fortune and come to the country, and he has never regretted it. He is tall, slim, with a direct but kindly air about him. Unlike some bankers with whom I've dealt, he never was sarcastic or unkind to us, even when he might have had reason to be. He earned our respect, and still has it.

Before the season was running smoothly, Swede got the mumps.

He had kissed his daughter Claudia good-bye one night before returning to camp, not knowing she was coming down sick. Three weeks later he got a sore throat but, like most men, who scoff at the idea of getting a child's disease, he went on working, getting wet and cold, until he became quite ill. By that time it was no laughing matter. He borrowed Sonny's pickup and went down to the doctor, twenty miles from camp. The doctor ordered him home at once. But our conscientious Swede was more worried about having our pickup than he was about his mumps, so he waited at the farm for a miserable hour or more, until I got home, so he could ask me to return to camp with the bad news—and the pickup, of course.

Swede warned me about the deep mudholes a mile or so out from Old Camp. He had left the four-wheel-drive rig a thousand feet or so beyond them, so I was to leave the light pickup up near the main logging road. That way, he told me, I'd have no trouble.

I minded him to the letter, and everything went fine. With a four-wheel-drive rig and a winch on the front end of it, no amount of mud (unless it's so deep it smothers the engine) can stop you. Swede's predicament was greeted with but a word or two of humor—mostly sympathy. I wondered—but didn't ask—how many of them had been exposed, or if they'd all had mumps. Nothing to do but wait three weeks and see if anything happened.

The next morning I set out early in the four-wheel rig again, heading for Tacoma with a fistful of orders. A mile and a half out from camp, the battery cable lost contact with the battery, and there I sat in the middle of a slight upgrade, "the fire gone out," as Swede would have said.

I took a wrench and pounded on the battery cable and the terminal, and jabbed viciously at the starter, but not a sound could I raise. There was nothing to do but abandon ship. It was another couple of miles to where I had left the pickup the night before, and I could hoof it, much as I hated to. But with those orders in my hand, I couldn't very well go back to camp. The crew was all out in the woods, and Sonny wasn't always too sympathetic when I couldn't use my own head to figure a way out of difficulties. So I walked.

A day in the busy, jostling town was enough to send me home to bed to sleep the clock around, and to drive seventy miles on top of it, and then fight my way through mud the last four miles of that journey was enough to make me wish again that I had married a white-collared businessman instead of a gyppo logger.

About two hours before dark, I reached the aforementioned mudholes. The prospect of walking in from there was not appealing. I decided to try driving alongside of the old rut (it had rained, and the mud looked pretty deep) so I revved up the motor of the little pickup and took off. I went the length of the pickup, and there I sat, mired down.

I spent the next two hours hauling pumice stone in a cigar box. I bruised my knees on the bumper, and generally had a bad time; but pumice stone gave excellent traction if I could get enough of it in the right place. The daylight dissolved slowly into the softness of a lovely June evening, but I didn't appreciate it. I was too busy trying to get out of the mud. The darker it became, the more desperate I got.

At last, with one great spinning lunge, we made

it to dry land, the little pickup and I. My troubles were over—or so I thought. At any rate, I made it up every steep little pitch and through every mudhole.

Coming down the slight hill to where the four-wheel rig was standing, a new thought entered my so-called brain. What if I couldn't start the four-wheel rig?

It took only a few minutes to determine that I couldn't start it, so I got back into the pickup. I tried to drive between the steep overhanging bank and the four-wheel rig, to get around and continue on into camp. And that was a mistake. The two vehicles locked bumpers, the rear end of the pickup slid into the front end of the rig, and there I was, with *two* trucks out in the middle of the deep woods, in the dead of night, and neither of the darned things could move in either direction!

I decided to wash my hands of the whole affair. Summoning what courage I could, I set out for camp —afoot. The bulldozer had left some cleated tracks along the road where Sonny had graded a day or so previously, so I walked along the rough path they made so I wouldn't get lost. There was little light where the hills came steeply down to the road, and the woods were dense, but after a while my eyes grew used to the darkness and I got along a bit better. However, my imagination went to work, conjuring a cougar behind every bush, a bear behind every fallen log. I whistled and I sang, with what little breath I had left over from treading the rugged road.

I got to within a thousand feet or so of camp without meeting sudden death from the wild beasts;

then I rounded a curve, and there, high on a stump, was the perfect silhouette of a cougar lying in wait. I stood paralyzed with fright, until that old common sense came back and told me to calm myself. There was a pale glimmer of moonlight through the clouds overhead, and if it were really a cougar its eyes would shine. I swallowed, and took a step forward; then another, and when nothing happened, I ran past the high stump and its menacing occupant, and made it to camp in nothing flat.

All the lights were out. The sound of the water from the overflow of the pressure tank near the cookhouse was a welcome one. I went down past Sonny's shack, between the bunkhouses, and into the cookshack, and felt my way carefully to the sink. There I had a good cry, verging on hysterics. When that was over, I washed my hands and face in cold water and dried them on a rough kitchen towel. Maybe I could face Sonny now.

Up at the shack, I stumbled over the grease gun and a cat roller on my way to the double bed, where Sonny made a solid shape under the covers. As I sat down on the edge of the bed to take off my shoes, he rolled over sleepily and asked "How'd you get here?" I gave him a few facts, including my walking in for two miles, and he murmured, "That's good," and went right back to sleep.

Suddenly the humor of the situation caught up with me, and I started to laugh.

"Sonny," I said. He woke up again, and grunted.

"I shouldn't have told you it was I," I said, chortling in anticipation of his discomfiture. "Maybe you would have thought it was Amy coming to visit you."

I should have known better. He pulled his pillow out from under his head, leisurely exchanged the cold side for the warm side, and said matter-of-factly, "Oh, I don't expect her over for a couple of nights yet." That man!

When I told Amy about it later, she roared with delight over the joke on me. So did Swede—after he recovered from his mumps and could find something to laugh about again.

The next day I went out to look at that high stump that had frightened me. The top of a fallen tree, complete with a heavy growth of moss, lay across the stump, making, with very little imagination (even in the broad daylight) the conceivable low-lying figure of a cougar in wait for its prey.

That season was the year of the final effort of the Supe to get rid of the gyppo outfit of Felt & Co. He had tried many times before, but fortunately for us, Mr. Midway had always interceded in our behalf. But Mr. Midway had reached retirement age, and when he left in July, the battle was on.

The Supe presented many reasons why we should be heaved out on our ear. We logged too many green trees. We logged too many rotten logs. We didn't log it clean enough. We cut trees marked for his logging operation (although his nearest setting was several miles away, and they had never mentioned doing any salvage logging). We had too many bad order loads. (We had fewer in comparison than did his logging operations.) There were various other charges, equally contradictory, and all intended to cover up the real reasons for his wanting to get rid of us.

First—we refused to lick his boots. We offered him the same hospitality we offered the fire wardens, or Mr. Cutting Rights, and refused to bow and scrape, or take his suggestions on how to log. Second—we went over his head. We forgot protocol in business when we asked Mr. Midway about various matters instead of consulting the Supe. This charge was true; but when he couldn't, or wouldn't help us, we did go over his head. He didn't keep his promises, and made his own company untruthful when he prevented us from boarding our men with his own in the Big Company camp, as per agreement, and had forced us to build a camp and maintain it at great expense and trouble to ourselves. Third— we didn't cut him in on our financial returns, therefore we got no breaks of any kind from him. He did receive many a bottle of whiskey for just seeing that we got our fair share of railroad logging flats, but we could have done better if we had anted up in cash, or given him a share in our outfit. Such practices are far from being unknown, but we just don't work that way. Lastly, gyppos were too much trouble. The Supe was no doubt right on that score. After all, we wanted a fair share of log cars, a decent scale on our loads, and a kind word once in a while—all of which we agreed were a lot of trouble to a man who hated gyppos.

We had always figured the gyppo logger had a definite place in the logging industry, but now the notion was creeping up on us that a gyppo logger's little outfit was like a ripe plum on a tree, to be squeezed dry of its value and then cast aside, and another gyppo employed until he, too went broke; and so on and on. Our seven years of work for that company seemed to count as nothing. They cared very little what happened to us, so long as they were not held liable for our taxes. To our jaundiced eye, they became the epitome of the big, cold, heartless corporation.

After barely getting a start on the 1953 season, the Fourth-of-July shutdown came to interrupt, as usual. It further shortened our season, but that couldn't be helped. The mills and logging companies who worked the year around let their men go on vacation, and the machinery was repaired in their absence; consequently, we couldn't deliver logs even if we *did* operate.

After the holiday, the season continued to advance without too much trouble. A strike in some of the neighboring companies brought us three good loggers who had been thrown out of work, which helped somewhat. Down at the farm, I ran the restaurant without much help, although my new cook was an excellent pie baker. Our nickel-a-cup coffee, homemade pie, and ample hamburgers gained widespread popularity, but we didn't get rich.

For an old friend of mine who owned the hotel in Eatonville I wrote a publicity brochure to advertise our highway as a route to Mount Rainier. My housework didn't get much attention, but the girls thoroughly enjoyed the brief summer with me at home more of the time.

The little chipmunks we had in a cage in the front yard turned up their toes and died. That was our last venture in caging wild beasties. I never did care for it much, anyway. They weren't meant to be locked in a cage for people to look at. But neither had I approved of the cat up at camp to keep the cookhouse cleared of chipmunks and little white-footed mice. I had always been willing to put up with the little rascals just for their sassy selves. My husband is a little on the tenderhearted side, too. We sometimes razzed him about putting off the burning of the remains of the Old Camp railroad cars. He took diesel one time (while waiting for me to come with the supply truck) intending to burn down the cars, but upon lifting a piece of board in one corner of the caboose, he found a small woods mouse and her tiny family of six pink babies. He gently replaced the board and tiptoed softly away. After all, he admitted, he couldn't disturb a family like that.

Nothing was sacred about our home if Sonny wanted or needed it at the logging camp. When we bought a new power lawn mower for the extensive lawn at the farm, I was elated. Now I could get that grass under control, and keep it that way! But I hadn't much more than caught up with the grass, and put the mower into the basement, when I caught Sonny stealing the motor!

I was coming down the basement stairs, and saw him dart around the corner of the outside door.

"Hey, Mister—whatcha got there?" I ran after

him to find out. It was the motor from my new lawn mower.

"But look, Honey, I've got to have the motor to run the refrigerator," he protested. "The old one's give out. Now, you don't want the meat to spoil, do you?"

I stood there tapping my foot in exasperation. "How long are you going to keep it?" I asked. "All summer?"

"Nope," my gyppo replied, grinning at his easy victory. "You figure out how to buy a new gasoline motor for the refrig, and I'll bring back your lawn mower motor." So I bought another motor for the mower. I couldn't see scything grass by hand when I owned a new power mower!

Shortly after the middle of July, Vicki went to northern California to visit her grandfather Felt for five weeks. Late in August I turned the management of the restaurant over to my cook, and drove down to get her, taking Kim and Midge Lloy with me. It was my first trip into southern Oregon and northern California, and I was disappointed at not being able to tear Sonny away from his logging operations long enough to go with us. All the way down, in addition to enjoying the scenery of our wonderful Pacific Coast country, I made special note of the number of mills, the stands of timber, the kind and quality of logs I happened to see on trucks, or dumped in millponds, and all the other evidences of logging prosperity, to tell my gyppo logger about upon my return. How good a judge I could be was open to question, but I tried.

We arrived back home at the farm exactly a week later, tired but happy. We had seen the redwoods, Crater Lake, museums, the Pacific Ocean, the Oregon and part of the California coastlines, criss-crossed the Oregon Cascades, and come home with the firm belief that our own spot in the shadow of "The Mountain," Mount Rainier, was the best of all. A fitting conclusion for provincial Pacific Northwesterners.

Then came that fateful letter from the Big Company, stating that after we had finished logging on the present setting, our services would no longer be required. We accepted the letter, and planned accordingly.

About three weeks later, the Supe came up and laid off our fallers. The forester had not as yet cleared our present setting as completed, and we had assumed we would at least be allowed to log as long as the other gyppos, so Sonny called him on it. But the Supe said he was calling it finished.

We told him we would accept this as a thirty-day notice, and would work accordingly. He seemed to be mollified for a week or two; then he came storming back again and ordered us out, with all our equipment to be moved within a week. October 15 would be the last day we would receive cars. We prepared to move out and take the matter up later with the Big Company officials.

It seemed rather odd that after seven years, and ten settings, the Supe should suddenly have the authority to declare a setting completed without the equal approval of the forester representing Mr. Cutting Rights. And then we learned from the lawyer for the Big Company that Mr. Cutting Rights had never had the authority to control our operations that he had exercised. We then asked a question, still unanswered: Why did all of our logging operations have to meet the approval of Mr. Cutting Rights and his forester for seven years, to the extent that we couldn't move from setting to setting without his approval and consent? Even the Supe had always told us our logging had to meet the requirements set forth by Mr. Cutting Rights, as well as those of the Big Company.

It was a very perplexing situation. We fought back by presenting our side of the case to both Big Company officials and their lawyer, but to no avail. We were eventually paid for one carload of logs in final settlement.

There was enough proof that personalities had entered into the deal and caused us this trouble, but what was the use of fighting any further? Lawsuits would only leave a bad taste in the mouths of all of us, big and little alike, and there were some people in the Big Company for whom I still have some respect, despite our treatment at the hands of some of the others. Our memories were bitter enough without adding more.

But there were compensations, too. Not the least of these was finding out who are your real friends and who are only of the fair-weather variety.

We went into business for the same reason that writers write, or lawyers take up the study of law, or farmers go farming for a living. Sonny was a logger, born of a logger father, and he would never have been happy doing anything else for a living. Neither was he happy working for someone else.

And I shared this aversion. I never could stand having a boss breathing down my neck. So we went into business for ourselves, hoping it would bring us a degree of security some time in the future; and we found that despite the grief and worry, there was a lot of satisfaction in proving it was still possible for young people, by hard work and considerable courage, to pull themselves up by their very boot-straps.

But according to many people (including some of our own relations) we did not have the correct attitude. They looked upon our zeal for pursuing the logging business as something for which there must be excuses made. Somewhere along the line, we came to the rude realization that some of our friends and relatives thought it something to be ashamed of—to be poor but ambitious, honest but minus a few of the superficial niceties they considered so important. When I sold my article to the *Post,* there was more than one excuse made for the wife of a gyppo logger.

Those excuses came from people to whom the material things are more important; the front you put on before society more to be judged than the earnest manner in which a man supports his family. So we came to the conclusion that the word "phoney" covered the lives and attitudes of a good many of those individuals who thought that being proud of being independent and earning your living the hard way was something that should be hidden from society's sight.

In business we found phoneys, too. In big business and small, in reputable places and in some not so reputable; we've met them all. With phoneys, money talks. When I had money they treated me like a queen, and when I was broke, they acted as if I had some sort of catching disease. We once took a check for eleven thousand dollars into a machinery house to buy a tractor. A. B. Joslyn was our benefactor, and went along with us to make the deal. That check caused a terrific commotion. My hand, and that of A. B., was almost wrung off by the president of the company himself. I even considered asking them to throw in a bottle of champagne to christen the new cat. Since that time, I've given the president of that concern many a bad time, but usually he forgave me as long as there was a chance of my digging up some money somewhere.

We found many phoneys on machinery row, who wouldn't hesitate a minute to cheat you in any deal if they thought they could get away with it—and they did. They are experts at putting on the screws anytime they happen to find a prospect in bad need of a piece of equipment that happened to be in scarce supply; one that would meet particular requirements, that is. One spring we were in the market for a cat, having just disposed of one of those peculiarities of the machinery world known as a lemon. We had looked at one not too far from home that would do the job without too much repair. As I look back on it, the entire deal meshed like the the gears in one of Sonny's favorite cats. This cat we wanted was priced at nine thousand dollars, and likely could have been obtained for less. We had about five thousand to pay as a down payment, and we went to a large finance company in Seattle to inquire about financing the balance. They sent a dealer out to look the cat over and appraise it. He came back and told us he had a much better cat for just a thousand dollars more, so we went to look at it. By the time we returned to the finance office, the price had gone from ten thousand to ten thousand five hundred—and the finance company told us they could finance this cat, but not the one we formerly wished to buy. So what could we do? We needed the cat, and we had to have financing. So we bought—and might as well have kept the original lemon we had just sold. We had nothing but trouble.

Two years later, we bought two cats of the same make, model, and year for thirty-five hundred; not thirty-five hundred apiece, but for both of them; and we were still paying for the ten-thousand-five hundred-dollar lemon! It wasn't the first time some phoney dealer foisted off a piece of haywire equipment on the gyppo, and it wasn't likely to be the last, either.

After being pushed around considerably by people in various important capacities, we came to the conclusion that the really big people always have time to say hello. They haven't withdrawn to the extent that the little drops of water in the great big bucket are too unimportant a part of the whole to so much as greet on the street. I have had the painful experience of having a man say he was too busy to see me, and then, when I went in to see a minor official of the company in an office directly across the hall from the big shot, have had the opportunity to watch him the better part of an hour doing nothing more important than read the morning paper, keep his stinking old pipe lit, and look out the window. There wasn't a phone call, a letter dictated, or a conference, in all that time, nor did he seem to mind my watching him. I have also been met with open arms and entertained by the hour, by an underling who made promises he never meant to keep, just to get me off the big shot's back.

On the other hand, we know a number of people who are quite well into the millionaire class, who are never too busy to say hello, or to sit down and chat over a cup of coffee, and have never let their business or social prominence go to their heads. They are real people.

Then there are those "dear old friends" who suddenly remember they knew you "when." One of these dropped in at our little restaurant one day in November, 1952, with a political acquaintance of mine, and renewed his friendship at great cost to us. We were still so naïve as to think that old friends could not possibly do us wrong.

But before we got through with the little deal *he* brought us, we were duped, took, hornswoggled, and sued.

At the court trial that came up some nine months later, at which we entered a counter suit for damages for the bridge and road we had built, we received what we thought to be little consideration from the judge. We later learned that the judge had once been in the position of a landowner "taken" by a gyppo logger! We were really up against a stacked deck.

It was my first experience in court, and if it had lasted more than the two and a half days, my nerves would have landed me in a padded cell. The court reporter paid me the compliment that I spoke plainly, so the words could be taken down by his recording machine. I should have told him my mother had taught me to speak out plainly whenever I had anything important to say. In that case, it didn't seem to matter much, although it turned out later that even though our testimony was deprecated, the opposition did prove us honest.

When the decision was handed down, it was more in the favor of the land owner than the gyppo logger. I muttered to myself that it evidently paid to be phoney, but actually I didn't mean it. If "dear old friend" can live with himself after committing such a breach of friendship and causing us so much trouble, then he is welcome to his own company.

Within the ranks of gyppo loggers we have met a few phoneys, too—but not many. They are the ones who are guilty of "big shot" tendencies. It takes time, and a few setbacks, but they eventually learn just how unimportant they are.

CHAPTER EIGHTEEN

Memories and Conclusions

DURING THE WINTER THAT FOLLOWED, WE FOUND
we had the general sympathy of the countryside, so
that was some consolation as we went on with the
rough job of removing seven years' accumulation of
"gyppo's junk" from the woods. There was the
plumbing and wiring to be taken out of the camp
buildings; equipment, large and small, to be moved
out. I went along with the four men who did the
work after the main crew left. I cooked for them,
and kept the coffeepot on while packing up the dishes
and kitchen utensils and remaining groceries. Once
I almost got a silver star for suggesting an easy way
to get that old monster of a refrigerator out of the
kitchen and into the dump truck our brother-in-
law was letting us use. I mentioned that it was too
bad Sonny hadn't dug a trench with the dozer for
the truck to back into, at the side of the building.
Swede snapped his fingers and went for the dozer
to carry out the idea. It worked.

The weather was wet several days in a row, although it occasionally cleared up and was lovely, as
only those woods can be when the sun shines. Each
night we would drag ourselves home with our loads
of stuff, wet, cold and hungry, and not a little sad-

dened at the destruction we were wreaking upon
our logging camp.

On one trip out we had trouble with the pickup,
so I sat alone while Sonny went back for the cat.
I had been feeling rather blue all day, and I found
myself seeing those hillsides through the eyes of a
homesick logger's wife. We had roamed and logged
over those ridges and flats, the whole length and
breadth of the big swamp, the creeks, the roads,
and they had all become dear to us. The face of
old Harrington Rock, with the autumn red of the
vine maples at its base, the blue spruce on its rocky
crown, I would see no more from the window of
the cookshack. I would miss seeing the play of misty
clouds across it in the early morn; the touch of a
light snow on its greater height, which had always
sent me into a paroxysm of worry in the early fall;
the full force of the noonday sun that brought out
the bold, craggy features of its rocky promontory.
I felt that I was looking for the last time at the
gold profile of old "Halibut Rock," as Amy said
Chub had called it.

I heard the raucous call of the blue jay as he
flitted through the forest; the hoarse sound of a
crow flying over the swamp; the frantic squeak of
the gray squirrel as it ran up a hemlock tree; and I
welcomed with a smile the silent shadow of the gray
and black camp robber who thought I might have
something to offer him to eat. How they used to
raise a fuss when they were too dumb to get themselves out of the kitchen, and I had to catch them.
No lunch in the woods would ever be complete without those squabbling little thieves.

The last few days were the worst for me, because
I couldn't bring myself to accept the ending of
another period of our lives. Perhaps it was my pride
that had been wounded, or my feeling of outraged
justice over what we deemed to be our mistreatment
at the hands of the Supe; but I knew that underlying my depression was a deep regret at leaving this
bit of country in the Cascades. Whatever we might
decide to do, wherever else we might go to log, I
knew I would never enjoy it quite as much as I
had there, or would I ever forget the many things
—sad, funny, joyful—that had happened to us while
gyppo logging those seven years around the big
swamp and below old Harrington Rock.

When the buildings were cleared of everything of
use, Sonny dozed the bunkhouse away from the
cookshack and shop and set it afire. The tar paper
building material with which it was lined, and the
dry shakes on the outside, made an exceptionally
hot fire. It made us thankful that we had never
had the misfortune to have a fire start in one of
the bunkhouses.

I took a whole roll of film, recording Felt's destruction of our little camp. He ran through and
over the cookshack with the dozer, leveling it to
the ground with great pleasure. The smaller bunkhouses and the washhouse were dismantled for the
lumber that could be salvaged. (A couple of weeks
later, one of the Supe's underlings set the wreckage
of the cookshack afire, giving credence to the Supe's
story about burning down the gyppo's camp. It
made good listening.) The remaining shack, our very
first camp building, the shop, we dragged out over

nearly four miles of rough road, to the main logging road, where it likely still stands.

That season of 1953 had been too good to be true,
that was for sure. We had a better crew than we'd
ever had, fewer breakdowns, less fire weather shutdown, and we had logged more logs. But that was
the catch—it *was* too good to be true. General business conditions were so poor that between the Supe
and these general economic recessions in the lumber
industry, we had worked only three months. But in
those three months we paid off all but a few hundred dollars of our outstanding mortgages against
our equipment. We owed fewer taxes at the end
of the year (in one department we were actually
paid ahead) but, as usual, we had nothing left over
for ourselves; not even employment security. We
added up the money we had borrowed from A. B.
Joslyn (it came to over fifty thousand dollars) and
repaid it with interest. That must have been a blow
to all his friends who had advised him against loan-
ing money to a couple of crazy people intent on
ruin in the logging business!

In the process of building our own business and
getting out of debt, we have come to a few con-
clusions that have proven interesting to me, because
they are not the ordinary or accepted concepts, even
of these times.

First, a woman's place is not necessarily in the
home. It is wherever she wants to be. Those are
my husband's words, and I think he is sincere in
his belief that women are more than homemakers.

They can also be business partners. I often regretted leaving my home for work at his side, where he wanted me to be, but I know in my heart I couldn't have done otherwise. Mine is too much the independent nature to keep quiet in a business which involves me and my children as much as it does my husband. I not only feel a strong sense of responsibility and partnership but a sincere interest in the business world. And what woman wouldn't be pleased and flattered when her husband openly declares his wife is smart enough to be deferred to for an opinion on business matters? I know I have taken advantage of him at times, but perhaps I will learn some day when to speak and when to keep still—if I live that long.

Sonny not only has faith in my judgment in business matters, but in my cat driving as well. Witness the spring of 1954, when we were trying to put a little cat together that hadn't run in over a year. I towed him all over most of the west twenty, and almost flung him off the cat a few times, and still he maintained his faith. Wonderful faith, I'd say.

Second, I think my dawning belief of ten years ago has been vindicated. A man should be happy in his work. My man loved his logging. His father before him loved logging—and still does. If I had demanded he follow some other kind of work to please me, his unhappiness would have broken up our marriage.

In June of 1952, we took Sonny's father with us when we made a trip around Mount Rainier with Gus Pasquarella. Gus and I listened while those two, father and son, logged all the way around that mountain. It was a wonder there was a piece of timber big enough for a toothpick left anywhere in the national park by the time they got home. They re-lived the old days at Fairfax, when Sam logged near the Carbon River Glacier in 1940. They drooled over the timber still left in the national park for-ests, logged it all around Ohanapecosh Hot Springs (where we love to go camping beneath the tall trees) and wished they still had—at present prices—the timber around Randle and Morton that they had logged there from 1936 to 1938.

Perhaps it was the challenge, or perhaps it was just the love of the logging woods that fascinated that man of mine, but he was happiest when he was having the most trouble in his gyppo logging show. No other way of life will ever totally replace it in his heart.

Third, we found that being in business for our-selves was a guaranteed risk of life, limb, and peace of mind. That should be enough said on that sub-ject. We have begun to feel we've served our time and proved our point in that direction. We could now sell off our equipment, get out of business, and be independent enough that we wouldn't owe any-one a penny. We might still have to work for a living, but at least we would no longer be beholden to anyone, or have to worry too much about where tomorrow's meals are coming from. We have been only moderately successful, and it has taken us twice as long to reach this point because we worked for a big timber corporation that gave us only about half a break at every turn.

I don't think I would advise a man who has a

good job to quit and go into business for himself. Except for that compulsion to be his own boss, why should he take on the worry about whether the equipment will run tomorrow, or how he's going to meet the payroll next week? When you work for someone, your taxes are paid, and if you find yourself without work for a few months, you can collect unemployment compensation. If you have some capital to invest, lend it to someone else at a nominal rate of interest and let *him* have the worry and responsibility. Not that I'm soured on business to the point of extreme bitterness, but it must be admitted that much of the incentive for small business is no longer in existence.

Congress has not, at this writing, come through with any actual aid for the small businessman, in the shape of either alleviation of the heavy tax burden or of easier financial backing. The little businessman might be the backbone of the nation, but from where I'm sitting, it looks as if he were cracking in the middle from too much pressure on all sides. To prove this, count up the number of businesses, mostly small ones, who are going broke every day.

Fourth, I've learned to appreciate my home and family. I've come a long, long way from the old tomboy days of my youth, when I couldn't be haltered long enough to learn how to bake a pie or a loaf of bread. Cooking, even for a logging crew or in my restaurant, is almost effortless to me now. I actually enjoy having a home, my family in it— and taking care of that home for all of us.

We like to do things together: camping, clam

digging, picnicking, and playing in the snow up on the mountain. We go swimming, shopping, traveling, or just visiting. Our parties for the girls include turning the house over to them, and they have a wonderful time—whether it is a Valentine party that Kim plans without telling us, or a Halloween party where everyone comes in costume.

An independent soul like myself finds it very difficult to accept the double harness of marriage. It took a dozen years for me to come to the place where I thought it the only way to happiness. Perhaps it is because my husband has been a most patient sort.

Fifth and last, we have reached an adjustment of our different viewpoints that dated back to before we were married. My idealistic one had to undergo a change, and I finally came to realize that timber is a crop, and should be harvested just as any other crop, when it is ripe. I still have that lost feeling whenever I see a tree leave that vacant place in the sky, but I also know that decay is waste, and in order to utilize our timber resources to the fullest extent, the management of our forests must be carefully carried out. So much of our timber was overripe when white men first came here a hundred years ago. Of course we cannot help what is past, but we can do better today and tomorrow. We can log that timber which is ripe, and replace what we remove by reforestation. Since better uses for wood products and by-products are being developed every day, I know the elimination of waste is furthering my idealistic viewpoint on our evergreen forests. I hope that our hills may forevermore be green.

I'm sure that Sonny's viewpoint has changed somewhat, too. He had long expressed his ideas on how timber should be logged in blocks of forty, sixty, or eighty acres—clear-cut logged—the slashing burned, and then the entire area reforested. When the new timber has grown to a certain point, then the remaining acreage could be logged in a similar manner. He claims that the winter winds wouldn't reap such devastation in the younger timber left unprotected under the present system of selective logging, and since the younger and smaller trees could be utilized for pulp, it wouldn't be a loss to log them, along with the ripe trees, by this method. They die when the wind blows them down anyway.

But a born gyppo never changes his spots, I find. Last winter, we took the children up to play in the snow at Longmire, in Mount Rainier National Park. Before we entered the park, we drove through a recently logged area that had been logged in the usual ugly manner—one that hadn't enhanced the appearance of the countryside. It was in brutal contrast to the virgin timber standing tall and straight inside the park boundary.

At once the quiet of the deep forest began to cast its magic spell. A light snow was falling on the lofty branches above us. The great brown trunks of the perfect trees that would make such wonderful peelers were tantalizing to the gyppo, I knew. I sighed. All the old love for the mighty forest was upon me again. The majesty of nature——

I heard Sonny sigh, too, and looked at him, smiling gently, thinking that at last he, too, was caught up in the magic spell. Then he breathed, in reverent tones:

"Ge-e-ez! Whatta loggin' show!"

Here We Go Again

LATE IN OCTOBER, 1953, WE ATTENDED THE LOGGING Congress in Seattle. Our feelings were bruised, our financial situation hovered on the brink of bankruptcy, and our prospects seemed practically nil. But we did have a promise of sorts; the kind of promise that we gyppos thrive upon, to which we were clinging with might and main. It had enough foundation to enable us to use it to stall off our creditors, and enough to convince the banker and finance company that our finances would change by early spring.

It was my first logging congress, and I found it tremendously interesting. Besides all the interesting people we met, old friends and new, there was a wealth of background material on old and new logging practices from the various machinery companies. Down in the basement of the huge building, three million dollars' worth of logging equipment and machinery were on display. Every time I lost my husband, I usually found him drooling over a big new tractor complete with logging arch and drum and air steering.

"Imagine that, Margaret—hydraulic steering on a tractor! And I thought a torque converter the best of the new improvements on a cat!" (The torque converter, I gathered, was the same as automatic transmission on an automobile.)

The second day, while we were eating lunch in the main-floor auditorium, an old friend of my husband's came over to our table. I liked the man immediately; although I had never met him before I felt I knew him from hearing so much about him. From a position as cruiser for a large timber company, he had advanced to the place where he was now known as a millionaire gyppo logger. Hardly a gyppo—but he had begun in a rather small way. With adequate financing, smart business acumen, and no few breaks, he had become a very important man in the lumbering world.

"Well, good to see you, Sonny," he said. "Been hearing you're in the logging business for yourself." They shook hands, and Sonny introduced me. "I read your article in the *Post*," he said, shaking my hand. "Congratulations." Then he sat down with us, and turned back to Sonny.

"I've got about six million feet of hemlock to finish logging to complete my contract with the Timber Company up your way, Sonny," he said. "Now, if my quota down south is more than last year's, I've got to get someone in there to finish the job for me. Have you got the equipment to do it?"

Sonny was slightly overwhelmed. Before the man left the table, they had an agreement of sorts, based on that all-powerful little word "if"; but it was good enough for us. Our immediate future was as barren as the logged-off hills at the foot of Mount Rainier. Our hearts were lighter from then on, and we clung to that nebulous promise like bark to a tree. We wore it out hoping upon it, but it never came to reality.

In the early spring of 1954, about the time we could have taken a logging job—*any* logging job— the word "strike" loomed its ugly, time-wasting head. None of the large timber companies wanted to clear out the roads, or call men back to work to get the equipment moved back to the woods, when a strike might be called any day.

One time I asked a labor leader, "Why is it that every spring, about the time the snow melts and the sun shines and we have a faint glimmer of be- ing able to resume logging earlier in the spring than we had the year before, the loggers or the union start talking strike?" He couldn't give me a defi- nite answer. He could see that such strike talk, and annual wage and hour negotiations, would have the effect of slowing down any plans for early resump- tion of logging, but he couldn't offer any solution.

The months wore on interminably, with no log- ging in sight for H. W. Felt & Co. and very little logging going on anywhere nearby for anyone else. Sonny talked again and again to superintendents and logging managers about getting a contract, large or small, but everyone expressed doubt about the labor situation. I warded off the creditors and wrote good- will letters expressing hope for the future. May came, and there was no work. June came, and rum- blings of a strike became more distinct; then, on the twenty-first, the entire logging woods industry went out on strike.

That settled something for us, anyway. Until the

strike was over, we could just jolly well whistle for work in the logging woods, like everybody else.

About this time, a neighbor who stopped in for coffee at our little restaurant told us what seemed to be a very tall tale. But tall or not, we were so desperate that Sonny went with Charley, the neighbor, to investigate.

A good half century ago, huge trees had been felled along the right-of-way for a water flume. Charley had discovered them the fall before, while hunting, and knowing something about logs, he became curious when he found the moss-covered timber, lying about like giant jackstraws, gave forth a ringing sound when he struck them with an ax or scuffed them with his caulked boots.

Sonny came home amazed. He could hardly believe what he had seen. Trees that had never been bucked, protected from the sunlight and air by overhanging brush and second-growth timber, were sound as a dollar. That ringing sound Charley had heard was to turn into a good, honest ringing of dollars into our bank account. But not right away. It took more than just a little cruising and exploratory work to bring this all about.

Number one obstacle: This timber lay on the right-of-way of the power company which owned the flume built fifty years before. No one knew if they would sell. In fact, everyone was certain that it was against their policy to sell any timber whatsoever.

Obstacle number two: The road belonged to Timber Company, a large outfit that owned and maintained most of the road in that area, and who didn't, as a rule, grant right-of-way to anyone, no matter how important.

Number three obstacle: The logging industry was on strike. Even if the timber could be bought and the right-of-way obtained, there was no telling when we could get in to log it.

But there were two wonderful advantages that kept us from becoming discouraged. One was that the operation would be close enough to home that no camp would be necessary. Second was that it would be an outright purchase deal, so profits would be doubled or tripled. True, we would have to go in hock for the money to buy the timber, but once we got it, we'd be able to pay it back with interest, and in short order.

Sonny did a little preliminary investigating. He got brushed off rather abruptly when he had climbed up a couple of rungs of the employees of the power company. So we took it to our own lawyer. He talked to the abrupt brusher-offer, and we then went over his head to a man whom our lawyer knew had more to say.

This negotiation took most of the summer. We got early promise of right-of-way over the road from our old friend Frank, who had earlier given us use of road when we worked for the Big Company in the upper country. Frank had recently taken over the management of the logging division of Timber Company, so his authority was genuine. Then we began making progress on buying the timber. It looked as if the entire thing was beginning to mesh just like the gears in a smooth-running cat.

But, like the cat, something went wrong with the transmission.

The strike ended about the middle of September. When it came to pinning down all the promises for right-of-way, there were evasions and legal technicalities brought up to delay us. By the time we had purchased the timber from the power company, and run down every lead on the right-of-way deal it was a whole month after the strike ended. Just a year and a week from the day we had left Big Company, we were again dusting off the rust and depreciation from our equipment and logging again.

Sonny was between two fires all that summer. He would make one of his many trips to Timber Company offices, either in the woods or down to Tacoma, and come home time after time with no news. Then I'd yak at him—"Why, why, why?" —in typical worried gyppo-logger's-wife fashion. I couldn't (and still can't!) understand why people can't go through with their promises. To me, it was to be yes or no; none of this "maybe" stuff, or passing the buck to someone else. I'd have loused up the deal for sure if I had handled it, but fortunately Sonny had put his foot down in time. At no time did *he* ever lose his temper—or his courage, either, for that matter. He used every bit of diplomacy he could muster, and it paid off.

One day he came home with that precious bit of paper that gave us right-of-way of Timber Company's road, at a cost of two dollars for every thousand feet of logs we hauled out over their road. It was one of the brightest days I can remember. We had to sell all timber to Timber Company, but since they paid market price, we were agreeable to that. To have no prospects at all, then to face a bright future, all within such a short span of time, made us almost deliriously happy.

The logging show was a tough one. It challenged all of Sonny's know-how to build a road, ford a swift, deep creek, and yard the logs a mile to a solid landing where they could be loaded on trucks. He bought a new power saw and hired one of our former fallers to buck the fallen trees. Said faller seemed to have forgotten how to run a saw, and within a few weeks transmission after transmission went out of that saw. We lost time; we lost several loads of logs, which was a serious matter when our time to take the timber off that particular piece of ground was limited to three months. Finally, we canned the faller, put one last new transmission in the saw, and things began to look up.

After so many years of lying on the wet ground, the logs naturally had no bark on them. They could be called "buckskin," for this reason, but they were more than 75 per cent sound and made excellent peelers. The Timber Company said that the yellow, fine-grained plywood they could peel from those logs was of excellent quality.

When we got our first check, we had to pinch ourselves. It didn't seem possible that at last we had gotten a break; the kind of break we had been praying for for so many years. We even began to change our minds about the Supe from the Big Company. Perhaps he had done us a favor by kicking us out of our salvage logging job, where we had just managed to keep going on a starvation profit margin for seven years. At the end of another month of logging, we were *certain* the Supe had done us a favor. An unintentional one, no doubt, but nonetheless a favor. If we hadn't been kicked out, we wouldn't have been so desperate as to look into such a remote possibility as Charley had told us about, and we wouldn't have pursued so diligently the task of obtaining it.

With the three-month deadline for logging on power company ground just ahead, Sonny began acquiring more patches in the same area; a little here, and a little there, to guarantee a continuance of this bonanza for as long as we could make it last. Some of our old crew began coming back: Teeko, who had set chokers for us; Gene, the cat driver— he who had never worn rain clothes or hat or gloves or wool socks, even in the fiercest of winter logging; Swede, who had gone into the garage business for himself east of the mountains but who came back to us for a couple of months; and Lennart, the Swedish logger. They had been pursuing their own lives, far from ours, during the year layoff, but it was like having part of our family come home when we saw them gathered about the table in the farm restaurant, having their early-morning coffee before catching the crew truck to the woods.

Swede was still careful to either get down on his knees to cross my linoleum, or to step carefully upon a couple of cedar shakes, to avoid chewing up my floors when he had his caulked boots on. Lennart had spent eight months in Alaska, falling timber on

Prince of Wales Island, and Gene had spent the whole year looking for work.

There were some new ones, of course. Clyde, built broad and husky, with laughing dark eyes and a merry joke told at the top of his lungs, worked on the power saw and set chokers. And George, who did all of our cruising, running of lines, and laying out of cat roads, occasionally filled in his winter months by setting chokers for us. He was a graduate forester, and did aerial survey work, so we knew he had a better future. We were not surprised to lose him, and speeded him on his way with our blessing—and regret—when he left us. And there was Shorty. He drove truck for a contract trucker who owned four of those big gray and red trucks, and we soon came to include Shorty for dinner and for early-morning coffee. He wasn't much over five feet, but what a husky five feet of truck driver he was! And how he could handle that big logging truck and tagalong, or gypsy four-wheeled trailer!

What Shorty lacked in height, he more than made up for in ingenuity, huskiness, and good humor. He really is a remarkable guy.   One day, a loading strap slipped off a log the crew was trying to put on his truck. It flew up twenty feet, hanging in the gin pole rigging. Swede and Clyde both tried to tong it down with poles, with no success.

Then Shorty came up with an unbelievable solution.

"Betcha I can get up on the truck and throw a log chain through the damned thing," he declared.

"You're crazy!" he was told.

"Betcha," he replied, and proceeded to roll up a

log chain—no mean feat in itself, for a twelve-foot
length of chain makes quite a parcel. Then he
climbed up on the truck and threw it at the hung-
up strap. The first time he missed, but the second
time the end of the chain passed directly through
the loop of the strap and brought it to earth, where
it could again be put back into service loading logs.

Shorty and Vicki carried on a running feud over
whether or not a piece of cocoanut cream pie should
be saved for his supper; but I noticed that whenever he left special orders for the day cook at the
farm restaurant, Vicki always relayed his message.

We were finally forced to decide that our original
estimate of twenty thousand feet of logs per day
was too high, and we'd do well to produce half
that amount. Those logs were not easily won. As
winter progressed, the water in the creeks and the
river through which we had to yard the logs came
up and washed over the tracks of the arch cats.
The mud got deep and gooey, the days got shorter.
Too short for a nine-hour day by daylight—especially
when things didn't always run smoothly. But our
checks were still rewarding enough to start paying
off our debts, and I had a gay time budgeting the
money. So much for this one that was two years
old; so much for that one that had gotten tough,
and only by the grace of God had been kept from
taking us to bankruptcy court; taxes; wages; gas
and oil; logging supplies; cat tracks; loan repay-
ments—on and on went the list. The girls got some
decent clothes, and Sonny and I refurbished our van-
ishing wardrobes. The front bedroom, which I made
into an office, got asphalt tile on the floor.

I had often dreamed of being able to meet a girl friend in town and leisurely have lunch, window-shop, and make like most small-town women with a day to themselves. Well, one day I tried it. I was on my way to Puyallup, the nearest town in the valley, to pick up a welding job at the garage, when I met Amy. She was on her way to the farm to see me, and was also supposed to buy herself a new coat; so we went into town together and proceeded to enjoy ourselves. We tried on all the coats in all six of the main stores in town. Then we looked at costume jewelry, and I bought each of us a pair of earrings, 50 per cent off, fifty cents a pair. Not a bad bargain. Then we had lunch, and I enticed her to go overboard on a special chef's salad in a certain restaurant where I liked to go.

Just as we were about to go "all out," as Sonny would say, we became a bit conscious-stricken. Amy had been on her way to the farm to use my adding machine on some income-tax figures as well as to visit; so I took her over to our lawyer's office, and we used his adding machine. I even helped her add up long columns in her cash book. Then I dropped in at the garage and picked up the car part that was being welded back into one piece, and we gave each other guilty little bye-byes and ended our positively luxurious day. I hadn't enjoyed myself so much in a long time.

I came out of the garage to find George and my husband had just driven up in George's car. My first thought was, "Dammit, one of the cats has broken down!" Then I took a second look at Sonny's face, and the peculiar way he was holding his left arm.

"Don't get panicky," he said. "I just broke my arm, or my shoulder, I don't know which. See if you can get ahold of Doc, willya? He's supposed to be here in town."

Thus ended my beautiful day. I located Doc, and arranged for Sonny to go immediately to the local hospital for repairs.

What happened was this: While walking through the woods, laying out a cat road, he had gone through a grove of alders. One of them he touched had moved slightly beneath his touch, so he moved on quickly, knowing all too well how tricky they can be when their roots are rotted off by high water. He had gone about twenty feet when Boom! It hit him. He heard his arm snap, and fell forward, clutching his small and deadly cruising ax to his bosom. Fortunately, the ax twisted sideways and instead of the bright blade being presented to his unarmored chest bone, the broad, harmless side lay against his body. After he came to, he picked himself up and walked a mile back to where the crew was working and informed them he was hurt.

For six weeks he carried his arm around tightly bound to his body with elastic bandage, and then in a sling; but even before that, he recovered enough to put the crew back to work getting logs out of the woods.

Three weeks later, on Saturday, George was falling a small alder along a cat road, and something —likely an alder—gave him a slashing blow across the face, laying his nose open to the bone. The new yellow panel crew truck we had just purchased got a fine workout under Shorty's capable hands, taking

George to the doctor. The doc took twenty-five
stitches in George's very handsome nose, shortened
it a bit, and within two weeks he was as good as new.

Such things happen in the logging woods, usually
so quickly that no one can ever actually tell just
exactly what did occur.

Whenever we had time, we liked to watch the
beavers at work. In fact, it got to the point where
we checked upon their daily progress in falling a
big old cottonwood tree across Kapowsin Creek.

"Look there! They're going to fall it just the
way it leans across the creek!"

"If they don't fall it the way it leans, they're
going to have to wedge," my logger husband replied
dryly.

Another time, Sonny reported they must be working a night shift, because now they had put in quite
a sizable undercut since the day before. It was quite
an undertaking for those little busy beaver fallers, for
that cottonwood tree was almost two feet through
at the stump, with moss-grown bark on the north
side, and it towered sixty or seventy feet into the
air. A minute's work for a power saw in the hands
of a good timber faller, but days and weeks for
those fat brown beavers.

We're waiting to see what happens when they get
the tree chewed through and felled across the creek.
Likely some mean old county man will report their
"destructiveness" to the government game warden,
and they'll have to pick up sticks and move again.

We logged happily for several months before we

became aware of a surprising attitude toward us in our own neighborhood. It was the old "He could fall into an outhouse and come out smelling like a rose" kind of thing, seeming to stem from the fact that we had gotten some timber of our own to log, and the right-of-way from the Timber Company to boot. The "lucky Felts" had gotten the breaks. No one seemed to remember that just a short time before we had been among the unemployed, and had just gone through a full year without work. And nothing could be farther from the truth than to say our good fortune could stem from *luck*. Certainly nothing could miss the truth farther than the assumption that we didn't work for what we got, every inch of the way. When I think of the knee-deep mud, the rising river, the rain, the breakdowns, the loss of time, the sheer hard labor and just plain guts it took to get each and every log out of the woods and loaded on the truck, I feel that luck has little to do with it.

A friend gave me this, saying it is her own creed: "What people call luck is merely the coinciding of preparation and opportunity." Certainly those seven years with the Big Company were preparation for anything the gyppo logging game may choose to throw at us in the future. Certainly we never had things easy enough to have our inner moral fiber softened. And when you hit bottom, there's only one way to go.

But how can you explain such things to people who, not having shared the depths of your despair, now cannot understand what appears to be such good fortune? I suppose it is not natural to expect others

to feel happy for you when you are getting ahead.
If this is true, then I am mighty unnatural. I *like*
to see folks get ahead by honest toil and sweat and
tears—and heaven knows that any gyppo logger gets
his share in ample measure!

In this logging game there are times when you
need the breaks; in fact, there is never a time when
you don't need them. All parts of a logging team
must work together; the weather must be just right,
the timber not too rotten, the scaler equipped with
a decent length thumb. Then—but *only* then—you
might get the production you've set for your goal.

The other day I overheard a truck owner say that
one of his trucks had made four trips on a certain
log haul.

"Good," said my gyppo, in all earnestness. "He
must really have had the breaks."

"Yes," the trucker agreed. "For once, everything
went perfectly. No hard luck with tires or truck,
perfect timing in loading and travel time and dumping." He had gotten "the breaks!"

I can think of no better way to end this than by
sharing the view from my farm office window. Outside, my gyppo is putting his new tractor through
its paces; this is much like the tractor he saw and
coveted at a recent logging congress. As he gyrates
happily about, that look is on his face again—that
look of a king on a throne, master of his cat, and
of his fate.

It's a beautiful hunk of machinery, thirty tons of
it, and it handles like a baby carriage. I know. I've
driven it.

But handling it is my gyppo's job. My job is to work and pray for the breaks to continue, so we can get it paid for!

AFTERWORD

FROM THE TIME I WAS SEVEN UNTIL I LEFT HOME FOR college, my mornings began with the predawn sound of logging trucks starting up at the Wilson and Sutton truck yard almost a half-mile from my house—that telltale whine of the air-powered motor that cranked the large diesel engines to a lumbering and uneasy start. Much later in the morning I trudged to the bus stop near the entrance to the truck yard and waited for the bus that made its way from Cougar, some sixteen miles east of my house, to the school in Woodland another sixteen miles west. The empty trucks would whoosh past me in a great gust of wind, dust, and diesel smoke as they headed back up the Lewis River (which separates Clark and Cowlitz Counties in southwestern Washington) toward Mount Saint Helens for a second load. As a small child, those blasts from the trucks would nearly knock me from the precariously narrow shoulder of the road into the beer bottle populated ditch. It got even more exciting when empty trucks heading upriver and full loads coming downriver crossed right where I was walking. When that happened, the ground shook and the noise level grew to the roar of a jumbo jet. It was exhilarating, and I'd madly make the motion indicating that the truckers should blow their horns (fist clenched above my head with a

violent downward yanking motion). Usually they'd com-
ply, though with fierce childlike loyalty, I was certain
that the independents' trucks honked more often than
those from the big corporations. (It's hard to avoid being
a populist in rural areas.) The Lewis River valley was his-
torically an antiunion place and tended to have more independent loggers than many other areas. Still, the big
firms like International Paper, Burlington Northern, and
especially Weyerhaeuser ran trucks up the river. Corporate or independent, the drivers pushed their trucks hard,
and when they'd passed my spot I was left in the midst of
a small and diminishing hurricane listening for the next
truck coming my way. All too soon, I'd reach the bus
stop at the entrance to the Wilson and Sutton truck yard.
With that, my morning ritual ended.

The Wilsons, of Wilson and Sutton Logging Company,
were our nearest neighbors, having blasted off the top of
a several hundred foot high knoll on their property to
build a sprawling split-level house within a few years of
my family's arrival in the area. From that high vantage
point, they overlooked much of Lake Merwin as well as
about ten acres of the carefully manicured grove of trees
they grew and the cattle they raised on the remaining
pastures of their eighty-acre parcel. Norm Wilson was
the logger. He had married Enid, one of the Sutton girls,
and with that extended family had built up a very successful independent logging operation, one of the largest
in the area. Enid, though she had no exceptional formal
education, made certain that the business ran. She kept
the books, argued with choker setters, machinery operators, mechanics, and truck drivers about their pay. She
not only held her ground with these tough men, but also
often put them in their place. She met deliveries and, I

am certain, went and got parts herself. Whatever needed to be done, she did it.

Enid also spent every summer spraying tansy, a task to which she mercilessly drove any of her children too young or unwise enough not to have found other employment. Sometimes she'd head into the hills north of her place with some of us kids in tow trailing large burlap sacks. We'd strip bark from chitum or cascara trees (it was used as a laxative), which Enid had us gather to make a little extra money. The lessons about working hard and using the resources around us must be why she dragged us out there. In retrospect, I can see that the logging families who hunted (and poached), or my family that went into the woods for edible mushrooms, were looking at the forests as a place full of many different resources, not just as trees for the harvest.

There were other logging families in the area besides a handful of successful independents. In some families, the men and older boys floated seasonally between marginal logging operations with one or two trucks, even more marginal stump farms, and, in some cases, commercial fishing. Women in these families worked too, but their unpaid labors supporting logging blurred with other domestic tasks and, in many cases, with part-time wage work outside the home.

This far-flung logging community that stretched for dozens of miles along the Lewis River was my primary home. As I came to read, research, write, and teach about the history of the Pacific Northwest, I found far too little available that reflected the lives of the logging families with whom I grew up. Their stories were much different than the "glory days" of isolated work camps, logging railroads, and steam donkeys. Their stories were different from those of the huge corporate entities that preyed on public lands whenever possible for timber, harvesting their own holdings as a last resort. I was at a loss as to how to convey the very different and significant stories of the families I had known to my students. I am particularly pleased, then, to have the opportunity to see Margaret Elley Felt's *Gyppo Logger* in the Columbia Northwest Classics reprint series. Felt gives readers an opportunity to see past the giant corporations and into the very real and earnest lives of Northwest logging families. She gives readers a palpable sense of being there and brings back to life an epoch that has received little treatment and even less understanding. Robert Walls's new foreword to the volume gave me, for the first time, an opportunity to bring today's sophisticated labor, gender, and environmental tools of analysis to bear on the topic. The combination is unbeatable. As I read through the volume again, not only can I feel the dust and smell the diesel smoke of my past, but I can also see that world more clearly than ever before. I thank both authors for their insights and hope that the logging families that I grew up with will too.

CHRIS FRIDAY
Bellingham, Washington
October 2001